ROUX TO DO

The Art of Cooking in Southeast Louisiana

The Junior League of Greater Covington

THE JUNIOR LEAGUE OF GREATER COVINGTON

ROUX TO DO
The Art of Cooking in Southeast Louisiana

Published by The Junior League of Greater Covington

Library of Congress Control Number: 2003104711
ISBN 10: 0-9740695-0-7
ISBN 13: 978-0-9740695-0-0

Edited, Designed, and Manufactured by
Favorite Recipes® Press
An imprint of
FRP
P.O. Box 305142
Nashville, Tennessee 37230
800-358-0560

Art Director: Steve Newman
Book Design: Jim Scott
Project Editor: Linda Jones

First Printing: January 2004
10,000 copies
Second Printing: July 2004
10,000 copies
Third Printing: September 2007
10,000 copies

Printed in China

Cookbook Committee

Co-Chairs
March 2002—Publication

Naz Butcher
Paula Kelly Meiners

Marketing Co-Chairs
August 2003—July 2004

Annette Dowdle
Allison Mercante

Co-Chairs
August 2001—March 2002

Dorothy Noriea
Gayle Wagner

Previous Cookbook Chairs

Wendy Bachrack   Leslie Martin

Cookbook Committee

Caroline Blossman
Annette Dowdle
Carolyn Dunn
Samantha Frost
Laura Galbreath
Beverly Gariepy

Liz Healy
Caroline Langdon
Allison Mercante
Christian Meredith
Amy Moreau
Anita North

Liz Norton
Lynda Pitts
Jessica Price-Boeh
Melissa Sproles

The Junior League of Greater Covington
Board of Directors 2002-2003

President
Phoebe F. Whealdon

President-Elect
Lisa Barnett

Community Vice President
Lisa Blossman

**Assistant Community
Vice President**
Sue Osbon

Membership Vice President
Leslie Martin

**Fund Development
Ways and Means
Vice President**
Misty Herpin

**Assistant Fund Development
Ways and Means
Vice President**
Amy Moreau

Treasurer
Cindy Leaber

Assistant Treasurer
Susan Meyers

Recording Secretary
Caroline Lightfoot

Corresponding Secretary
Rebecca Dougherty

Sustainer Advisors
Patsy Bonneau
Donna Paciera
Beth Heintz
Nancy Anderson

Contents

Preface

The Northshore, the parishes north of Lake Pontchartrain and New Orleans, has long been known as an artists' community. Just as we appreciate beautiful art, Southeast Louisianians also relish our food. Like any good artist, a southern cook uses instinct and heart to create a pièce de résistance. The Junior League of Greater Covington invites you to share our love of art and food with our first cookbook, *Roux To Do*.

The following members of the Junior League of Greater Covington honor their Favorite Cooks—the people who have inspired us to love cooking and, of course, eating, but most of all creating memories with our families and friends.

Pamela Brown honors her Mother, Norma Sloan.

Naz Nawas Butcher honors her Mother, Sue Nawas.

Naz Nawas Butcher honors her Father, Rifat Nawas.

Naz Nawas Butcher honors her Mother-in-Law, Judy Butcher.

Naz Nawas Butcher honors her Grandmother-in-Law, Jackie Thurmon.

Cory and Jeanne Crotty honor their Mother, Jeanne Crotty.

Annette Dowdle honors her Mother, Joyce Lavender.

Annette Dowdle honors her Mother-in-Law, Charlie Dowdle.

Tara Dragon honors her Mother, Kathy Dragon, as the greatest cook ever!

Paula Kelly Meiners honors her Niece, Leah Kennedy Vaughan.

Paula and Mike Meiners honor their friends, Julia Ann and Richard Hodgson.

Allison Mercante honors her Mother, Kathryn G. Croft.

Allison Mercante honors her Mother-in-Law, Josie Mercante.

Amy Moreau honors her Mother, Sue Wertz.

Amy Moreau honors her Mother-in-Law, Mary K. Moreau.

Camille Romero Reed honors her Mother, Hazel Romero.

Melissa Sproles honors her Mother, Gale Taylor.

Melissa Sproles honors her Mother-in-Law, Frances Sproles.

Leigh Anne Walls honors her Mother, Dorothy Wall.

The Junior League of Greater Covington is an organization of women committed to promoting volunteerism, developing the potential of women, and improving the community through the effective action and leadership of trained volunteers. Its purpose is exclusively educational and charitable. With close to two hundred active members, the Junior League of Greater Covington provides over $75,000 and over 10,000 volunteer hours to the Greater Covington community annually. Our members are committed to reaching out to provide quality educational and cultural opportunities, which enrich the lives of the citizens of our community. Through numerous fundraisers, including the Harvest Cup Polo Classic, *Roux To Do* cookbook, The Junior League Showhouse, Walk of Art, and our Annual Attic Sale, the League is able to continue its financial support of designated Greater Covington volunteer programs for child advocacy, public education, the elderly, and the arts.

Ah Roux, The Ubiquitous Roux

Roux: Simply a combination of oil and flour stirred slowly and constantly to make a brown-colored mixture that is the basis for many south Louisiana dishes such as gumbo, stew, sauce piquante (pEE-kawnt), and court-bouillon (COO-bee-yawn).

I am constantly amazed that such a simple preparation is a subject that continues to be debated by both the locals and the newcomers who find themselves trying to learn the ins and outs of Louisiana cuisine. It appears that just about every cook and chef in Louisiana has his or her style of preparation, and there are really no hard-and-fast rules about making a roux. Some cooks tell you that a roux is made by combining equal parts of oil (usually vegetable or corn oil, and in the old days, lard was used) and all-purpose flour in a heavy pot, then stirring slowly and constantly on medium heat until the desired color is reached (and that is yet another feature of roux—the color—which will be explained later). Then again, some cooks choose to heat the oil a bit before adding the flour and continuing with the cooking. And yet others may prefer heating the pot before adding the oil-flour mixture. There is also debate about the ratio of oil to flour. Some like more oil; others prefer more flour. It is simply a matter of taste and what you learned at your mother's knee. Of course, Louisianians are fond of constantly experimenting, so you may want to do some testing and research on your own to get the taste that makes YOU happy.

It really doesn't matter how it is made. What does matter is that, should it burn (you can tell when that happens because it separates and has tiny globs of browned or burned bits of flour floating in the oil), it's best to throw it out and begin again. A burnt roux will make whatever dish you are preparing taste awful.

The color of the roux can range from blond (the color of sandpaper) to medium (the color of peanut butter), to dark (the color of chocolate), depending on what type of dish you are preparing. For example, a delicate crab stew may be made with a medium-brown roux, while a dark roux is used for most gumbos and other hearty dishes that demand a richer taste.

So prolific is roux in the cuisine of south Louisiana, a recipe for it is usually incorporated into just about every cookbook about Acadian (Cajun) and Creole cooking.

And I'll tell you how I make mine. I learned to make roux when I was old enough to drag a kitchen stool and perch on it near Mama's stove. She always added the room-temperature oil and flour to the pot at the same time over medium heat.

"Chère, once you start your roux, do not leave it. You must watch it carefully as you slowly stir and stir, just until it reaches just the right color," she explained seriously.

She liked a rich medium-brown roux, and it usually took about 30 minutes to get it to her liking. On the other hand, I learned an alternative method from Papa, an avid sportsman, Boy Scout leader, newspaper editor/publisher, and all-around bon vivant and raconteur. He preferred cooking over a wood fire, especially when he was at the family camp located right outside the levée that contains the Atchafalaya Basin. There he had his campfire site, properly constructed according to the Boy Scout handbook of the time—the 1950s. While he managed the heat of the wood fire, moving his pot to the intensity of the heat he wanted, I sat on a small wooden stool watching with admiration and respect. "T-Black [my nickname], heat the oil just a little bit, not much, before you add the flour," he would say softly.

He was of the school of less oil to flour to make a thicker roux. By the time he had downed two cold beers (about 20 minutes), the dark-brown roux was done since we were cooking on a higher heat than Mama. I couldn't wait until I was old enough to be able to time my roux by drinking two cold beers!

Depending on what I'm cooking, the color and time changes. I agree with Mama about the lighter-colored roux when making a shrimp stew or crawfish stew. I like the golden color of the finished product. But if I'm hankering for a rich duck gumbo, or a chicken and smoked sausage gumbo, I'll opt for a darker-colored roux. I've been known to go through three beers to get that color! As I said before, you may want to experiment with your roux, and I offer these tips:

Don't use canola oil!

Never use self-rising flour!

Focus on the task at hand!

Throw away burnt roux!

Be patient!

Have fun!

After all, cooking is a form of entertainment in Louisiana and there is nothing like spending the better part of the day fooling around in the kitchen. Personally, it's my best therapy! Enjoy!

—Marcelle Bienvenu
Cookbook Author and Co-Author
Times Picayune *Contributor*

Roux Do's and Don'ts

Roux Do's

DO read recipes carefully and all the way through before starting a recipe to make sure you have all the ingredients and understand all the steps. Also, always have your ingredients pre-measured and within arm's reach before starting your recipes, especially when timing is key in properly preparing a recipe.

DO buy extra ingredients for unexpected mistakes or if it's the first time you have made a recipe.

DO sharpen knives frequently; believe it or not, more kitchen accidents occur with dull knives.

DO add a few grains of rice to salt to keep it from clumping.

DO chill your grater in the freezer for a few minutes to make shredding cheese easier.

DO cook meat fat side up for maximum flavor and moisture.

DO rub hands with lemon, then salt, and rinse with cold water to remove garlic, onion, and other cooking odors from your hands. This also works on wooden cutting boards.

DO freeze or dip popcorn kernels in ice water before popping for fewer unpopped kernels or "old maids."

DO add onions first when sautéing onions and garlic. Add the garlic when the onions are just about done.

DO add cinnamon to your coffee grounds when placing them into your coffeemaker for a little spice in the morning.

DO store herbs in a cool, dark place in containers with tight-fitting lids. Glass containers are best because some herbs' characteristics can be altered if they are stored in plastic containers.

DO bring eggs to room temperature for easier separating.

DO plan on serving about 8 different types of appetizers, for a party with more than 45 guests; for less than 45 guests, plan on serving 6 different appetizers; for 14 to 16 guests, plan on serving 4 or 5 different appetizers; and for 8 to 10 guests, plan on serving 3 types of appetizers.

DO use fresh ginger immediately after it has been sliced as the flavor will quickly begin to fade.

Roux Don'ts

DON'T beat eggs in an aluminum bowl as they will darken. Always beat eggs in glass, stainless steel, or porcelain bowls.

DON'T store herbs directly above the stove as heat exposure can change the flavor of herbs.

DON'T make a recipe for the first time for a special occasion. If you want to make a new recipe or dish for a party or special occasion, do a "dry run" by making the recipe earlier in the week to make sure it turns out properly.

DON'T store cooking oils and vinegars in a cupboard over the oven or stove. Store them in a dark, cool cupboard for maximum color and flavor.

DON'T overcook or brown garlic when sautéing. Overcooked garlic will become bitter. Minced garlic usually cooks in less than 1 minute.

DON'T stir rice while it's cooking or it will be sticky. Stirring breaks the grains and releases more starch, which is what makes rice sticky. Instead, just fluff rice when it is done cooking.

DON'T panic if you forgot to soak your beans overnight when making red beans and rice. Here's a quick rescue. Place the dried beans in a pot, cover with water and bring to a boil. After they boil, remove from heat and let them sit for 1 to 2 hours. Drain and use the beans as desired.

Rouxles to Live By—Food for Thought

Anything worth doing is worth overdoing.

"Wine is proof that God loves us and wants us to be happy."
—Benjamin Franklin

—this also applies to chocolate and shoes.

"In matters of style, swim with the current; in matters of principle, stand like a rock."
—Thomas Jefferson

For beautiful lips, say only kind things. For beautiful eyes, look for the good in others.

Even the cheapest wine tastes better when served in good crystal.

Even if you have to lock yourself in the bathroom, try to take 10 minutes every day for yourself, to get your thoughts together, and to reflect on what is going on in your life.

"Cookery is not chemistry. It is an art. It requires instinct and taste rather than exact measurements."
—Marcel Boulestin

Use your silver every day. It will tarnish less and you won't believe how much pleasure you will get from eating your morning cereal or oatmeal with a silver spoon!

Remember, your guests aren't coming to rate your cooking. They are coming to spend time with you.

"What is beautiful is good, and who is good will soon be beautiful."
—Sappho, c.610 B.C.

"There's no love sincerer than the love of food."
—*George Bernard Shaw*

"Wear a smile and have friends; wear a scowl and have wrinkles."
—*George Eliot*

"Nobody can make you feel inferior without your consent."
—*Eleanor Roosevelt*

"Laughter is more contagious than tears."
—*Balinese saying*

Always remember the value of time, the virtue of patience,
and the power of kindness.

It takes good manners to put up with bad ones.

The most important thing you can do for your children is tell them
you love them every day and be sure your actions reflect it.

You will never be sorry if you think before acting and speaking.

Try to be courteous and kind to others. What Mama said about bees and honey really is true.

Never be afraid to try different things and to think outside the box.
After all, Rouxles are meant to be broken!

About Our Authors

Tim Allis is a Senior Editor with *In Style* Magazine.

Marcelle Bienvenu is a native of St. Martinville, Louisiana. Her weekly column, "Creole Cooking," is published in the *Times Picayune* of New Orleans and syndicated throughout Louisiana. Her cookbook *Who's Your Mama, Are You Catholic, and Can You Make a Roux?"* is a compilation of Cajun/Creole recipes and wonderful family stories. Marcelle and Chef Emeril Lagasse co-authored *Louisiana Real and Rustic, Emeril's Creole Christmas, Emeril's T.V. Dinners,* and *Every Day's A Party.* She is currently Editor-in-Chief for the cooking section on Emeril's website. She lives with her husband, Rock Lasserre, on Bayou Teche in St. Martinville.

Sheila Bosworth is the author of *Almost Innocent* and *Slow Poison*, novels set in New Orleans and Covington. Sheila lived in Covington for fifteen years and is now a resident of New Orleans.

Corinne Cook, born and raised in Churchpoint, Louisiana, has been a contributing writer for the Food section of the *Advocate* of Baton Rouge since 1975. Her gourmet columns appear weekly in the *Advocate* under the byline the "Gourmet Galley." Corinne is also the author of her own cookbook, *Extra! Extra! Read All About It.*

Pat Hazell is a regular guest on the *Tonight Show*, one of the original writers for the series *Seinfeld*, and the co-creator of NBC's sitcom *American Pie.* As a playwright, his comedy hits include *The Wonder Bread Years, Bunk Bed Brothers, My Life in 3D,* and *Grounded For Life.* He is referred to as "The Go-To-Guy for Corporate Entertainment" and was recently selected by *New Orleans Magazine* as one of the people to watch in 2003.

Pat and his wife, Sydney, are the parents of two of the brightest shining stars in the universe. The Hazell family resides in Mandeville.

Metsy Hingle is a native of New Orleans who now resides in Covington. Metsy is the award-winning, best-selling author of twenty-one novels. Her current and upcoming romantic suspense novels set in Louisiana include *Behind the Mask, The Wager,* and *Flash Point.*

John R. Kemp is associate director of the Louisiana Endowment for the Humanities and a former staff writer for the New Orleans *Times-Picayune*. He also previously served as associate commissioner for public affairs for the Louisiana Board of Regents for Higher Education and director of news services and publications at Southeastern Louisiana University. John currently writes about the visual arts and historic preservation for a number of regional and national magazines and publications, including *Art & Antiques, ARTnews, American Artist, Louisiana Cultural Vistas, Country Roads, Fodor Guides, Louisiana Life,* and *New Orleans Magazine.* He also has written for *France Magazine, Travel-Holiday, Southwest Art, Southern Magazine, Southern Traveler,* and *Southern Accents.* He covers the regional art scene for *Steppin' Out* on WYES public television in New Orleans. His books include *Alan Flattmann's French Quarter Impressions, Manchac Swamp: Louisiana's Undiscovered Wilderness, New Orleans: An Illustrated History, Lewis Hine: Photographs of Child Labor in the New South, Martin Behrman of New Orleans: Memoirs of a City Boss,* and *Louisiana Images, 1880-1920: A Photographic Essay by George Francois Mugnier.* He resides in Covington with his wife, Betty.

Elizabeth Moore is a Sustaining member of the Junior League of Greater Covington. She has co-authored four children's and young adults' books with Alice Couvillon. They are *Louisiana Indian Tales, Mimi's First Mardi Gras, Mimi and Jean-Paul's Cajun Mardi Gras,* and *Evangeline for Children.* She is a freelance writer for the Covington and Mandeville sections of the *Times-Picayune.* Her column, "North Shore Notables," documents parties and fundraising events in West St. Tammany. Elizabeth also writes feature articles.

Ken Wells, who grew up in Bayou Black near Houma, is an author of Cajun novels and a senior editor and writer for "Page One" of the *Wall Street Journal.* Ken's Cajun novels include *The Catahoula Bayou Trilogy* comprised of *Meely LeBauve, Logan's Storm,* and *Junior's Leg.* When he isn't busy with journalism or pecking away at novels, Wells plunks around on a blues and jazz guitar and often wishes he were fishing.

About Our Cover Artist

Sarah Dunn was born in New Orleans, Louisiana, and raised in an environment surrounded by art. The rich history, vivid stories, and old-time architecture of New Orleans were her first inspirations to create. She explores all aspects of her creativity through sculpture, drawing, woodworking, metal, and glass.

Sometimes oils, pastels, or watercolors are incorporated into her paintings, but it is acrylic which conveys her ideas most fluidly. Her work has been described as full of movement and shape with a great understanding of color. Her subject matter explores the human figure, landscapes, still life, and the purely abstract. Dunn pulls her inspiration from many places such as nature, architecture, music, and literature.

Most recently her work has been featured in Chicago and Los Angeles. After hurricane Katrina she returned home to open the Sarah Dunn Art contemporary gallery in downtown Covington, where she strives to bring new and interesting art to the public.

More of her work can be viewed at Sarah Dunn Art Studio Gallery, 609 East Boston Street, Covington, Louisiana 70433, or on-line at www.sarahdunnart.com.

About Our Photographer

Timothy Dunford is one of the Northshore's premiere commercial photographers. He is a regular contributor to *Inside Northside* magazine and is recognized for producing dynamic images of art, architecture, and people. Tim welcomes visitors to his new website, www.timothydunford.com.

He married a local Louisiana girl and transplanted from southern California to battle humidity and rising cholesterol. He is a proud father and makes the best homemade pizza in St. Tammany Parish.

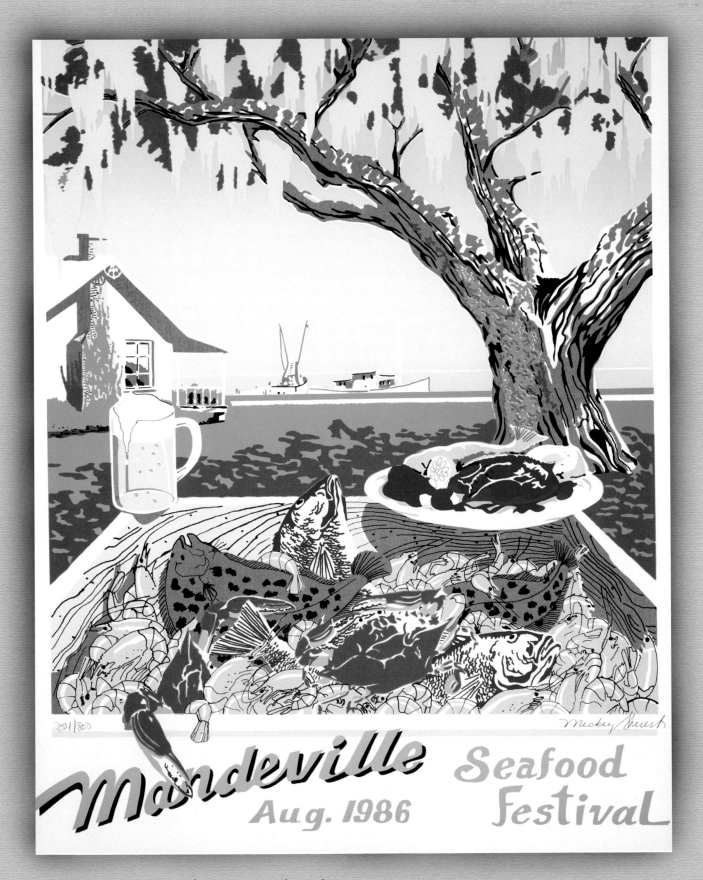

The Prelude...Appetizers

Being Sent to Mandeville

"If you keep acting like that, they will send you to Mandeville!" For years this has been a threat to anyone growing up in Louisiana that was behaving unusually.

When my father-in-law married a woman from Mandeville, his friends told him, "You must be crazy." This was the same thing my show business associates declared when I transferred to the sleepy hamlet of Mandeville from the thriving metropolis of Los Angeles. They slung phrases around like, "You're nuts," "You're out of your mind," and "You should have your head examined."

Yes, one must be a little crazy to survive in Old Mandeville, with restaurants like Juniper, Nuvolari's, Vianne's Tea Salon, and The Broken Egg Café. Suffering through all the family entertainment at the Mandeville's Trailhead. Experiencing a night of jazz revival in the restored Dew Drop Social & Benevolent Hall. Viewing original productions at The North Star Theatre. Riding bikes on the Trace or watching fireworks explode over the north shore of Lake Pontchartrain. We are all insane.

Now that I am a resident, or rather an inmate, I warn people to stay away from this area. Why ruin a good thing? A cry of "Don't send me to Mandeville!" is an updated version of "Don't throw me in the briar patch!"

If living in the heart of Old Mandeville makes me completely certifiable, then tighten the buckles on my straightjacket and fluff up the padded walls because I'm staying awhile. In fact, I am willing to commit my entire family to enjoying this crazy town as long as we all live here.

Everyone knows that in all great institutions it's the real nuts that last the longest and have the best time.

What does this have to do with the Junior League's cookbook? Try a recipe with pecans in it... They're nuts, too.

—Pat Hazell
Author, Playwright,
and Comedian

Mrs. Hays' Stuffed Chicken Wings

Courtesy of Emeril Lagasse, Nola Restaurant

CHICKEN WINGS
¼ cup chopped green onions
¼ cup finely chopped celery hearts
2 tablespoons sugar
¼ cup plus 1 tablespoon finely chopped
uncooked shrimp
2 cups finely chopped white onions
¼ cup finely chopped fresh cilantro
2 ounces wood ear black mushrooms, chopped
1 pound ground pork
Salt and pepper to taste
Fish sauce to taste
12 to 18 chicken wings
3 tablespoons Creole seasoning
½ cup flour
Vegetable oil for deep-frying

HOISIN SAUCE
3 jalapeño chiles, seeded and finely chopped
½ cup sugar
4 cups (1 quart) hoisin sauce
2 cups water
Juice of 2 small limes
2 tablespoons minced garlic

GARNISHES
2 tablespoons finely chopped parsley
¼ cup chopped roasted peanuts

For the chicken wings, combine the green onions, celery, sugar, shrimp, white onions, cilantro, mushrooms and pork in a mixing bowl and mix thoroughly. Season with salt, pepper and fish sauce. Slice the wings along the bone in order to leave the skin and meat attached. Sever the first joint of the chicken wings and remove the bones. Slide the knife along the underside of the skin and separate to the joint, holding tightly to keep the joint intact. Season the chicken wings inside and out with 1 tablespoon of the Creole seasoning. Roll back the skin and remove the bones. Cut the edges of the skin and stuff the shrimp mixture into the cavity. Lay the leftover meat and skin over the top to enclose the filling. Place on a baking sheet.

Bake at 325 degrees for 20 minutes. Remove from the oven and cool completely. Season the flour with 1 tablespoon of the Creole seasoning. Dredge the cooled wings in the flour mixture.

Preheat oil to 360 degrees in a wok or large stockpot. Arrange the wings carefully in batches in the hot oil. Fry each batch for 3 to 4 minutes or until golden brown and crispy. Drain on paper towels. Season with the remaining 1 tablespoon Creole seasoning.

For the hoisin sauce, purée the jalapeño chiles with the sugar in a food processor. Add the hoisin sauce, water, lime juice and garlic. Purée until fully incorporated. Pour into a 2-quart container. Let stand for 1 hour or until the sugar dissolves, stirring occasionally.

To serve, arrange the chicken wings on a lettuce-lined platter. Drizzle the hoisin sauce over the top. Garnish with the parsley and peanuts.

Makes 12 to 18 stuffed wings and 1½ quarts sauce

Mandeville Seafood Festival

No, we don't have a Fourth of July parade, silly; parades in Louisiana are for Mardi Gras and St. Patrick's Day. Our Independence Day tradition is—what else—a festival! We celebrate America's birthday at the Mandeville Seafood Festival held on the scenic Mandeville lakefront. Live music and dancing, fireworks, and lots of delicious fresh Louisiana seafood highlight the festival, which can be enjoyed from land or while floating in your boat on the waters of Lake Pontchartrain.
The Mandeville Seafood Festival is held on the weekend closest to the Fourth of July at the Lakefront Harbor in Mandeville. For more information, go to www.seafoodfest.com.

Andouille Puff with Roasted Peppers

2 teaspoons olive oil
12 ounces chicken or pork andouille,
cut into 1/2-inch pieces
2 1/4 cups milk
3/4 cup finely ground cornmeal
Salt and freshly ground pepper to taste
3/4 cup thinly sliced roasted red bell peppers
1/2 cup sour cream
1/2 cup chopped green onion tops
3 egg yolks, lightly beaten
5 egg whites
Pinch of salt
1 cup (4 ounces) crumbled firm ricotta cheese

Heat the olive oil in a large skillet over medium-high heat. Add the sausage. Sauté for 3 to 4 minutes or until light brown.

Bring the milk to a simmer in a medium saucepan over medium heat. Add the cornmeal in a slow steady stream, whisking constantly. Season with salt and pepper to taste. Reduce the heat to medium-low. Cook for 10 to 12 minutes or until thickened and slightly stiff, whisking constantly. Fold in the sautéed sausage, bell peppers, sour cream, green onion tops and egg yolks until mixed. Remove from the heat. Cover the pan tightly with plastic wrap.

Beat the egg whites in a mixing bowl until frothy. Add a pinch of salt. Beat until stiff peaks form. Stir 1/2 cup of the beaten egg whites into the cornmeal mixture until smooth. Fold in the remaining egg whites. Fold in the cheese. Pour immediately into a buttered 10-inch braiser pan.

Place on the oven rack in the lower third of the oven. Bake at 425 degrees for 10 minutes. Reduce the oven temperature to 375 degrees. Bake for 25 to 30 minutes longer or until the top is golden brown and the puff is more than doubled in height. Cool slightly before serving.

Serves 6

NOTE: You may substitute queso fresco for the ricotta cheese if available.

Chicken and Shrimp Potstickers

POTSTICKERS
1 pound ground chicken
1 pound ground shrimp
4 teaspoons chopped fresh gingerroot
4 cups finely shredded white cabbage
2 cups finely cut shiitake mushrooms
1/4 cup chopped cilantro
2 medium red onions, finely chopped
Salt and pepper to taste
24 dumpling wrappers
4 egg yolks, lightly beaten
1/4 cup sesame seed oil
1/4 cup water

GINGER SAUCE
2 teaspoons crystallized ginger
2 tablespoons soy sauce
1 1/2 tablespoons rice wine vinegar
1 tablespoon toasted sesame oil
1 tablespoon minced green onions
1 teaspoon sesame seeds, toasted

For the potstickers, mix the chicken, shrimp, gingerroot, cabbage, mushrooms, cilantro and onions in a bowl. Season with salt and pepper. Cover and chill for 1 hour.

Place the dumpling wrappers on a flat surface. Brush the edges of the wrappers with the egg yolks. Place 1 tablespoonful of the chicken mixture in the middle of each wrapper. Fold the wrappers to enclose the filling and press the edges to seal. Sauté in the sesame seed oil in a large skillet until golden brown. Add the water. Cook, covered, for 5 minutes.

For the ginger sauce, purée the ginger in a food processor. Combine the ginger purée, soy sauce, vinegar, sesame oil, green onions and sesame seeds in a small saucepan and mix well. Cook over medium-low heat for 1 to 2 minutes or until bubbles appear around the edge. Remove from the heat. Let stand for 20 to 30 minutes.

Serve the potstickers with the ginger sauce.

Serves 12

NOTE: To toast sesame seeds to bring out their nutty flavor, sauté in a small sauté pan over medium heat for 2 minutes or until golden brown.

Chafing Dish Duck

3 ducks (more if using teal)
Salt and black pepper to taste
Worcestershire sauce to taste
3 tablespoons vegetable oil
3 tablespoons flour
1 cup chopped onion
1 cup chopped bell pepper
1 cup sliced celery
2 garlic cloves, minced
1/2 cup water
Apple or orange quarters
1 cup jelly (any flavor)
3 slices bacon, cut into halves
1 cup red wine
6 small green onions, finely chopped
1/4 cup (1/2 stick) butter
3/4 cup dry red wine
1 cup Franco-American gravy, or brown gravy
Dash of lemon juice
2 (6-ounce) cans sliced mushrooms, drained
Red pepper to taste

Rinse each duck and pat dry. Season each duck inside and out with salt, black pepper and Worcestershire sauce. Arrange in a baking pan. Bake at 500 degrees until brown. Remove from the oven. Reduce the oven temperature to 300 degrees.

Cook the oil and flour in a saucepan to make a roux, stirring constantly. Add 1/2 of the vegetables to the roux. Cook until the vegetables are wilted. Blend in the garlic and water. Remove from the heat. Mix the remaining vegetables in a bowl.

Stuff the cavities of the ducks with apple quarters. Season with salt and black pepper. Spread the jelly over the duck breasts. Place in a deep roasting pan. Spoon the uncooked vegetable mixture over the ducks. Spoon the roux mixture over the uncooked vegetables. Criss-cross the bacon halves over the ducks and vegetables. Pour 1 cup wine over the ducks.

Bake, covered, for 2 to 3 hours or until the duck is almost falling off the bone, basting frequently with the wine and drippings. Remove the ducks from the pan, reserving the drippings. Let the duck cool slightly. Shred the ducks, discarding the skin and bones.

Sauté the green onions in the butter in a skillet until soft. Add 3/4 cup wine. Cook until the liquid is reduced by 1/2. Add the gravy, lemon juice, reserved pan drippings and mushrooms. Add the shredded duck and mix well. Season with salt, black pepper and red pepper. Spoon into a chafing dish. Serve with party rolls or melba toast.

Serves 10 to 12

NOTE: For an entrée, serve over fluffy white rice.

The Art of Sportsman's Paradise

How do you know it's duck season in South Louisiana? Suddenly, every pickup truck has a pet porter in the back because duck hunting just wouldn't be the same without the faithful Labrador to bring back the quarry. Louisiana lies on one of the main flyways used by migrating ducks and offers a great habitat for the winter. Successful conservation efforts have made it a hunter's— and a duck eater's—paradise.

Sponsored by Resource Bank

34366000022673

Duck Spring Rolls with Dipping Sauce

SPRING ROLLS
1 duck, cut into quarters
8 cups (2 quarts) water
1 cup sliced celery
1 bay leaf
8 peppercorns
1 onion, cut into quarters
2 cups shredded green cabbage
¼ cup shredded carrots
2 tablespoons chopped green onions
1 teaspoon grated fresh gingerroot
1 tablespoon cornstarch
1 tablespoon dry sherry
1 tablespoon soy sauce
1 tablespoon sesame oil
1 egg yolk
1 teaspoon water
14 to 16 (7×7-inch) egg roll skins
4 cups vegetable oil

DIPPING SAUCE
½ cup ketchup
¼ cup white vinegar
¼ to ½ cup sugar
2 to 6 dashes of hot sauce, or to taste

For the spring rolls, combine the duck pieces, 8 cups water, celery, bay leaf, peppercorns and onion in a 6-quart Dutch oven or stockpot with a heavy bottom. Bring to a boil over medium-high heat. Reduce the heat to medium. Cook for 20 to 25 minutes or until the duck is tender, skimming off the foam occasionally. Drain the duck, reserving the broth. Let the duck cool slightly. Shred the duck, discarding the skin and bones. Strain the reserved broth into a freezer-safe container, discarding the solids. Freeze the broth for future use.

Combine the shredded duck, cabbage, carrots, green onions, gingerroot, cornstarch, sherry, soy sauce and sesame oil in a large bowl and mix well. Blend the egg yolk and 1 teaspoon water in a bowl.

To assemble, place an egg roll skin on a lightly floured surface with 1 point of the square pointing toward you. Place about 2 heaping tablespoons of the duck mixture just below the center of the egg roll skin. Fold the bottom point of the egg roll skin over the mixture and roll up, folding in the sides. Brush the top point with the egg yolk mixture and continue rolling to complete the seal. Repeat with the remaining duck mixture, egg roll skins and egg yolk mixture.

Heat the oil in a 12-inch nonstick skillet or wok over medium-high heat. Fry the rolls 3 or 4 at a time for 3 to 4 minutes or until golden brown, turning once. Drain on paper towels.

For the dipping sauce, combine the ketchup, vinegar, sugar and hot sauce in a bowl and blend well.

Serve the spring rolls hot or at room temperature with the dipping sauce.

Makes 14 to 16 spring rolls

Beignets de la Mer

¹/₃ pound fresh tilapia
1 egg
¹/₄ cup heavy cream
1 tablespoon fresh lemon juice
2 dashes of hot sauce
1 teaspoon salt
¹/₂ teaspoon cayenne pepper
¹/₂ teaspoon white pepper
1 teaspoon chopped green onions
1 tablespoon dill weed
4 ounces small shrimp, peeled and deveined
4 ounces crawfish meat
4 ounces lump crab meat, shells removed
8 cups (2 quarts) vegetable oil
1 egg
1 egg white
6 ounces beer
2¹/₄ cups self-rising flour

Cut the fish into 1-inch pieces. Purée the fish, 1 egg, heavy cream, lemon juice, hot sauce, salt, cayenne pepper and white pepper in a food processor. Pour into a bowl. Fold in the green onions, dill weed, shrimp, crawfish meat and crab meat. Chill for 30 minutes.

Heat the oil to 325 degrees in a heavy bottomed stockpot or cast-iron pot. Whisk 1 egg, the egg white and beer in a bowl. Add 1¹/₄ cups of the flour and mix well. Shape the seafood mixture into 2-ounce cakes. Sprinkle with the remaining 1 cup flour. Dip into the beer batter. Place the beignets carefully in the hot oil. Fry for 2 minutes on each side. Serve with Jeanne's Rémoulade Sauce (page 191).

Serves 6 to 8

Cajun Curry Bundles

¹/₃ cup plain yogurt
¹/₂ cup shredded coconut
¹/₃ cup finely chopped cashews
¹/₄ cup mango chutney, chopped
1¹/₂ teaspoons curry powder
¹/₂ teaspoon grated fresh gingerroot
2 ounces lump crab meat, shells removed
2 ounces crawfish meat, fat removed and coarsely chopped
2 ounces shrimp, cooked, peeled, deveined and coarsely chopped
12 sheets phyllo
1 cup (2 sticks) butter, melted

GARNISH
18 fresh chives

Combine the yogurt, coconut, cashews, chutney, curry powder and gingerroot in a bowl and mix well. Fold in the crab meat, crawfish meat and shrimp. Unfold the phyllo. Place 1 phyllo sheet on a large cutting board lined with waxed paper. Cover the remaining phyllo with a damp paper towel to prevent the phyllo from drying out. Brush the phyllo sheet generously with melted butter. Top with 3 more phyllo sheets to form a 4-layer stack, brushing each layer with butter. Cut the stack into 6 squares. Place 1 to 1¹/₂ tablespoons of the seafood mixture in the center of each square. Bring the 4 corners of each square together over the center of the filling and pinch and twist to enclose and form bundles. Repeat with the remaining phyllo and filling. Arrange the bundles on an ungreased baking sheet. Bake at 375 degrees for 18 to 20 minutes or until golden brown. Tie a chive around the neck of each bundle for garnish. Serve warm.

Makes about 18 bundles

NOTE: To freeze, prepare the bundles as directed, but do not bake. Freeze on the baking sheet and then place in an airtight freezer container. Do not thaw before baking.

Caviar Pie

DON'T PASS THIS ONE UP. EVEN PEOPLE
WHO DON'T LIKE CAVIAR END UP LOVING
THIS ONCE THEY TRY IT.

6 hard-cooked eggs
2 to 3 tablespoons mayonnaise
1 tablespoon pepper
2 tablespoons finely chopped parsley
1 cup finely chopped green onions
3 (4-ounce) jars black caviar, drained
Juice of 1 lemon, strained
2 cups sour cream

GARNISHES
1 (4-ounce) jar orange caviar
Parsley sprigs

Mash the hard-cooked eggs in a bowl. Add the
mayonnaise, pepper, parsley and green onions
and mix well. Butter a 9- to 10-inch plate or
cake stand with a small lip. Spread the egg
mixture on the plate to form a crust. Chill for
4 hours.

Place the black caviar in a colander and
sprinkle with the lemon juice. Place the
colander in a bowl big enough to catch the
liquid but deep enough that the caviar is not
sitting in the drained liquid. Chill for at least
1 hour to allow the caviar to drain well. Blot
the bottom of the colander with paper towels
to soak up any excess liquid.

Spread the caviar over the egg crust, being
careful not to break the caviar. Stir the sour
cream until creamy. Spread over the caviar
layer. Chill, covered, for 1 hour. Spoon some of
the orange caviar in the center and along the
edge of the pie for garnish. Garnish with
parsley sprigs. Serve with a basket of melba
rounds or Triscuits. For individual servings, cut
into small wedges and serve on individual
plates with toast points.

Serves 10 to 12

Deviled Eggs Luziane

12 eggs
1 tablespoon olive oil
12 ounces medium shrimp,
cooked, peeled and deveined
$1/2$ cup mayonnaise
2 tablespoons minced parsley
1 tablespoon capers, drained and chopped
1 medium shallot, minced
1 garlic clove, finely minced
2 teaspoons fresh dill weed, chopped
Kosher salt and freshly ground pepper to taste
1 (4-ounce) jar black caviar (optional)

GARNISH
24 small sprigs of dill weed

Place the eggs in a large saucepan and cover
with cold water. Bring to a boil over medium
heat. Reduce the heat to low. Simmer for
5 minutes. Remove from the heat and cover
with a tight-fitting lid. Let stand, covered, for
15 to 20 minutes; drain. Place the eggs in a
large bowl of ice water and chill thoroughly.
Peel the eggs and cut into halves lengthwise.
Carefully remove the yolks from the eggs,
being careful not to tear the egg whites. Place
the yolks in a bowl and mash lightly with a
fork. Arrange the egg whites on a serving platter.

Reserve 12 shrimp for garnish and cut into
halves. Chop the remaining shrimp coarsely.
Fold the chopped shrimp, mayonnaise, parsley,
capers, shallot, garlic and dill weed into the
egg yolks. Season with kosher salt and pepper.
Mound a heaping rounded tablespoonful of
the mixture into each egg white half. Spoon
about $1/8$ teaspoon of caviar on the top of each.
Garnish each with a shrimp half and sprig
of dill weed.

Serves 12

ROUX DO: Do pack deviled eggs, egg salad, or
other egg-based food with ice in an insulated
bag or ice chest to keep chilled if you are
taking them to a picnic or outdoor event.

Mandeville Marinated Oysters

1 gallon oysters
½ cup vinegar
½ cup olive oil
½ cup ketchup
½ teaspoon horseradish
1 teaspoon salt
Pepper to taste
½ cup thinly sliced green onions

GARNISH
6 thin lemon slices

Drain the oysters well and place in a medium bowl. Mix the vinegar, olive oil, ketchup, horseradish, salt, pepper and green onions in a bowl. Pour over the oysters to cover completely. Marinate, covered, in the refrigerator for 12 hours, turning the oysters gently every few hours. Fill a large serving bowl half full with ice. Insert the bowl of oysters into the ice. Garnish with the lemon slices. Serve with crackers using cocktail forks.

Serves 12 to 14

NOTE: You may double or triple this recipe.

All around Lake Pontchartrain, sailors await the first breezes and clear days that signal it's time to hoist up the sails. On any day, sailboats such as baby Optimists and Lasers can be seen heading out of Northshore marinas alongside their bigger cousins, sixty- and seventy-foot cruisers. The sight of the sailboats skimming along the water makes the daily trip across Lake Pontchartrain an enjoyable commute.

Sponsored by Melinda's

Fried Oysters with Brie

1 egg, beaten
¾ cup ketchup
2 tablespoons Worcestershire sauce
2 teaspoons Louisiana hot sauce
1 teaspoon celery salt
1 quart oysters, drained
2 cups cornmeal
2 tablespoons Creole seasoning
½ teaspoon white pepper
½ teaspoon black pepper
Vegetable oil for frying
8 ounces Brie cheese
1 package mixed salad greens
3 lemons, quartered

Mix the egg, ketchup, Worcestershire sauce, hot sauce and celery salt in a bowl. Add the oysters. Marinate in the refrigerator for 1 hour. Mix the cornmeal, Creole seasoning, white pepper and black pepper in a shallow dish.

Pour oil into a large deep skillet to a depth of at least 3 inches. Heat the oil to 350 degrees. Drain the oysters, discarding the marinade. Roll each oyster in the cornmeal mixture to coat, shaking off the excess. Fry the oysters in small batches in the oil until golden brown. (Do not overcrowd the skillet or the oysters will become soggy.) Drain the oysters on paper towels and keep warm in a 250-degree oven.

Cut the rind from the cheese and discard. Cut the cheese into cubes and place in a microwave-safe bowl. Microwave on High at 30-second intervals until melted and smooth, stirring after each interval.

Divide the salad greens among 6 serving plates. Arrange the fried oysters on the salad greens and drizzle with the melted cheese. Serve with the lemon quarters.

Serves 6

ROUX DO: Do sprinkle salt in your skillet to prevent splattering.

Shrimp and Tasso with Five-Pepper Jelly

Courtesy of Commander's Palace, New Orleans

FIVE-PEPPER JELLY
1½ cups light corn syrup
1¼ cups cane vinegar or white vinegar
½ teaspoon red pepper flakes
Salt and freshly ground black pepper to taste
1 red bell pepper, seeded and finely chopped
1 yellow bell pepper, seeded and
finely chopped
1 green bell pepper, seeded and finely chopped
4 jalapeño chiles, finely chopped

LOUISIANA HOT SAUCE BEURRE BLANC
⅓ cup Louisiana hot sauce or
hot sauce of choice
2 tablespoons minced shallots
6 medium garlic cloves, minced
¼ cup heavy cream
6 tablespoons unsalted butter, softened
Kosher salt to taste

SHRIMP AND TASSO
24 jumbo shrimp, peeled and deveined
1 ounce boneless tasso, cut into 1-inch strips
½ cup sifted flour
Creole seasoning to taste
½ cup vegetable oil

ASSEMBLY
12 pickled okra, cut into halves lengthwise

NOTE: Sometimes tasso will have a lot of bone, resulting in a poor yield of meat.

For the jelly, combine the corn syrup, vinegar and red pepper flakes in a small saucepan. Season with salt and black pepper. Cook until thickened and reduced by ⅔. Remove from the heat. (The mixture will become even thicker as it cools. This is called a gastrique.) Sauté the bell peppers and jalapeño chiles in a hot skillet for 30 seconds or until their color is brightened. Add to the gastrique with a slotted spoon.

For the beurre blanc, combine the hot sauce, shallots, garlic and heavy cream in a small saucepan. Simmer over medium heat until reduced by ½, stirring frequently. Add the butter a small amount at a time, whipping constantly and being careful not to let the sauce break. (The cream acts as a stabilizer.) Strain the warm sauce into a bowl, discarding the solids. Season with kosher salt.

For the shrimp and tasso, make a ¼-inch-deep slit down the back of each shrimp. Insert 1 tasso strip into each incision and secure with a wooden pick. Mix the flour and Creole seasoning together. Lightly dust the shrimp with the seasoned flour.

Fry the shrimp in the oil in a large skillet over medium heat for about 30 seconds on each side or until the shrimp are firm with a nice red-brown color. Remove the shrimp to drain on paper towels for a few seconds. Toss the shrimp and beurre blanc in a bowl to coat thoroughly. Remove the wooden picks.

To assemble and serve, place a portion of the jelly on each of 8 appetizer plates. Arrange 3 shrimp on each plate, alternating with 3 pieces of pickled okra.

Serves 8

Marinated Chèvre

2 (5-ounce) logs chèvre, or goat cheese
Freshly ground pepper to taste
1/2 teaspoon chopped garlic
3 tablespoons thinly sliced canned or
fresh-roasted red bell peppers
2 tablespoons sun-dried tomato strips
8 kalamata olives, pitted and sliced
1/2 cup sliced red onion or Vidalia onion
1 tablespoon fresh rosemary, basil or
oregano, chopped
3/4 cup extra-virgin olive oil

Cut the cheese into rounds about 1 inch thick. Place in a shallow dish large enough for the slices to fit comfortably. Sprinkle with pepper. Top each round equally with the garlic, bell peppers, sun-dried tomatoes, olives, onion and rosemary. Pour the olive oil over the top to barely cover. Marinate, covered, in the refrigerator for 1 to 2 days before serving. Serve with crackers or toast rounds.

Serves 8

Roux Do: Do use dried sun-dried tomatoes if you cannot find sun-dried tomatoes packed in oil. To soften them for use, pour hot water over them and let stand for 15 to 20 minutes.

Rosemary Chèvre

2 (3-ounce) logs chèvre, or goat cheese
1 tablespoon fresh rosemary leaves, chopped
1/2 cup extra-virgin olive oil
3 tablespoons lemon juice

Place the cheese logs in a shallow dish. Sprinkle evenly with the rosemary. Pour the olive oil and lemon juice evenly over the top. Serve immediately or let stand until the flavors meld.

Serves 8

Marinated Chèvre is a favorite of ours and borrowed from Barrie Aycock, who, with her husband, Bobby, owns Glen-Ella Springs Inn in Clayton, Georgia. Clayton is ninety miles north of Atlanta, tucked away in the Northeast Georgia mountains. The charming inn dates back to 1890 and is surrounded by the lovely Chattahoochee National Forest. It's a great place to relax in rocking chairs on the porch, listen to birds sing, and enjoy gourmet Southern cuisine. On a visit several years ago, a guest of the inn was speaking with Bobby about some high school heroic exploits while Bobby tended the front desk. For no apparent reason, the lights in the inn blinked off and on again. The guest was somewhat taken aback when Bobby chirped, "Every time somebody tells a lie in this place, the lights go out!"

—*Mr. and Mrs. Michael A. Meiners*

Checkerboard Cheese

½ cup extra-virgin olive oil
½ cup white wine vinegar
1 (2-ounce) jar diced pimento, drained
¼ cup parsley, chopped
3 tablespoons minced green onions
3 garlic cloves, minced
1 teaspoon sugar
1 teaspoon basil
½ teaspoon salt
½ teaspoon freshly ground pepper
8 ounces sharp Cheddar cheese, chilled
8 ounces cream cheese, chilled
8 ounces Monterey Jack cheese, chilled

Combine the olive oil, vinegar, pimento, parsley, green onions, garlic, sugar, basil, salt and pepper in a jar with a tight-fitting lid. Secure the lid to the jar and shake to mix well.

Cut the Cheddar cheese into halves lengthwise. Cut each half into slices ¼ inch thick. Repeat with the cream cheese and Monterey Jack cheese. Arrange the Cheddar cheese, cream cheese and Monterey Jack cheese alternately on edge in a shallow baking dish or lipped serving tray to form a checkerboard pattern. Shake the marinade and pour over the cheese arrangement.

Marinate, covered, in the refrigerator for at least 8 hours before serving.

Serves 24

Nord du Lac Bruschetta

1 baguette with sesame seeds
4 to 6 tablespoons extra-virgin olive oil
1 tablespoon minced garlic
½ teaspoon freshly ground pepper
1 tablespoon freshly grated pecorino
Romano cheese
1 green, yellow or red bell pepper,
cut into thin strips
2 plum tomatoes, cut into ¼-inch slices
3 green onions, cut into ¼-inch slices
½ cup (2 ounces) shredded mozzarella cheese,
asiago cheese, Saga blue cheese or crumbled
Gorgonzola cheese
4 ounces fresh mushrooms,
cut into ⅛-inch slices
4 ounces thinly sliced prosciutto or smoked
ham, cut into ½-inch strips
Freshly grated pecorino Romano
cheese to taste

Cut the baguette into halves lengthwise and place cut side up on a baking sheet. Mix the olive oil, garlic, pepper and 1 tablespoon Romano cheese in a bowl. Spread over the cut sides of the baguette. Arrange the bell pepper, tomatoes and green onions on each half. Sprinkle with the mozzarella cheese. Top with the mushrooms and prosciutto.

Bake at 350 degrees for 5 to 10 minutes or until the cheese melts. Broil for 2 to 3 minutes or until the cheese begins to brown. Cut into 2-inch slices. Sprinkle with Romano cheese to taste.

Serves 8

Bacon Cheese Bites

3 cups (12 ounces) shredded sharp
Cheddar cheese
1 (4-ounce) can sliced black olives
1 cup finely chopped green onions
¼ to ½ cup chopped jalapeño chiles
1 cup mayonnaise
1 cup crumbled crisp-cooked bacon
1 package cocktail rye bread

Combine the cheese, olives, green onions, jalapeño chiles, mayonnaise and bacon in a bowl and mix well. Spread on the bread. (At this point, you may freeze on baking sheets, stack in sealable plastic bags and store in the freezer.)

Place on a baking sheet. Bake at 300 degrees for 15 to 20 minutes or until bubbly.

Serves 8

NOTE: Make ahead and store in the freezer so you can pop as many as you need into the oven to serve unexpected guests or for a little snack.

Cheese Straws

1 pound extra-sharp Cheddar cheese, shredded
¾ cup (1½ sticks) butter, softened
¾ cup (1½ sticks) margarine, softened
1 teaspoon cayenne pepper, or to taste
4 cups (1 pound) flour, sifted

Mix the cheese, butter, margarine and cayenne pepper with dough hooks in a mixing bowl. Add the flour 1 cup at a time, mixing well after each addition. Place the dough in a cookie press fitted with a large star tip. Press in strips onto a lightly greased baking sheet. Bake at 350 degrees for 10 to 15 minutes or until light brown. Cool on the baking sheet.

Makes about 8 dozen

The Art of the Oak

A Mandeville landmark is the Seven Sisters Oak, a live oak estimated to be over 1,200 years old. The tree is located in the Lewisburg area of Mandeville on the shores of Lake Pontchartrain and measures forty feet in circumference. The Seven Sisters Oak is the President of the Live Oak Society, a very exclusive club comprised only of live oak trees having a girth, or "waistline," of eight feet or greater, and one human member, a chairman who is responsible for registering and recording its members. The Seven Sisters Oak is the largest live oak tree known in the United States, thus its office as President of the Society. Some say the tree got its name because at one time it was thought to be seven trees that had grown closely together. In actuality, it is one tree with seven separate trunks. Others say that it was named by its owner, who was one of seven sisters. Regardless of how it came to be called the Seven Sisters Oak, this majestic tree is truly one of the Northshore's greatest treasures.

Sponsored by Beau Chêne Country Club

Friendship Bread

EVERYONE LOVES THIS AND ALWAYS ASKS FOR THE RECIPE.

1 large round loaf Hawaiian bread
4 cups (16 ounces) shredded sharp
Cheddar cheese
8 ounces cream cheese, softened
8 ounces sour cream
1/2 cup finely chopped green onions
2 (4-ounce) cans chopped green chiles, drained
1 to 1 1/2 cups chopped ham, crumbled crisp-cooked bacon, chopped cooked turkey or a combination

Cut the top from the bread and scoop out the center to form a bread bowl, reserving the top and center. Tear the reserved bread center into bite-size pieces.

Combine the Cheddar cheese, cream cheese, sour cream, green onions, green chiles and ham in a bowl and mix well. (The mixture will be stiff.) Spoon into the bread bowl. Replace the top and place on a baking sheet. Bake at 350 degrees for 1 hour and 10 minutes. (The outside of the bread may blacken a little, but this won't affect the taste.) Serve with the reserved bread pieces or tortilla chips for dipping.

Serves 8

NOTE: You may substitute light ingredients, but do not substitute fat-free ingredients.

Gougères

1 cup water
5 tablespoons butter
1 teaspoon salt
1/4 teaspoon freshly ground pepper
1/4 teaspoon freshly ground nutmeg
1 cup flour
1 cup (4 ounces) shredded Gruyère cheese
5 eggs, at room temperature
1 1/2 teaspoons water

Combine 1 cup water, the butter, salt, pepper and nutmeg in a medium saucepan. Bring to a boil over medium-high heat. Cook until the butter melts. Reduce the heat to low. Add the flour. Cook for 1 minute or until the mixture pulls away from the side of the pan, beating constantly with a wooden spoon. Remove from the heat. Add the cheese and beat with a wooden spoon until the cheese is incorporated. Add 4 of the eggs 1 at a time, beating well after each addition. Continue to beat until the mixture is smooth, shiny and firm.

Drop the batter by small spoonfuls onto a lightly greased baking sheet. Brush with a mixture of the remaining egg and 1 1/2 teaspoons water. Place on a rack in the upper third of the oven. Bake at 425 degrees for 15 to 20 minutes or until golden brown and doubled in size. Remove from the oven. Serve hot or cool to room temperature.

Makes 3 dozen

Variation: Add 4 ounces smoked salmon to the batter and prepare as above. Fill a pastry bag fitted with a tip with a wide opening with a mixture of sour cream and chopped fresh dill weed. Pipe into the cooled Gougères.

Pesto and Sun-Dried Tomato Torta

5 garlic cloves
1½ cups packed fresh basil leaves
¼ cup pine nuts
2 tablespoons extra-virgin olive oil
1 teaspoon fresh lemon juice
2⅔ cups (about 21 ounces) cream cheese, softened
¼ cup (1 ounce) freshly grated Parmesan cheese
1⅓ cups drained oil-packed sun-dried tomatoes
⅓ cup tomato paste
¾ cup (1½ sticks) butter, softened
Salt and pepper to taste

GARNISHES
Sprigs of fresh basil
Toasted pine nuts

Process the garlic in a food processor until finely chopped. Add the basil, ¼ cup pine nuts, olive oil and lemon juice and process until blended. Add ⅓ cup of the cream cheese and the Parmesan cheese and pulse until blended. Spoon the pesto into a medium bowl.

Process the sun-dried tomatoes in the food processor until coarsely chopped. Add the tomato paste. Process until almost smooth. Add ⅓ cup of the cream cheese and blend well.

Beat the remaining 2 cups cream cheese and butter in a large mixing bowl until fluffy. Season with salt and pepper.

Spray a 6-cup soufflé dish with nonstick cooking spray. Line with plastic wrap, leaving an overhang over the side. Spread ¾ cup of the butter mixture evenly over the bottom of the prepared dish. Layer ½ of the tomato mixture, ½ cup of the remaining butter mixture and ½ of the pesto over the butter layer. Continue to layer with ½ cup of the remaining butter mixture, remaining tomato mixture and remaining pesto. Spread the remaining butter mixture over the top. Cover with the plastic wrap. Chill for 8 to 12 hours.

Uncover the torta and invert onto a serving platter. Remove the plastic wrap. Garnish with sprigs of fresh basil and toasted pine nuts. Serve with toasted baguette slices.

Serves 20

Mandeville: The Art of Balance

In 1834, New Orleanian Bernard Xavier de Marigny de Mandeville purchased 5,000 acres on the north shore of Lake Pontchartrain with the specific goal of developing a prosperous new town. At the time, the Marigny family owned nearly a third of the city of New Orleans, and Bernard himself owned and operated a profitable sugar plantation on the property that is now Fontainebleau State Park. Due to the national depression of 1837 and then the Union occupation during the Civil War, Mandeville never evolved into a thriving community during Bernard's lifetime.

It was not until the late nineteenth century that Mandeville gained popularity with its Southshore neighbors as being a charming lakeshore resort town. By steamship-ferry service and by railroad from New Orleans through eastern St. Tammany Parish, people flocked to Mandeville for its beautiful lakefront, gorgeous trees, and summer homes.

Once the Causeway Bridge opened in 1956, the population boomed, and Mandeville grew into a thriving, prosperous city. Only twenty-four miles from the Southshore, Mandeville offers both cosmopolitan access and historical charm. As the "Gateway to the Northshore and St. Tammany Parish," the city of Mandeville invites all to enjoy its natural beauty, historical significance, emphasis on the arts, and relaxed family atmosphere.

Smoked Gouda Crawfish

2 tablespoons butter
½ cup chopped green onions
½ cup fresh parsley, chopped
4 garlic cloves, pressed
1 pound crawfish tails, cooked and peeled
1½ teaspoons Creole seasoning
⅓ cup heavy cream or milk
½ teaspoon pepper
Salt to taste
8 ounces smoked Gouda cheese, shredded
¼ cup dry vermouth

Melt the butter in a large nonstick skillet over medium heat. Add the green onions, parsley and garlic. Sauté until the vegetables are tender. Add the crawfish, Creole seasoning, heavy cream, pepper and salt.

Cook until heated through, stirring constantly. Add the cheese and vermouth. Cook until the cheese melts, stirring constantly. Serve warm as a dip with chips or melba toast.

Serves 8

Variation: Spoon the mixture into pastry shells. Bake at 350 degrees for 10 minutes or until heated through. You may make the filling ahead of time. Makes 4 main-dish servings.

Crab Mold

1 tablespoon unflavored gelatin
3 tablespoons cold water
1 (10-ounce) can cream of mushroom soup
6 ounces cream cheese
1 cup mayonnaise
1 cup finely chopped celery
2 green onions, finely chopped
6 to 8 ounces crab meat, shells removed and flaked, or shrimp, cooked, peeled and chopped
Cayenne pepper to taste

Soften the unflavored gelatin in the cold water in a bowl. Combine the softened gelatin, soup and cream cheese in a saucepan. Cook until the gelatin is dissolved and the mixture is smooth, stirring constantly. Remove from the heat to cool. Stir in the mayonnaise, celery, green onions, crab meat and cayenne pepper. Spoon into a mold. Chill for 12 hours or until set.

Serves 8

I was visiting my parents in rural Titus, Alabama, when my then-boyfriend and now-husband, Mike, came up to visit me and meet my parents for the first time. Mike thought it might be a treat to bring a hamper of Lake Pontchartrain crabs to boil and share with my relatives during his visit. Of course, he was trying to make a good impression on my parents. Mike had no idea how little people who live in rural Alabama know about eating boiled crabs. My uncle Raymond, who owned Ward's Slo-Check, the general store in Titus, proudly displayed a crab (that had died on its way from Louisiana) on one of his two gas pumps. The fun really began when Mike boiled the crabs and served them on the picnic table at my cousin Sylvia's lake house. Nobody knew how to eat them! Poor Mike spent the rest of the afternoon picking crab meat for my crab-ignorant relatives, but he certainly made an impression on them!

—Paula Kelly Meiners

Elegant Grapes

2½ cups pecan halves
8 ounces cream cheese, softened
5 ounces Camembert cheese, rind removed
1 tablespoon heavy cream
1 pound green or red seedless grapes

Spread the pecans on a baking sheet. Bake at 300 degrees for 15 minutes or until toasted and golden brown. Watch carefully to prevent burning. Remove from the oven to cool. Chop the pecans coarsely.

Beat the cream cheese, Camembert cheese and heavy cream in a mixing bowl until smooth. Coat the grapes with the cheese mixture and roll in the chopped pecans. Place on a plate lined with waxed paper. Chill until ready to serve.

Serves 8

Spinach Amuse-Bouche

1 cup flour
1 teaspoon salt
2 teaspoons baking powder
2 eggs
1 cup milk
½ cup (1 stick) butter, melted
1 (10-ounce) package frozen chopped spinach, thawed and drained
½ onion, chopped
1 pound sharp Cheddar cheese, shredded

Sift the flour, salt and baking powder together. Beat the eggs in a mixing bowl. Add the flour mixture, milk and butter and stir to mix well. Stir in the spinach, onion and cheese. Spoon into a greased 9×13-inch baking dish.

Bake at 350 degrees for 30 to 35 minutes or until set. Remove from the oven to cool. Cut into squares.

Makes 20 squares

NOTE: This recipe may be frozen and reheated. Drain well on paper towels.

St. Tammany Trace and Trailhead: The Art of the Outdoors

The St. Tammany Trace is Louisiana's first Rails to Trails conversion. Following old railroad tracks for thirty-one miles, the trail winds its way though five communities in St. Tammany Parish. The St. Tammany Trace is a scenic route for cycling, hiking, jogging, walking, in-line skating, and horse riding. Mandeville's Trailhead is easily identified by "The Green Caboose," the information and ranger office for the Trace. The Trailhead serves as a rest stop with water fountains, playground, pavilion, and picnic tables, as well as a local arts center with an amphitheatre, hosting local plays, town celebrations, musical performances, and brown bag series.

Sponsored by Coldwell Banker-Tec Real Estate

Pesto Dip and Chips

8 ounces cream cheese, softened
1 (6-ounce) package pesto sauce or
homemade pesto sauce
1 garlic clove, chopped
1 French baguette, sliced and baked

Place the cream cheese in a small baking dish
sprayed with nonstick cooking spray. Spread
the pesto sauce over the cream cheese. Sprinkle
with the garlic.
    Bake at 350 degrees for 20 minutes.
Spread on the bread chips.

Serves 8

Sweet Potato Cheese Pâté

8 ounces cream cheese, softened
2 cups cold mashed sweet potatoes
1/4 cup finely chopped onion
1 garlic clove, minced
2 tablespoons finely chopped jalapeño chile
1 teaspoon seasoned salt
1 teaspoon Worcestershire sauce
2 teaspoons Louisiana hot sauce
1/4 cup chopped pecans

Beat the cream cheese and sweet potatoes
in a mixing bowl until smooth. Add the
onion, garlic, jalapeño chile, seasoned salt,
Worcestershire sauce, hot sauce and pecans
and mix well. Chill, covered, for 4 hours or
until easy to handle. Shape into a ball. Chill,
covered, for 4 hours or until firm. Serve with
assorted crackers, breadsticks or vegetables
for dipping.

Makes about 3 cups

NOTE: When cutting or seeding hot chiles, use
rubber or plastic gloves to protect your hands.

You've Got the Rhythm Red Bean Dip

1 pound dried red beans
2 tablespoons butter
8 ounces andouille, chopped
1 cup chopped celery
1 cup chopped onion
1 cup chopped green bell pepper
1 garlic clove, minced
1 teaspoon fresh thyme, chopped
2 bay leaves
1 1/2 tablespoons Creole seasoning
1 (10-ounce) can beef broth
1 (10-ounce) can tomatoes with green chiles
6 cups (1 1/2 quarts) water

Rinse and sort the beans. Soak in water to
cover in a saucepan for 8 to 12 hours; drain.
Melt the butter in a large stockpot. Add the
sausage. Cook until the sausage is brown.
Add the celery, onion, bell pepper, garlic,
thyme, bay leaves and Creole seasoning.
Cook for 5 minutes. Add the beans, beef broth,
tomatoes with green chiles and water. Cook
over medium-high heat for 1 hour or until
the beans are tender, stirring frequently to
prevent sticking. Mash or purée the beans in
a food processor until smooth. Return to the
stockpot. Simmer for 2 hours or until of a dip
consistency. Serve warm with potato chips.

Serves 8

NOTE: You may use rinsed and drained canned
red beans to save time.

Wooden Boat festival

Madisonville, Louisiana
2000

Feast de Résistance…Salads and Soups

Salads and Soups

In 1975, I left Louisiana for graduate school at the University of Missouri, slipping out of town never having accomplished one of my goals, which was to learn to cook my Momma's gumbo. My first winter away, it snowed like crazy and was bitterly cold and I was homesick, not to mention starved for gumbo. But gumbo was not to be found in Columbia, Missouri, a place where chicken-fried steak was considered gourmet cooking. Desperate, I called my mom one weekend and asked her to give me her recipe. She said, "First, you make roux."

Hmm, a roux, huh?

So there was my poor mother trying to walk her roux-ignorant son through a roux over the phone. Well, I later realized this was like trying to tell somebody who's never done it before how to have sex over the phone…It just can't turn out well.

I went ahead and made that roux, and it was by far the worst gumbo that God ever let be made. I called it "telephone gumbo." Even my cat wouldn't eat it.

I went home that Christmas and spent several occasions watching my mother make her roux. Eventually, I got the hang of it. Of course, I've never cooked a gumbo that I thought lived up to my mother's. But when I serve it to people in New Jersey, where I now live, they fall down and weep in joy. Of course, in New Jersey, a lot of things make you fall down and weep…

—Ken Wells
Author and Senior Editor/Writer,
"Page One" of the *Wall Street Journal*

Hmm, a roux, huh?

Caesar Chicken Summer Salad

3 cups chopped cooked boneless skinless chicken breasts
3 cups hot cooked penne pasta
2 cups thinly sliced fresh spinach
1½ cups cherry tomato halves
½ cup thinly sliced fresh basil
½ cup chopped green onions
⅓ cup Caesar salad dressing
4 ounces feta cheese, crumbled
1 garlic clove, minced

Combine the chicken, pasta, spinach, tomatoes, basil, green onions, salad dressing, cheese and garlic in a large bowl and toss to coat. Serve warm or cold.

Serves 4

Madisonville Wooden Boat Festival

A sign recently sighted on one of the prize boats at the Madisonville Wooden Boat Festival read, "If God had wanted man to have fiberglass boats, he would have made fiberglass trees." This quote captures the feeling and inspiration behind the Madisonville Wooden Boat Festival, a two-day event benefiting the Lake Pontchartrain Basin Maritime Museum and Research Center. The mission of the Museum and Research Center, also located in Madisonville, is to protect and preserve the area's maritime, naval, and marine history; as well as the culture related to that history. Each year, more than one hundred boats, ranging in size from ten to seventy feet, line the shore of the picturesque Tchefuncte River in Madisonville, giving wooden boat owners an opportunity to show off the work and craftsmanship that goes into their beautiful vessels. Almost 40,000 people come to this event every year, turning the tiny town of Madisonville into one big party.

The Madisonville Wooden Boat Festival is held on a weekend in mid-October on Water Street in Madisonville. For more information, go to www.lpbmaritimemuseum.com.

Curried Chicken Salad

CURRIED MAYONNAISE
3 tablespoons mayonnaise
1 tablespoon curry powder, or to taste
1 tablespoon Dijon mustard
1 teaspoon lemon juice
1 garlic clove, minced

SALAD
¼ to ½ cup slivered or sliced almonds
Butter for sautéing
2 envelopes Italian salad dressing mix
10 boneless skinless chicken breasts, cooked and chopped
1 cup crumbled crisp-cooked bacon
1½ to 1⅓ cups green grape halves
2 large ribs celery, thinly sliced
½ to 1 cup chopped fresh parsley

ASSEMBLY
Red leaf lettuce
Cut-up fruit of choice

For the curried mayonnaise, mix the mayonnaise, curry powder, Dijon mustard, lemon juice and garlic in a bowl and blend well. Store in the refrigerator until ready to use.

For the salad, sauté the almonds in a small amount of butter in a skillet until brown and toasted. Prepare the salad dressing using the package directions. Combine the hot chicken and salad dressing in a large bowl and toss to coat. Marinate, covered, in the refrigerator for 3 hours or longer.

Drain the chicken, reserving 1 to 2 tablespoons of the marinade. Combine the chicken, bacon, grapes, celery, parsley, toasted almonds and reserved marinade in a large bowl and toss to combine. Add the curried mayonnaise 1 tablespoon at a time, tossing to mix well after each addition. Chill, covered, for a few hours to enhance the flavors.

To assemble and serve, spoon the chicken salad onto individual serving plates lined with red leaf lettuce and surround with cut-up fruit.

Serves 6 to 8

ROUX DO: Perk up wilted lettuce and celery by soaking them in ice water.

Gourmet Chicken Salad

CHICKEN SALAD
4 to 6 boneless skinless chicken breasts
1 (14-ounce) can chicken broth
Dry white wine
1 red onion, cut into halves and quartered
2 ribs celery, cut into quarters
3 garlic cloves
1/2 large red onion, finely chopped
3 ribs celery, finely chopped
Mayonnaise to taste
Salt and 3-pepper mix to taste

TOSSED SALAD
Lettuce mix of choice, such as
European spring mix and romaine
2 tomatoes, cut into halves and sliced
Tops from 1 bunch green onions, chopped
1/2 red bell pepper, cut into strips and halved
1/2 green bell pepper, cut into strips and halved
1/2 yellow bell pepper,
cut into strips and halved
1/2 large cucumber, peeled, halved,
seeded and sliced
2 ounces feta cheese, finely chopped
Homemade Italian salad dressing

For the chicken salad, place the chicken and chicken broth in a stockpot. Add enough wine to cover. Add the red onion quarters, 2 ribs celery and garlic. Bring to a boil over high heat. Cover and reduce the heat to low. Poach for 40 minutes or until the chicken is cooked through. Remove the chicken to a platter to cool. Strain the liquid, discarding the solids. Freeze the liquid in 2-cup portions for later use. Chop the chicken. Combine the chicken, finely chopped red onion and finely chopped celery in a large bowl. Add enough mayonnaise to bind the ingredients together and mix well. Season with the salt and 3-pepper mix. Chill, covered, for 8 to 12 hours.

For the tossed salad, combine the lettuce mix, tomatoes, green onion tops, bell peppers, cucumber and cheese in a large bowl and toss to mix. Add enough salad dressing to coat and toss to mix. Place the tossed salad in individual salad bowls. Mound a large scoop of the chicken salad on top of each. Serve with hot bread and white wine.

Serves 4

Sesame Chicken and Bean Salad

SESAME DRESSING
3/4 cup fat-free Italian salad dressing
2 tablespoons sesame oil
3 tablespoons reduced-sodium tamari
soy sauce
1 1/2 teaspoons grated gingerroot, or
3/4 teaspoon ground ginger

SALAD
2 (15-ounce) cans pinto beans or
black beans, rinsed and drained, or
3 cups cooked dried pinto beans
1 pound boneless skinless chicken breasts,
grilled and shredded
1 pound asparagus, cut into 1-inch
pieces, cooked
4 green onions, sliced

ASSEMBLY
6 cups spinach leaves
2 tablespoons sunflower seeds

For the sesame dressing, combine the salad dressing, sesame oil, soy sauce and ginger in a small bowl and blend well.

For the salad, combine the pinto beans, chicken, asparagus and green onions in a large bowl and mix well. Drizzle with the sesame dressing and toss to coat.

To assemble and serve, arrange the spinach on individual salad plates. Spoon the salad over each. Sprinkle with the sunflower seeds.

Serves 6

Smoked Turkey Rémoulade Salad

TURKEY SALAD
1½ pounds smoked turkey, cut into cubes
½ medium onion, chopped
1 rib celery, chopped
¾ cup mayonnaise
¼ cup Creole mustard
½ teaspoon hot sauce
Salt and pepper to taste

MIXED GREEN SALAD
1 teaspoon Creole mustard
½ teaspoon sugar
Pinch of salt
Pinch of freshly ground pepper
¼ cup apple cider vinegar
½ cup vegetable oil
1 pound mixed salad greens

SWEET POTATO NESTS
2 sweet potatoes
Vegetable oil for frying
Cajun seasoning to taste

For the turkey salad, combine the turkey, onion, celery, mayonnaise, Creole mustard, hot sauce, salt and pepper in a bowl and mix well.

For the mixed green salad, combine the Creole mustard, sugar, salt, pepper and vinegar in a bowl and stir until the sugar and salt are dissolved. Add the oil in a slow steady stream, whisking constantly. Place the salad greens in a large bowl. Add just enough of the dressing to lightly coat.

For the sweet potato nests, peel the sweet potatoes. Process in a food processor until shredded. Pour oil into a skillet to a depth of about 3 inches. Fry the sweet potatoes in small batches until the sweet potatoes begin to brown slightly. Remove from the oil and season with Cajun seasoning.

To assemble and serve, divide the mixed green salad among 4 serving plates. Top with the turkey salad. Mound a handful of the fried sweet potatoes to resemble nests on the turkey salad. (The presentation looks better the higher you can mound the sweet potatoes.)

Serves 4

Roux Don't: Don't peel the whole onion if you only need a small portion. Cut only the amount you need, and store the remaining onion with skin on in the refrigerator.

Lobster Salad with Lemon Verbena Dressing

Courtesy Executive Chef Gerard Maras, Artesia Manor

1 (1½- to 1¾-pound) lobster
3 or 4 sprigs of fresh lemon verbena
1 egg yolk
1 teaspoon water
1 cup blended olive oil (80% olive oil, 20% vegetable oil)
Juice of ½ lemon
Salt and pepper to taste
1 large vine-ripened tomato, peeled, seeded and cut into ¼-inch strips
Pea shoots, sunflower shoots or mesclun
2 radishes, julienned

Steam the lobster for 6 to 8 minutes. Remove to a platter. Chill for 30 minutes. Remove the lobster from the shell, leaving the tail and claw meat intact.

Chiffonade 5 or 6 of the lemon verbena leaves. Chop the remaining verbena. Whisk the egg yolk and water in a stainless steel bowl. Drizzle in enough of the oil gradually to make an emulsified dressing thick enough to coat a spoon, whisking constantly. Whisk in the chopped verbena, lemon juice, salt and pepper. Let stand for 10 minutes. Adjust the seasonings to taste.

Cut the meat from 1 lobster claw and ½ of the tail meat into disks and place in a bowl. Add the tomato strips and 1 tablespoon of the dressing and toss to coat. Place in the center of a serving plate.

Toss the pea shoots with a few drops of the remaining oil and salt in a bowl. Place above the lobster on the plate. Drizzle about 1 tablespoon of the dressing on the plate around the lobster. Sprinkle the radishes and chiffonade of verbena around the lobster to finish the plate.

Serves 1

Shrimp Salad with Green Goddess Dressing

GREEN GODDESS DRESSING
¾ cup mayonnaise
½ cup strained fresh lemon juice
2 cups firmly packed fresh parsley leaves
1 bunch green onions, chopped
1 (2-ounce) can anchovy fillets, drained
1 tablespoon sugar
½ teaspoon pepper

SHRIMP AND SALAD
3 pounds large shrimp, peeled and deveined
4 heads hearts of romaine
2 ripe avocados, peeled, pitted and chopped

For the dressing, pulse the mayonnaise, lemon juice, parsley, green onions, anchovy fillets, sugar and pepper in a food processor until liquefied. Chill in the refrigerator.

For the shrimp and salad, boil the shrimp in water to cover in a saucepan for 3 minutes or until the shrimp turn pink; drain. Chill, covered, in the refrigerator. (To save time, have the shrimp steamed at the seafood market.) Separate the romaine leaves and rinse well. Spin dry in a salad spinner. Wrap the leaves in a cloth or paper towel. Chill for 1 hour before serving.

To assemble and serve, tear the romaine into bite-size pieces and place in a salad bowl. Add the avocados. Pour the desired amount of dressing over the salad and toss to coat. Divide among 6 to 8 serving plates. Top each with the shrimp.

Serves 6 to 8

Moroccan Shrimp Salad

DRESSING
3/4 cup olive oil
6 tablespoons lemon juice
Pinch of sugar
Paprika, salt and pepper to taste

SALAD
1 cup cooked couscous
1 (14-ounce) can chick-peas,
drained and rinsed
1 pound shrimp, cooked and peeled
3 green onions, thinly sliced
4 small to medium tomatoes, peeled,
seeded and chopped
1 bunch fresh mint, chopped

For the dressing, blend the olive oil and lemon juice in a bowl. Season with sugar, paprika, salt and pepper.

For the salad, combine the couscous, chick-peas, shrimp, green onions, tomatoes and mint in a large salad bowl. Pour the desired amount of dressing over the top and toss to coat well. Serve with lemon wedges.

Serves 4

ROUX DO: For easy tomato peeling, bring a large saucepan of water to a boil. On the bottom of each tomato, cut an "X" through the skin with a sharp paring knife. Drop 2 to 3 tomatoes at a time into the boiling water. Boil for 10 to 15 seconds. Remove the tomatoes with a slotted spoon and immediately plunge into a bowl of ice water to cool and stop the cooking process. Remove the tomatoes from the ice water. The skin should easily slip off each tomato.

Shrimp on a Half Shell

Shrimp boil seasoning
8 ounces fresh shrimp, peeled and deveined
1/4 cup mayonnaise
1 teaspoon Dijon mustard
1 tablespoon tarragon vinegar
1/2 teaspoon minced garlic
1 teaspoon minced shallots
1 tablespoon minced bell pepper
1 tablespoon minced pimento
2 tablespoons capers, drained and minced
Creole seasoning, salt and pepper to taste
2 ripe avocados
Lime juice for sprinkling

Season water in a stockpot with the shrimp boil seasoning. Bring to a boil. Add the shrimp. Boil until the shrimp turn pink; drain and cool. Mince the shrimp.

Whisk the mayonnaise, Dijon mustard and vinegar in a bowl. Add the garlic, shallots, bell pepper, pimento and capers and mix well. Fold in the shrimp. Season with Creole seasoning, salt and pepper.

Peel the avocados. Split into halves and discard the pits. Sprinkle immediately with lime juice to prevent discoloration. Divide the shrimp mixture among the avocado halves.

Serves 4

Greens with Roquefort Vinaigrette

CAJUN CROUTONS
5 thick slices white bread, cut into cubes
1/2 cup (2 ounces) freshly grated
Parmesan cheese
1/4 cup (1/2 stick) butter, melted
1 1/2 teaspoons Creole seasoning
1/4 teaspoon cayenne pepper (optional)

ROQUEFORT VINAIGRETTE
1/4 cup white wine vinegar
2 tablespoons fresh lemon juice
2 teaspoons Dijon mustard
1 garlic clove, minced
1/2 teaspoon pepper
2/3 cup olive oil
2 ounces Roquefort cheese, crumbled
2 ounces blue cheese, crumbled

SALAD
1 package fresh baby spinach or spring mix
1 cup grape tomatoes or cherry tomato halves
1/2 small red onion, thinly sliced

For the croutons, combine the bread, Parmesan cheese, butter, Creole seasoning and cayenne pepper in a large sealable plastic bag. Seal the bag and shake to coat. Arrange on a foil-lined baking sheet. Bake at 300 degrees for 30 minutes or until the croutons are crisp and golden brown. Remove from the oven to cool. Store in a sealable plastic bag.

For the vinaigrette, process the vinegar, lemon juice, Dijon mustard, garlic and pepper in a food processor. Add the olive oil gradually, processing constantly. Stir in the Roquefort cheese and blue cheese gently with a spatula.

For the salad and assembly, combine the baby spinach, grape tomatoes and red onion in a salad bowl. Add the desired amount of vinaigrette and toss to coat. Sprinkle with the croutons. Serve immediately.

Serves 4 to 6

Mardi Gras Salad

1 1/2 cups mayonnaise
1/2 cup white vinegar
1 1/2 heads romaine, torn into bite-size pieces
1 head purple cabbage, sliced
1 yellow onion, sliced
1 yellow bell pepper, sliced
2 cucumbers, peeled, halved and sliced
2 avocados, cut into pieces
3/4 cup Italian bread crumbs
3/4 cup (3 ounces) freshly grated
Parmesan cheese
3/4 teaspoon salt
1 1/2 teaspoons freshly ground pepper

Mix the mayonnaise and vinegar in a bowl and blend well. Chill until ready to serve.

Combine the romaine, cabbage, onion, bell pepper, cucumbers and avocados in a large bowl. Sprinkle with the bread crumbs, cheese, salt and pepper. Add the mayonnaise mixture and toss to coat. Serve immediately.

Serves 12

Christmas Spinach Salad

Seeds of 1 pomegranate
10 ounces spinach leaves, rinsed and torn
1 ripe avocado, sliced
1 cup fresh mushrooms, thinly sliced
1/2 cup coarsely chopped walnuts or pecans
Salt and freshly cracked pepper to taste
3 slices bacon
1/4 cup packed brown sugar
1/2 cup cider vinegar
1/3 cup olive oil

Reserve some of the pomegranate seeds for garnish. Place the spinach leaves, avocado slices, remaining pomegranate seeds and sliced mushrooms in a large bowl. Toast the walnuts in a large skillet over high heat for 1 minute, stirring constantly. Sprinkle over the salad. Season with salt and pepper.

Fry the bacon in a skillet until crisp. Remove the bacon to paper towels to drain. Drain the skillet, reserving 1 tablespoon of the drippings in the skillet. Add the brown sugar, vinegar and olive oil. Cook over medium heat until the brown sugar is dissolved, stirring constantly.

Crumble the bacon over the salad. Pour the hot dressing over the top and toss to coat. Sprinkle with the reserved pomegranate seeds and serve immediately.

Serves 4 to 6

Cranberry Gorgonzola Spinach Salad

DRESSING
1/4 cup olive oil
1/4 cup seasoned rice vinegar
3/4 teaspoon Dijon mustard
1/2 teaspoon horseradish
1 teaspoon crushed garlic
2 tablespoons chopped parsley

SALAD
3 (6-ounce) bunches fresh spinach
2 small cans mandarin oranges, drained
1 Granny Smith apple, chopped
1/3 cup dried cranberries
1 cup pecan halves or walnut halves
Butter for sautéing
1/3 cup Gorgonzola cheese

For the dressing, whisk the olive oil, rice vinegar, Dijon mustard, horseradish, garlic and parsley in a bowl. Chill, covered, in the refrigerator until ready to serve.

For the salad, combine the spinach, mandarin oranges, apple and dried cranberries in a large bowl and toss to mix. Sauté the pecans in a small amount of butter in a skillet. Pour the dressing over the spinach mixture and toss to coat. Sprinkle with the toasted pecans and cheese. Serve immediately.

Serves 4 to 6

NOTE: You may substitute Citrus Vinaigrette (page 194) for the dressing. You may also substitute 1 pint grape tomatoes, halved, for the apple.

Cantaloupe Salad with Andouille and Pistachio Goat Cheese Balls

1 link andouille
¼ cup balsamic vinegar
⅓ cup pistachios
1 (5-ounce) container goat cheese
½ cantaloupe
⅓ cup olive oil

Remove the casing from the sausage. Process in a food processor until finely chopped. Brown in a skillet until crisp. Remove to paper towels to drain, reserving the drippings in the skillet.

Heat the reserved drippings in the skillet over high heat. Stir in the balsamic vinegar. Cook over high heat, stirring to deglaze the skillet. Cook until the mixture is reduced slightly. Remove from the heat.

Process the pistachios in a food processor until processed to a rough powder. Shape the cheese into teaspoonful-size balls. Roll ½ of the cheese balls in the sausage to coat. Roll the remaining cheese balls in the pistachio powder.

Cut the cantaloupe into thin slices and arrange on 4 plates. Place 1 of each kind of goat cheese ball on each plate. Mix the vinegar mixture with the olive oil in a bowl. Drizzle over the cantaloupe slices. Sprinkle with the remaining sausage and pistachio powder.

Serves 4

Northshore Mardi Gras

In St. Tammany Parish, Mardi Gras is a family event. Northshore creativity abounds at Carnival, including Mandeville's Krewe of Paws, a dog parade on the Lakefront, and Abita Springs's Krewe of Push Mow, which features artfully decorated wagons, bicycles, and riding and push lawn mowers. Traditional Carnival parades include Covington's Krewe of Olympia and the Lion's Parade, as well as Mandeville's all-female Krewe of Eve and the Original Krewe of Orpheus. Madisonville's Krewe of Tchefuncte features anchored boats along the scenic Tchefuncte River, Lacombe's Krewe of Skunks invites motorcycles, trucks, and four wheelers to participate, and the Krewe of Folsom features fire trucks and antique cars.

Sponsored by Fairway Medical Center

Fruit Ambrosia Salad

1 golden pineapple
1 medium cantaloupe
1 honeydew melon
1 orange, sectioned
2 red apples
1 pear
1 bunch seedless red grapes
2 cups coconut, toasted
1 teaspoon vanilla extract
3½ cups whipped cream

GARNISH
Coconut shavings

Chop the pineapple, cantaloupe, honeydew melon, orange, apples and pear into ½-inch pieces and place in a large bowl. Add the grapes, coconut and vanilla and mix well. Fold in the whipped cream. Garnish with coconut shavings.

Serves 12

NOTE: You may also add sliced strawberries and fresh mint sprigs.

Fresh Greens with Pears and Goat Cheese

GOAT CHEESE MEDALLIONS
4 (3-ounce) logs goat cheese
1 cup olive oil
1 tablespoon dried whole basil
1 tablespoon chopped fresh chives
¾ cup soft bread crumbs, toasted

CHAMPAGNE VINAIGRETTE
¼ cup extra-virgin olive oil
1 garlic clove, pressed
1 tablespoon minced shallots or
minced green onion bulb
2 tablespoons Champagne vinegar
1 teaspoon good quality sherry vinegar
2 teaspoons fresh lime juice
¼ teaspoon kosher salt
¼ teaspoon freshly ground pepper

SALAD AND ASSEMBLY
4 cups torn Bibb lettuce
4 cups torn radicchio
4 cups romaine
2 (16-ounce) cans pear halves,
drained and chopped
1 medium green bell pepper, chopped
¾ cup chopped walnuts

For the goat cheese medallions, chill the cheese logs for 15 minutes before slicing. Cut the cheese into 24 rounds by using unflavored unwaxed dental floss. Combine the olive oil, basil and chives in a large shallow dish. Arrange the cheese slices in the olive oil mixture. Chill, covered, for 6 hours or longer. Drain the cheese, discarding the marinade. Coat the cheese slices with the bread crumbs. Arrange on a baking sheet. Bake at 400 degrees for 10 minutes or until light brown. Remove from the oven to cool.

For the vinaigrette, mix the olive oil and garlic in a small bowl. Let stand at room temperature for 30 minutes. Whisk in the shallots, Champagne vinegar, sherry vinegar, lime juice, kosher salt and pepper.

For the salad and assembly, toss the Bibb lettuce, radicchio and romaine together. Place 1 cup of the lettuce mixture on each salad plate. Arrange 2 cheese medallions on each. Sprinkle with the chopped pears, bell pepper and walnuts. Drizzle with vinaigrette.

Serves 12

Spring Sensation Salad with Sweet Spicy Pecans

BALSAMIC VINAIGRETTE
1/2 cup balsamic vinegar
3 tablespoons Dijon mustard
3 tablespoons honey
3 garlic cloves, pressed
3 green onions, minced
1/4 teaspoon salt
1/4 teaspoon pepper
Extra-virgin olive oil

SWEET SPICY PECANS
1 cup water
1/4 cup sugar
1 cup pecan halves
3 tablespoons sugar
1 tablespoon chili powder
1/4 teaspoon ground red pepper

SALAD
8 ounces spring mix greens
1 head red leaf lettuce, rinsed and
torn into bite-size pieces
4 ounces feta cheese, crumbled
2 (11-ounce) cans mandarin oranges, drained
1 pint strawberries, sliced

For the vinaigrette, whisk the balsamic vinegar, Dijon mustard, honey, garlic, green onions, salt and pepper in a 2-cup measure until blended. Whisk in enough olive oil gradually to make 2 cups. Chill, covered, until ready to serve.

For the pecans, microwave the water in a small microwave-safe glass bowl until the water boils. Add 1/4 cup sugar and stir until dissolved. Add the pecans. Soak for 15 minutes; drain. Combine 3 tablespoons sugar, the chili powder and red pepper in a sealable plastic bag. Add the pecans and shake to coat. Arrange in a single layer on a lightly greased baking sheet. Bake at 350 degrees for 15 minutes, stirring once.

For the salad, toss the spring mix greens, red leaf lettuce, cheese and balsamic vinaigrette in a large salad bowl. Add the mandarin oranges and strawberries and toss gently. Sprinkle with the sweet spicy pecans just before serving.

Serves 10 to 12

ROUX DO: Store fresh berries in a colander in the refrigerator so that the cold air can circulate around them.

ROUX DON'T: Don't leave a moldy berry next to a good one, as mold in berries spreads quickly. Remember, it only takes one bad berry to ruin the pint.

Broccoli, Walnut and Blue Cheese Salad

VINAIGRETTE
1 cup vegetable oil
1/2 to 1 cup sugar
1/2 cup red wine vinegar
3 tablespoons soy sauce
Salt and pepper to taste

SALAD
1 (6-ounce) package chow mein noodles
1 cup chopped walnuts
1/4 cup (1/2 stick) butter, melted
2 cups chopped broccoli
1 head romaine, torn into bite-size pieces
4 green onions, chopped
1 package sliced mushrooms
1/2 to 3/4 cup crumbled blue cheese

For the vinaigrette, combine the oil, sugar, vinegar, soy sauce, salt and pepper in a jar with a tight-fitting lid. Cover the jar and shake well. (The vinaigrette may be made ahead of time to let the flavors blend more, but it is not necessary.)

For the salad, place the chow mein noodles and walnuts in a baking dish. Pour the butter over the top and toss to coat well. Bake at 325 degrees for 25 minutes or until roasted. Watch carefully to prevent burning. Mix the broccoli, romaine, green onions, mushrooms, cheese, roasted noodles and walnuts in a large salad bowl. Add the desired amount of vinaigrette and toss to coat.

Serves 4 to 6

Blue Cheese Coleslaw

3 tablespoons cider vinegar
2 tablespoons finely chopped onion
1 tablespoon sugar
3/4 teaspoon celery seeds
1/4 teaspoon salt
1/8 teaspoon dry mustard
1/4 teaspoon pepper
1 garlic clove, minced
1/4 cup vegetable oil
1 pound cabbage, finely shredded
4 ounces blue cheese, crumbled

Combine the vinegar, onion, sugar, celery seeds, salt, dry mustard, pepper and garlic in a small bowl. Add the oil in a fine steady stream, whisking to blend. Chill, covered, for 1 hour or longer.

Combine the cabbage and cheese in a bowl and toss to mix. Chill, covered, for 1 hour. Drizzle the vinegar mixture over the cabbage mixture and toss gently. Serve immediately.

Serves 6

NOTE: For crisp coleslaw, first soak the shredded cabbage in ice water for 1 hour. Drain the cabbage and pat dry. Place in a plastic bag and store in the refrigerator until ready to use.

Roux Don't: Don't wash fruits and vegetables until ready to use.

Summer Corn Salad

3 cups fresh or frozen cooked corn, or
2 (12-ounce) cans Shoe Peg corn, drained
2 tomatoes, peeled, chopped and drained
1 bell pepper, chopped
1 purple onion, chopped
1 cucumber, chopped
½ cup sour cream
¼ cup mayonnaise
2 tablespoons vinegar
½ teaspoon celery seeds
½ teaspoon dry mustard
2 teaspoons salt
½ teaspoon pepper

Combine the corn, tomatoes, bell pepper, onion and cucumber in a large bowl and mix well. Stir in the sour cream, mayonnaise, vinegar, celery seeds, dry mustard, salt and pepper. Chill, covered, for 8 to 12 hours before serving. You may store in the refrigerator for several days.

Serves 8

NOTE: If using fresh corn, remove the ears of corn from hot water and plunge into ice water to stop the cooking process. Stand 1 ear at a time on a plate and cut off the kernels with a sharp knife, scraping the "milk" from the cobs. Add to the salad.

Roux Do: Do add a teaspoon of sugar to the boiling water for sweeter corn.

Roux Don't: Don't overcook the corn. It only takes 3 to 5 minutes per ear to cook.

The Art of Maritime

Madisonville, Louisiana, is one of the oldest communities in the state and as such has had a full history. Originally called "Cokie" from the French word coquille, *meaning shell, the town's name was changed in 1811 to honor President James Madison. At the turn of the century, Madisonville was an important shipbuilding town and still has shipyards. It was also a popular resort town from the 1920s to the 1940s for New Orleanians who crossed Lake Pontchartrain via large steamers to spend summer weekends. In addition to the Wooden Boat Festival, Madisonville hosts two other annual boating events. The first is the New Year's Eve Crew of Lights. Each New Year's Eve, a lighted boat parade proceeds down the Tchefuncte River, which runs through Madisonville. Madisonville also hosts the annual Mardi Gras Boat Parade on the Sunday before Mardi Gras. The "floats" in this parade actually float, as the parade is made up entirely of boats that parade down the Tchefuncte. Then they tie up along Water Street, where spectators gather to catch throws and watch the parade. Given its location on the Tchefuncte River, water and maritime have played an important part in Madisonville's history, which makes it the ideal location for the Lake Pontchartrain Basin Maritime Museum and Research Center.*

Creoles with Spicy Crawfish Egg Salad

10 ripe Creole tomatoes
2 tablespoons unsalted butter
1 cup finely chopped sweet onion
1 tablespoon minced garlic
1/2 teaspoon chili powder
1/8 to 1/2 teaspoon cayenne pepper, or to taste
1 pound crawfish tails with fat
12 hard-cooked eggs, peeled and
coarsely chopped
3/4 cup mayonnaise
1/2 cup finely chopped red onion
2 small ribs celery, finely chopped
1 tablespoon finely chopped dill pickle
1 tablespoon fresh lemon juice
2 tablespoons Dijon mustard
1/4 cup minced parsley
1/2 teaspoon paprika
1/2 to 1 teaspoon Louisiana hot sauce, or
to taste
Kosher salt and freshly ground
black pepper to taste
2 packages spring mix salad greens

GARNISH
Paprika to taste

Cut the tops from the tomatoes and reserve. Scoop out the pulp to form a shell, reserving 2 cups of the tomato pulp. Arrange the tomato shells on a baking sheet and cover with plastic wrap. Place the reserved tops in a sealed container. Chill the tomato shells and reserved tops for 2 to 8 hours.

Melt the butter in a large skillet. Add the sweet onions and garlic. Sauté over high heat until the onions are tender but not translucent. Add the chili powder and cayenne pepper. Cook for 1 minute. Add the reserved tomato pulp. Cook for 10 minutes or until the mixture is reduced by 1/2. Add the crawfish and mix thoroughly. Cook over medium heat for 5 to 8 minutes or until the crawfish are cooked through. Spoon into a bowl and cover with plastic wrap. Chill in the refrigerator.

Combine the hard-cooked eggs, mayonnaise, red onion, celery, dill pickle, lemon juice, Dijon mustard, parsley, paprika and hot sauce in a bowl and mix well. Fold in the chilled crawfish mixture. Season with kosher salt and black pepper. Stuff into the tomato shells.

Divide the salad greens evenly among 10 salad plates. Place a stuffed tomato in the center of each plate and lean a reserved cut tomato top against the tomato. Sprinkle the egg salad with paprika to garnish.

Serves 10

Roux Don't: Never store fresh tomatoes in the refrigerator, as cold temperatures will destroy the flavor of the tomatoes.

Roux Do: Do serve egg dishes within 2 hours when entertaining.

Creole Tomato and Vidalia Onion Stacked Salad

16 ounces buttermilk blue cheese or
Roquefort cheese, crumbled
½ cup lemon juice
2 teaspoons Worcestershire sauce
4 to 8 dashes of Louisiana hot sauce, or
to taste
1 teaspoon kosher salt
1 teaspoon freshly ground black pepper
½ teaspoon white pepper
2 cups olive oil
½ cup buttermilk
32 (½-inch-thick) slices Creole tomatoes
(about 8 large)
32 (¼-inch-thick) slices Vidalia onions
(about 4 medium)
24 plain or garlic-flavored whole bagel chips

GARNISH
2 tablespoons finely chopped fresh parsley
8 slices bacon, cooked and crumbled

ROUX DO: Always serve tomatoes at room
temperature for the best flavor.

Mash the cheese, lemon juice, Worcestershire
sauce, hot sauce, kosher salt, black pepper and
white pepper in a medium bowl to form a thick
paste. Scrape into a food processor or blender.
Add the olive oil in a steady stream, processing
constantly. Continue to process until the
mixture is creamy. Pour into a large jar with a
tight-fitting lid. Add the buttermilk. Seal the jar
and shake vigorously until the dressing is
thoroughly mixed. Chill for 1 hour or longer.
Shake the dressing well before serving.

To serve, spoon about 1 tablespoon of the
dressing onto the center of each of 8 serving
plates. Place a tomato slice over the dressing.
Drizzle some more dressing over each of the
tomatoes. Place an onion slice on top. Drizzle
with more dressing and top with a whole bagel
chip. Repeat the process, using 4 slices of
tomatoes, 4 onion slices and 3 bagel chips for
each stack. Each stack should end with a
tomato slice, topped with an onion slice and
with dressing drizzled over the top. Garnish
each plate with chopped parsley and crumbled
bacon.

Serves 8

Creole Tomatoes and Satsumas: Nature's Art

*Fresh produce is a St. Tammany staple, and two favorites are grown in our own
backyard. Creole tomatoes are large, sweet, vine-ripened tomatoes grown in southeast
Louisiana and known for their unusual shape and rich color. They are a local treat
in the late spring and early summer. To be true Creole tomatoes, they have to be grown in
Plaquemines or St. Bernard Parish. The unique flavor of Creole tomatoes is attributed to the mix
of sand and heavy clay soil that was deposited by the Mississippi River in these two
parishes before the levees were built to protect New Orleans from the rising river. Satsumas
are seedless mandarin oranges that grow on small trees and ripen in the early fall. The
majority of satsumas are also grown in Plaquemines Parish. Satsumas are juicy, sweet, and easy
to peel; as such, they are especially popular with children of all ages. Southeast Louisiana
is the primary source of satsumas in the United States.
Both Creole tomatoes and satsumas can be found in local grocery stores,
farmer's markets, and roadside fruit stands.*

Sponsored by Copeland's Restaurants

Famous New Orleans
Restaurant and Bar

Mushroom Medley

2 cups cremini mushroom halves
2 cups portobello mushroom pieces
1 cup button mushroom halves
1/4 cup olive oil
1 teaspoon minced garlic
1 cup chopped seeded tomatoes
1/4 cup fresh lemon juice
2 teaspoons balsamic vinegar
Salt and pepper to taste
3 tablespoons chopped fresh basil

Toss the mushrooms, olive oil and garlic in a large bowl. Spread on a large baking sheet. Bake at 400 degrees until roasted and brown. Return to the bowl. Add the tomatoes, lemon juice, balsamic vinegar, salt and pepper and toss to mix. Let stand, covered, at room temperature until ready to serve. Add the chopped basil just before serving and toss well.

Serves 6

Fried Okra Salad

8 slices bacon
Vegetable oil for frying
Cornmeal for coating
Salt and pepper to taste
4 cups sliced okra
1/2 cup chopped Vidalia onion or
other sweet onion
1/2 cup chopped green bell pepper
2 cups chopped tomatoes

Fry the bacon in a skillet until crisp. Remove the bacon to paper towels to drain. Crumble the bacon. Drain the skillet, reserving some of the drippings in the skillet. Add enough oil to the skillet to fry the okra.

Mix the cornmeal, salt and pepper in a sealable plastic bag. Add the okra and shake to coat. Fry the okra in the hot oil mixture in the skillet until golden brown. Remove to paper towels to drain. Combine the fried okra, onion, bell pepper and tomatoes in a large bowl and toss to mix. Sprinkle with the crumbled bacon. Serve at room temperature.

Serves 4

Santa Fe Salad

1 cup sour cream
1/2 small bottle Italian salad dressing
1 1/2 tablespoons chili powder
1 teaspoon garlic salt
Salt and pepper to taste
4 avocados
Lemon juice for dipping
1 package grape tomatoes, cut into halves
1 (15-ounce) can kidney beans,
rinsed and drained
1 to 2 heads iceberg lettuce
1 large package corn chips, crushed

Mix the sour cream, Italian salad dressing, chili powder, garlic salt, salt and pepper in a bowl. Cut the avocados into slices and dip in lemon juice. Add the avocado slices, tomatoes and kidney beans to the sour cream mixture and mix well. Marinate, covered, for 3 to 12 hours.

To serve, tear the lettuce into bite-size pieces in a salad bowl. Add the desired amount of avocado mixture 1 spoonful at a time, tossing well after each addition. Add the crushed corn chips and toss well to mix.

Serves 8

Roux Do: For a more flavorful salad, pierce the tomatoes to absorb the salad dressing.

Chilled Avocado Soup with Ginger and Lime

2 tablespoons butter
3 shallots, minced (about ½ cup)
1 tablespoon minced fresh gingerroot
2 (14-ounce) cans low-salt chicken broth
2 tablespoons fresh lime juice
¼ teaspoon cayenne pepper
2 (13-ounce) avocados, peeled, cut into halves
and mashed (about 2¼ cups)
½ cup half-and-half
Salt and black pepper to taste

GARNISHES
Chopped fresh cilantro
Lime slices

Melt the butter in a medium saucepan over medium heat. Add the shallots and gingerroot. Sauté for 1 minute. Add the chicken broth, lime juice and cayenne pepper. Bring to a boil and reduce the heat to medium-low. Simmer for 3 minutes. Spoon into a large bowl.

Purée the avocados and half-and-half in a blender. Whisk into the soup. Season with salt and black pepper to taste. Chill, covered, for 3 to 24 hours.

To serve, ladle into soup bowls. Garnish with cilantro and lime slices.

Serves 6 to 8

Roux Do: If your avocados are not ripe, place in a brown paper bag and roll the top of the bag down to seal. Place in a dark cupboard overnight. The avocados should be ripe the next day.

To remove the avocado pit, cut the avocado into halves. Hold ½ of the avocado in the palm of your hand and place a spoon at one edge of the pit. Scoop out the pit.

Roux Don't: Don't use avocados unless they are fully ripe. Don't store avocados in the refrigerator, as they will not ripen.

Chilled Cucumber Soup

1 long English cucumber, or
2 slender unwaxed cucumbers
Salt to taste
2 garlic cloves, minced
½ teaspoon salt
1 tablespoon white wine vinegar
2 tablespoons extra-virgin olive oil
1½ cups plain yogurt
1 tablespoon fresh dill weed
1 cup chilled chicken broth, skimmed

Peel and slice the cucumber. Place the cucumber slices in a bowl. Add salt to taste and toss well. Let stand for 15 minutes or longer to draw some of the liquid from the cucumber.

Mash the garlic and ½ teaspoon salt in a large bowl to form a paste. Stir in the vinegar and olive oil. Add the yogurt, dill weed and chicken broth and mix well.

Pour the cucumber slices into a colander and rinse well. Pat dry with a clean kitchen towel. Fold into the yogurt mixture. Chill until ready to serve.

Serves 6

NOTE: You may top with lump crab meat or peeled cooked shrimp. If the cucumber contains a lot of seeds, cut into quarters lengthwise and remove the seeds.

Creole Gazpacho

ONLY MAKE THIS RECIPE IN THE SUMMERTIME WHEN YOU CAN PURCHASE FRESH TOMATOES—
CREOLE TOMATOES FROM PLAQUEMINES PARISH ARE THE BEST, IF YOU CAN GET THEM. THIS GAZPACHO
IS WONDERFUL AND SO REFRESHING FOR LUNCH ON A HOT SUMMER DAY.

2 cucumbers
8 Creole tomatoes
3 red bell peppers, seeded
2 red onions
6 garlic cloves, minced
6 cups tomato juice
1/2 cup white wine vinegar
1/2 cup olive oil
1 tablespoon kosher salt
1 1/2 teaspoons freshly ground pepper

Cut the unpeeled cucumbers into halves lengthwise and remove the seeds. Chop the cucumbers, tomatoes, bell peppers and red onions separately into 1-inch pieces. Pulse 1 vegetable at a time in a food processor until coarsely chopped. Do not overprocess.

Combine all of the processed vegetables in a large bowl. Add the garlic, tomato juice, vinegar, olive oil, kosher salt and pepper and mix well. Chill, covered, for 8 to 12 hours to enhance the flavor.

Serves 4

NOTE: You may add 1 pound medium shrimp, cooked, peeled and deveined, just before serving.

Roux Don't: Don't place the tomatoes in the sun to ripen, as this will soften them. The best way to ripen tomatoes is to place them in a brown paper bag and store in a dark spot for 3 to 4 days or until ripe.

Roux Do: Try to buy locally grown tomatoes whenever possible, as they will be riper and taste better than those you can buy in the grocery store.

2002–2003 Junior League of Greater Covington Board

As a new board, we came together in May 2002. We spent a weekend at a retreat coming up with our game plan for the year, figuring out our similarities and our differences, and basically just getting to know one another. More than any of the planned workshops and targeted discussions gave us insight into our group dynamic, the meals told the tale of our ladies. We were all responsible for some portion of the shared "three squares" for two and a half days. Each person brought things to share and sample with the group, and we marveled at all the new tastes and recipes.
As the weekend progressed, we found out who liked to cook, who didn't, who followed the recipe to the letter, and who "winged it." Our cooking styles told a lot about our board as a whole. We were a great mixture of people coming together, appreciating and embracing the differences within. Who knew we'd ever find that in a bowl of gazpacho?

Creamy Chicken Tortilla Soup

2 or 3 boneless skinless chicken breasts
1 tablespoon olive oil
½ teaspoon Creole seasoning
1 teaspoon cilantro
6 tablespoons butter
1 large onion, chopped
2 or 3 ribs celery, chopped
1 teaspoon minced garlic
3 tablespoons flour
5 tablespoons tomato sauce
9 cups chicken broth
2 tablespoons taco seasoning mix
½ teaspoon chili powder
1 teaspoon cumin
2 or 3 slices Velveeta cheese or
American cheese
½ to ¾ cup half-and-half
Fried flour tortilla strips or tortilla chips
Chopped avocados
Shredded Cheddar cheese or
Monterey Jack cheese

Sauté the chicken breasts in the olive oil in a skillet until cooked through. Sprinkle with the Creole seasoning and cilantro.

Melt the butter in a 4- to 5-quart saucepan. Add the onion, celery and garlic. Sauté until the vegetables are tender. Add the flour. Cook for 1 minute, stirring constantly. Add the tomato sauce. Cook for 3 to 4 minutes. Stir in the chicken broth. Bring to a boil. Add the taco seasoning mix, chili powder and cumin. Cook, covered, over medium heat for 20 minutes. Cut the chicken into pieces. Stir into the soup. Add the Velveeta cheese. Cook until melted, stirring constantly. Stir in the half-and-half. Ladle into soup bowls. Top with fried flour tortilla strips, chopped avocados and Cheddar cheese.

Serves 6 to 8

Chicken Tortilla Soup

2 tablespoons vegetable oil
1 green bell pepper, chopped
1 onion, chopped
2 garlic cloves, minced
1 (4-ounce) can chopped green chiles
6 cups chicken broth
3 cups chopped cooked chicken
1 (10-ounce) can tomato soup
1 (14-ounce) can stewed tomatoes
2 cups frozen whole kernel corn
2 teaspoons Worcestershire sauce
1 teaspoon cumin
1 teaspoon chili powder
¼ cup wine
Salt and pepper to taste
Hot pepper sauce to taste
5 tortillas, cut into bite-size pieces, or
tortilla chips
Shredded Cheddar cheese, Monterey Jack
cheese or Colby cheese
Sour cream
1 or 2 avocados, chopped

Heat the oil in a large heavy stockpot. Add the bell pepper, onion, garlic and green chiles. Sauté until the vegetables are tender. Add the chicken broth, chicken, tomato soup, tomatoes, corn, Worcestershire sauce, cumin, chili powder and wine. Season with salt, pepper and hot pepper sauce. Simmer over low heat for 3 hours.

To serve, place the tortilla pieces in soup bowls. Ladle the soup over the tortilla pieces. Top with cheese, sour cream and avocados.

Serves 6 to 8

Chicken and Wild Rice Soup

1 tablespoon vegetable oil
8 ounces boneless skinless chicken breasts,
cut into bite-size pieces
1 medium onion, chopped
8 ounces sliced fresh mushrooms
2 garlic cloves, finely chopped
1 (6-ounce) package long grain and
wild rice, cooked
2 (14-ounce) cans chicken broth
1/2 teaspoon tarragon
1/2 teaspoon thyme
Salt and pepper to taste
2 tablespoons cornstarch
1 (12-ounce) can evaporated milk
1/2 cup white wine

Heat the oil in a large saucepan. Add the
chicken, onion, mushrooms and garlic. Sauté
until the chicken is brown and cooked through
and the vegetables are tender. Add the cooked
rice, chicken broth, tarragon, thyme, salt and
pepper. Bring to a boil. Dissolve the cornstarch
in a small amount of the evaporated milk in a
bowl. Whisk into the chicken mixture. Add the
remaining evaporated milk, whisking constantly.
Whisk in the wine. Cook for 5 minutes or until
thickened, stirring constantly. Serve with
French bread.

Serves 4 to 6

NOTE: You may use fat-free evaporated milk,
if desired.

Roux Do: If your soup is too salty, add a
quartered potato to absorb the salt and then
discard the potato.

Crab Meat and Brie Soup

4 fish bouillon cubes
4 cups boiling water
2 (14-ounce) cans vegetable broth
1/4 cup brandy
1 cup white wine
4 cups (1 quart) heavy cream
1/2 cup (1 stick) butter
1/2 cup flour
8 to 10 ounces Brie cheese
Pinch of salt
Pinch of white pepper and cayenne pepper
1 pound jumbo lump crab meat or white crab
meat, cooked and shells removed

Dissolve the fish bouillon cubes in the boiling
water in a saucepan. Add the vegetable broth,
brandy and white wine. Bring to a simmer over
medium heat. Simmer for a few minutes. Stir
in the heavy cream. Return to a simmer over
low heat.

Melt the butter in a skillet. Blend in the
flour. Cook until smooth and creamy, stirring
constantly. Simmer over low heat for 1 minute.
Add to the cream mixture, stirring constantly.
Cook for 4 to 5 minutes or until thickened,
stirring constantly.

Cut the cheese into 1-inch cubes and the
rind into smaller pieces. Add to the soup. Cook
until the cheese is completely melted, stirring
constantly. Season with salt, white pepper and
cayenne pepper. Stir in the crab meat just
before serving.

Makes 3 quarts

Crawfish Corn Bisque with Spicy Red Pepper Cream

SPICY RED PEPPER CREAM
1 (7-ounce) jar roasted red peppers, drained and patted dry
3 tablespoons sour cream
2 tablespoons cayenne pepper sauce

BISQUE
½ cup (1 stick) butter
½ cup chopped onion
½ cup chopped green onions
2 tablespoons flour
½ teaspoon salt
½ teaspoon black pepper
½ teaspoon cayenne pepper
1 tablespoon Worcestershire sauce
10 dashes of Tabasco sauce
4 cups (1 quart) milk or half-and-half
8 ounces Cheddar cheese, shredded
2 pounds crawfish, cooked, peeled and cut into halves
3 cups fresh corn, blanched and drained (optional)

GARNISH
Chopped fresh parsley

For the red pepper cream, process the roasted red peppers, sour cream and cayenne pepper sauce in a blender or food processor until puréed.

For the bisque, melt the butter in a large saucepan. Add the onion and green onions. Sauté until translucent but not brown. Add the flour gradually, stirring constantly to prevent lumps. Add the salt, black pepper, cayenne pepper, Worcestershire sauce and Tabasco sauce. Add the milk gradually, stirring constantly to prevent lumps. Bring to a gentle boil and reduce the heat. Add the cheese. Cook until the cheese melts. Add the crawfish and corn. Stir in the red pepper cream. Ladle into soup bowls. Garnish with parsley.

Serves 6 to 8

The Art of Advice to Children

Be creative in the kitchen; don't be afraid to make mistakes and take risks, and never eat a home-cooked meal alone. If you have to eat alone, eat out!

Cream of Crawfish Soup

1 pound crawfish tails with fat, peeled
1/2 cup chopped green onions
1 cup chopped mushrooms
2 cups chicken stock, heated
1/4 cup (1/2 stick) butter
1 onion, finely chopped (about 1 cup)
1/2 cup flour
2 cups heavy cream, heated
2 cups milk, heated
2 teaspoons salt
2 teaspoons cracked pepper
2 teaspoons Creole seasoning
2 teaspoons garlic powder

GARNISH
Paprika

Process the crawfish tails, green onions and mushrooms in a food processor until ground, adding 1 cup of the chicken stock if needed. Melt the butter in a heavy 3-quart saucepan over medium-high heat. Add the onion. Sauté for 5 minutes. Stir in the flour. Cook for 1 to 2 minutes, stirring constantly. Add the remaining chicken stock and mix well. Add the ground crawfish mixture and mix well. Simmer over medium heat for 5 minutes, stirring constantly. Add the heavy cream, milk, salt, pepper, Creole seasoning and garlic powder and mix well. Bring to a boil and reduce the heat to the lowest setting. Simmer for 5 minutes, stirring constantly. Remove from the heat. Ladle into soup bowls. Garnish each lightly with a pinch of paprika.

Serves 6 to 8

Oyster Artichoke Soup

2 quarts oysters
2 bunches green onions, chopped
8 ounces mushrooms, chopped
10 whole bay leaves
Pinch of thyme
1/2 cup (1 stick) butter
1/4 cup white wine
3 tablespoons flour
2 (14-ounce) cans chicken broth
2 (14-ounce) cans artichoke hearts
(not marinated), drained and chopped
6 sprigs of fresh parsley, chopped
2 cups heavy cream
Pinch of basil
Pinch of salt and pepper

Simmer the undrained oysters in a large saucepan until the edges curl. Remove from the heat. Drain the oysters, reserving the liquor. Chop the oysters.

Sauté the green onions, mushrooms, bay leaves and thyme in the butter in a skillet until the vegetables are tender. Add the wine and flour. Cook until thickened but not brown, stirring constantly. Add the chicken broth and reserved oyster liquid. Simmer for 15 minutes. Add the chopped oysters, artichoke hearts and parsley. Simmer for 10 minutes. Remove from the heat. Stir in the heavy cream, basil, salt and pepper. Discard the bay leaves before serving.

Serves 8 to 12

Shrimp and Corn Soup

1/3 cup vegetable oil
3 tablespoons flour
2 onions, finely chopped
1 bell pepper, finely chopped
2 ribs celery, finely chopped
Salt to taste
1/2 teaspoon thyme
1/2 teaspoon black pepper
1/2 teaspoon white pepper
1/8 teaspoon cayenne pepper
1 pound uncooked medium shrimp,
peeled and deveined
2 tablespoons parsley, chopped
1/2 to 1 teaspoon liquid shrimp and crab boil
1 (14-ounce) can whole peeled
tomatoes, chopped
1 (14-ounce) can whole kernel corn
2 cups (or more) shrimp stock or
chicken stock, heated

Heat the oil and flour in a stockpot to form a blond roux, stirring constantly. Add the onions, bell pepper, celery, salt, thyme, black pepper, white pepper and cayenne pepper. Cook for 10 minutes or until the vegetables are tender. Add the shrimp, parsley and liquid shrimp and crab boil. Simmer for 5 to 10 minutes. Add the undrained tomatoes, undrained corn and hot shrimp stock. Simmer for 1 hour or until the desired consistency, adding additional shrimp stock as needed.

Serves 4 to 6

Golden Split Pea Soup

1 1/2 cups dried yellow or green split peas
1 medium onion, chopped
2 medium sweet potatoes, peeled and chopped
6 cups low-sodium chicken broth or water
2 teaspoons chicken bouillon granules
2 teaspoons cumin
1/2 teaspoon ginger
1/2 teaspoon pepper

Sort and rinse the peas. Combine the peas, onion, sweet potatoes, chicken broth, bouillon granules, cumin, ginger and pepper in a stockpot and mix well. Bring to a boil and reduce the heat to low. Simmer, covered, for 1 hour or until the peas are soft and the soup thickens, stirring occasionally.

Serves 8

Zesty Broccoli Cheese Soup

2 cups water
2 chicken bouillon cubes
1 (10-ounce) package frozen broccoli
1/2 cup chopped celery
1/4 cup chopped onion
2 tablespoons flour
1 1/2 cups milk
8 ounces Velveeta cheese, cubed
Dash of Tabasco sauce
Dash of Worcestershire sauce

GARNISH
Chopped chives

Bring the water and bouillon cubes to a boil in a saucepan. Add the broccoli, celery and onion. Cook until the vegetables are tender. Mix the flour with 1/2 cup of the milk in a bowl. Add the remaining milk to the broccoli mixture. Bring to a boil. Add the flour mixture. Cook until slightly thickened, stirring constantly. Add the cheese. Cook until the cheese melts, stirring constantly. Stir in the Tabasco sauce and Worcestershire sauce. Ladle into soup bowls. Garnish with chives.

Serves 6

Summer Squash Lemon Soup

2 onions, chopped
2 tablespoons olive oil
4 to 6 garlic cloves, chopped
1 leek, chopped
6 summer squash, chopped
5 cups chicken broth
Pinch of chopped fresh thyme, or
dried thyme to taste
Tabasco sauce to taste
2 strips of lemon peel

GARNISHES
Freshly grated Parmesan cheese
Pine nuts

Sauté the onions in the olive oil in a saucepan until translucent. Stir in the garlic and leek. Add the squash and chicken broth. Bring to a simmer. Simmer for 25 minutes. Add the thyme, Tabasco sauce and lemon peel. Purée in a blender or food processor. Pour into soup bowls. Garnish with cheese and pine nuts.

Serves 5

ROUX DO: Do store unbroken garlic bulbs for up to 3 to 4 months in a cool, dark, dry location. Individual cloves keep 5 to 10 days.

ROUX DON'T: Don't store garlic near or above the stove or sink, as heat and/or dampness will ruin the garlic.

Wild Yam Soup with an Attitude

6 sweet potatoes
2 onions
2 garlic bulbs
Olive oil for drizzling
1/4 cup olive oil
1 onion, chopped
2 ribs celery, chopped
1 teaspoon poultry seasoning
2 teaspoons cumin
1/2 teaspoon white pepper
4 (14-ounce) cans vegetable broth, or 6 cups
homemade chicken broth
Salt to taste
Cream or milk

GARNISHES
Sour cream
Sliced green onions
Chopped toasted pecans

Place the sweet potatoes and unpeeled whole onions on a lightly greased baking sheet. Bake at 400 degrees for 30 minutes.

Cut off the tops of the garlic bulbs. Drizzle with a small amount of olive oil. Wrap in foil. Place on the baking sheet with the sweet potatoes. Bake for 30 minutes or until the sweet potatoes are soft.

Heat 1/4 cup olive oil in a stockpot. Add chopped onion and celery. Sauté until the vegetables are translucent. Add the poultry seasoning, cumin and white pepper. Cook for 2 minutes, stirring constantly.

Peel the roasted sweet potatoes and roasted onions when cool enough to handle. Squeeze the pulp from the garlic bulbs. Purée the sweet potatoes, roasted onion, garlic pulp and sautéed vegetables in a food processor, adding a small amount of the vegetable broth to facilitate puréeing. Return the puréed mixture to the stockpot. Stir in the remaining broth and season with salt. Bring to a boil and reduce the heat. Simmer gently for several minutes to allow the flavors to blend. (The soup may be prepared up to this point and frozen.)

To serve, place the frozen soup in a stockpot. Heat over low heat until thawed. Cook over medium heat until heated through, adding enough cream or milk to make the desired consistency. Ladle into soup bowls. Garnish with sour cream, sliced green onions and toasted pecans.

Serves 8 to 12

Covington
THREE RIVERS
ART FESTIVAL

2001

NOVEMBER 10 & 11 • 10–5 • FREE ADMISSION
HISTORIC DOWNTOWN COVINGTON, LOUISIANA

Bravo, Bravo…Breads and Brunch

Breads and Brunch

"What this book about?"

"It's a cookbook. Read me a recipe...."

"...But what you fixing to cook? What recipe must I read?"

"Nothing. I don't care. I just want to hear a recipe."

A recipe was a consoling thing. Not all recipes, not the ones out of, say, *The Joy of Cooking*, that sounded scientific, but the ones in the ladies' cookbooks. These were the cookbooks that told the treasured family recipes and featured the names of the ladies who'd contributed them. "Tante Andrée Daube Glacé," and then at the recipe's end: "Mrs. Ernest Bouligny (Nancy Elise)" or "Maque Choux, Mrs. Charles R. Lee ('Kitten')." This was the kind of information that was as good as a dollhouse for creating entire scenes, in your mind. This Kitten Lee and Nancy Elise Bouligny were some of the women Rory thought of as the ones who knew what to do. They ran the high-ceilinged houses with waxed wood floors, where nobody's mother died. The men who owned these houses rewarded the women for their general competence and good health and fine recipes by giving them dresses and cars and jewels. There was a catch, though, to reading these cookbooks: every few pages you ran the risk of seeing a recipe supplied by an unmarried lady. These recipes were mainly for appetizers and main-dish accompaniments—the old maids knew their place—and they could frighten and sadden you. "Angel Biscuits (Miss Verolyn Colomb)" or "Pantry Shelf Tomato Wow (Miss Ruth Hoefield)." Rory didn't want to picture that pantry, and sometimes she was afraid to picture the old maids themselves—Miss Marguerite Crain, for example, of *The Bayou Teche Roll-Out-The-Barrel Cookbook*, with her prize recipe entitled "Liverwurst Ball."

"Mirliton with Shrimp Dressing," said Cato. "Six small mirliton. Four to five slice bacon, chop."

Excerpt from *Slow Poison* used with permission of the
author, Sheila Bosworth. Publisher: Alfred A. Knopf

Crawfish Blues Corn Bread

1 cup blue, white or yellow cornmeal
1 cup buttermilk
1 cup flour
2 tablespoons sugar
1 teaspoon baking powder
1/2 teaspoon baking soda
2 eggs, beaten
1/4 cup (1/2 stick) butter, melted
1 cup cream-style corn
1/2 cup (2 ounces) shredded
Pepper Jack cheese
1/2 cup (2 ounces) shredded sharp
Cheddar cheese
1 (4-ounce) can chopped mild
green chiles, drained
1/4 to 1/2 cup chopped jalapeño chiles (optional)
1 pound crawfish tail meat

Mix the cornmeal and buttermilk in a large bowl. Let stand for 30 minutes. Add the flour, sugar, baking powder, baking soda, eggs and butter and mix well. Stir in the corn, Pepper Jack cheese, Cheddar cheese, green chiles, jalapeño chiles and crawfish. Pour into a greased 9×13-inch baking pan. Bake at 375 degrees for 30 minutes or until golden brown. Serve hot or at room temperature.

Serves 6 to 8

Hot Water Corn Bread

1 cup stone-ground cornmeal
1/2 cup flour
1 teaspoon salt
1/2 teaspoon garlic powder
1 to 1 1/2 cups boiling water
Vegetable oil for deep-frying

Mix the cornmeal, flour, salt and garlic powder in a bowl. Stir in enough of the boiling water to make a batter thick enough to stick to a spoon.
Heat oil to 360 degrees in a deep fryer. Drop the batter by spoonfuls into the hot oil. Deep-fry for 10 minutes or until golden brown.

Serves 6 to 8

NOTE: You may order stone-ground cornmeal from War Eagle Mill in Arkansas.

Three Rivers Art Festival

The fun starts with art and just keeps going for two wonderful days at the Covington Three Rivers Art Festival held every November in historic downtown Covington. See photography, sculpture, pottery, paintings, glass, woodwork, jewelry, and more as 160 artists sell their work in colorful tents along Columbia Street. Enjoy music, food, and lots of activities for kids. There is also a 5K Race, a Student Art Exhibition, and an Arts Alive! Stage where artists actually demonstrate their work. This art festival has become a major attraction of St. Tammany Parish and its arts community. It strives to enhance and build upon tourism by bringing artists as well as festival attendees into our parish. Call 985-871-4141 or visit www.threeriversartfestival.com.

Aunt Joyce's Mexican Corn Bread

3 eggs, beaten
1½ cups yellow cornmeal
1 tablespoon baking powder
1 teaspoon salt
1 cup buttermilk
½ cup vegetable oil
3 jalapeño chiles, finely chopped
4 slices bacon, crisp-cooked and crumbled
1 (4-ounce) jar chopped pimentos
1 (14-ounce) can cream-style corn
3 tablespoons finely chopped onion
1 cup (4 ounces) shredded sharp
Cheddar cheese

Combine the eggs, cornmeal, baking powder, salt, buttermilk, oil, jalapeño chiles, bacon, pimentos, corn, onion and cheese in the order listed in a large bowl and mix well. Pour into a greased 9×12-inch baking dish. Bake at 400 degrees for 45 minutes or until brown.

Serves 6 to 10

This recipe is taken from The Aunts' Cookbook, *developed by my sister, Phyllis Kelly Kennedy, as a fiftieth anniversary gift to my parents, Mr. and Mrs. R. L. Kelly of Titus, Alabama. My sister explained our appreciation for the wonderful food prepared by our mother and aunts, "As a little girl, I figured that I was rich. They always talked in Sunday School about poor people who didn't have enough to eat. The logical conclusion was that since we had such good food, and so much of it, we certainly must be rich. Obviously, I learned better eventually, but I still feel that a heritage of bountiful food, fresh and lovingly prepared, is as fine a gift as a family could give to me." I am thankful for all the warm memories and wonderful recipes passed on to me from my mother, sister, and aunts.*

—Paula Kelly Meiners

Spinach Bread

1 (10-ounce) package frozen chopped spinach
4 to 6 garlic cloves, chopped
¼ cup olive oil
1 loaf French bread
1 (14-ounce) can artichoke hearts,
drained and chopped
½ cup parsley, chopped
4 cups (16 ounces) shredded
mozzarella cheese
1 cup (4 ounces) shredded Swiss cheese

Cook the spinach using the package directions; drain. Sauté the garlic in the olive oil in a small skillet for 2 to 3 minutes or until light brown.

Cut the top from the bread and reserve. Remove the center from the bread to form a shell. Tear the removed bread into small pieces and place in a large bowl. Add the artichoke hearts, spinach, undrained garlic, parsley, mozzarella cheese and Swiss cheese and mix well. Pack into the bread shell and replace the reserved top. Wrap in foil. (You may chill or freeze until ready to bake. If frozen, thaw before baking.) Bake at 350 degrees for 20 minutes.

Serves 6 to 8

NOTE: If you have any extra filling, spoon into a baking dish and sprinkle with bread crumbs. Bake as directed above.

Herb Focaccia

3 tablespoons olive oil
1 cup packed minced yellow onion
2 medium garlic cloves, minced
1/4 cup fresh basil, minced
1 tablespoon fresh thyme, minced
2 tablespoons fresh rosemary, minced
Freshly ground pepper to taste
1 1/2 cups (105 to 115 degrees) water
1 cup (105 to 115 degrees) milk
1 tablespoon salt
2 teaspoons sugar
2 1/2 teaspoons dry yeast
Pinch of sugar
6 1/2 cups bread flour
Olive oil for brushing
Cornmeal for dusting
Coarse salt for sprinkling

Heat 3 tablespoons olive oil in a medium skillet over medium heat. Add the onion and garlic. Reduce the heat to low. Sauté for 3 minutes or until the onion is softened and fragrant. Add the basil, thyme, rosemary and pepper. Cook for 1 minute. Spoon into a large bowl. Stir in 1 cup of the water, the milk, salt and 2 teaspoons sugar.

Dissolve the yeast and a pinch of sugar in the remaining 1/2 cup water in a small bowl until the mixture is creamy and begins to bubble. Add to the onion mixture. Add the bread flour 1 cup at time, stirring until the dough becomes too thick to stir. Place on a lightly floured surface. Knead in enough of the remaining bread flour to keep the dough from sticking. Knead for 5 minutes or until the dough is smooth and elastic.

Place in a large bowl generously greased with olive oil, turning to coat the surface. Cover the bowl with plastic wrap and a clean kitchen towel. Let rise for 1 to 2 hours or until doubled in bulk. Punch the dough down. Let rise, covered, for 1 hour or until doubled in bulk.

Brush olive oil over the bottom and sides of a 13×17-inch heavy aluminum baking sheet. Sprinkle with cornmeal and tap to remove any excess.

Punch the dough down and turn out onto a work surface sprinkled with cornmeal. Turn the dough over and coat lightly with cornmeal. Shape into a rough rectangle. Lift the dough and place on the prepared baking sheet. Pat and gently pull the dough to cover the baking sheet. Let rise, uncovered, in a draft-free place for 45 to 60 minutes or until almost doubled in bulk. Dip your fingers in flour and make many deep indentations in the dough. Brush lightly with olive oil and sprinkle with coarse salt.

Place on an oven rack positioned in the bottom third of the oven. Toss ice water on the oven floor. Bake at 450 degrees for 30 minutes or until the edges are crisp and deep golden brown. Slide the focaccia onto a large rack to cool using a long metal spatula. To serve, cut into pieces with a serrated knife.

Serves 12

ROUX DO: Do store bread at room temperature. It will stay fresher longer than if stored in the refrigerator.

Jazz Fest Crawfish Braided Bread

THIS TASTES LIKE THE WORLD-FAMOUS CRAWFISH BREAD SOLD AT THE NEW ORLEANS JAZZ FEST.
IT'S JUST AS DELICIOUS, BUT THE BEST PART IS THAT YOU WON'T HAVE TO WAIT IN A LONG
LINE IN NINETY-PLUS-DEGREE WEATHER TO GET IT.

1 pound crawfish tails, coarsely chopped
1 (4-ounce) jar pimentos, drained and chopped
¾ cup chopped green onions
½ cup (2 ounces) shredded
Pepper Jack cheese
½ cup (2 ounces) shredded Cheddar cheese
Salt, pepper and Creole seasoning to taste
2 (8-count) cans refrigerator
crescent roll dough
½ teaspoon thyme, chopped (optional)
½ teaspoon oregano, chopped (optional)
½ teaspoon sweet basil, chopped (optional)
1 egg white, lightly beaten
Sesame seeds (optional)

Combine the crawfish, pimentos, green onions, Pepper Jack cheese and Cheddar cheese in a large bowl and mix well. Season with salt, pepper and Creole seasoning.

Unroll the crescent roll dough. Place in a large bowl. Add the thyme, oregano and basil. Knead until the herbs are combined with the dough. Roll into a 10×14-inch rectangle on a floured surface. Spoon the crawfish mixture lengthwise down the center. Cut the dough into 1- to 1½-inch strips from the edge to the filling on each side with a sharp paring knife. Fold the strips alternately across the filling to form a braid. (You may cover the braid at this point and refrigerate until ready to bake.)

Brush the braid with the egg white. Sprinkle with sesame seeds. Bake at 400 degrees for 30 to 35 minutes or until golden brown. Cut into slices before serving.

Serves 10

Global Wildlife Center:
The Art of Safari

Was that a giraffe you just saw in Robert, Louisiana? Yes, and a baby one at that. The Global Wildlife Center, located in Robert, Louisiana, is home to over 3,000 exotic, endangered, and threatened animals from all over the world and is the largest free-roaming wildlife preserve in the country. The Global Wildlife Center is dedicated to educating children and adults alike on the importance of ensuring the conservation of endangered species. Visitors are able to view animals and, most exciting of all, feed and pet them while on a guided Safari Wagon Tour. Every spring, the Center holds its annual fund-raiser, Starry Safari, featuring live music, food from local restaurants, a silent auction, and artwork from Louisiana artists to benefit the Animal Care Program at the Center. For more information on the Global Wildlife Center, call 985-624-WILD or go to www.globalwildlife.com.

Moggie's Angel Biscuits

5 cups flour
1 tablespoon baking powder
1/4 teaspoon sugar
1 teaspoon salt
1 cup shortening
1 envelope dry yeast
2 tablespoons warm water
2 cups buttermilk
Melted margarine for dipping

Mix the flour, baking powder, sugar and salt in a large bowl. Cut in the shortening until crumbly. Dissolve the yeast in the warm water in a bowl. Stir in the buttermilk.

Add to the flour mixture and mix well; let rise 20 minutes. Knead on a lightly floured surface. Divide into 2 equal portions. Roll each portion into an 8- to 10-inch circle. Cut with a biscuit cutter. Dip each biscuit in melted margarine and fold over. Place on a baking sheet. Bake at 400 degrees for 12 to 15 minutes or until light brown.

Makes 2 1/2 dozen

Roux Do: Always start at the outer edge of the dough when using biscuit or cookie cutters, and always flour the cutters before using.

The Art of Southern Cooking

Southern cooking is a multi-sensory experience—it involves your senses of smell, taste, touch, sight, and sound. The sizzle of the skillet as you fry chicken, the smell of freshly baked cobbler, the feel of bread dough in your palms—it is all part of the whole experience.

—*Allie Pierson*

Cheddar Biscuits

2 cups flour
1 tablespoon baking powder
1 teaspoon baking soda
1 teaspoon salt
1 teaspoon sugar
1/2 cup (1 stick) unsalted butter, chilled
1 cup buttermilk
1/2 cup (2 ounces) coarsely shredded
Cheddar cheese

Mix the flour, baking powder, baking soda, salt and sugar in a bowl. Cut in the butter until the mixture resembles cornmeal using a pastry cutter or 2 knives. Make a well in the center of the mixture. Pour the buttermilk into the well and add the cheese. Stir quickly for 1 to 2 minutes or until the dough pulls away from the side of the bowl. Place the dough on a floured surface. Knead gently and quickly for 4 turns or until the dough is no longer sticky. Roll or pat the dough 1/2 inch thick. Dip a 2 1/2-inch biscuit cutter in flour and cut the dough into 12 circles. Place on an ungreased baking sheet. Bake at 400 degrees for 12 to 15 minutes or until golden brown.

Makes 1 dozen

Roux Do: Only buy biscuit or cookie cutters with sharp edges.

Blueberry Scones

SCONES
2¼ cups flour
½ cup sugar
2 teaspoons baking powder
½ teaspoon salt
½ cup (1 stick) unsalted butter, chilled
2 eggs
¼ cup milk
1 teaspoon vanilla extract
¼ teaspoon lemon zest
1½ cups fresh or drained thawed frozen
blueberries or a mixture of favorite berries

CRUMB TOPPING
¾ cup flour
¼ cup packed light brown sugar
⅛ teaspoon cinnamon
¼ cup (½ stick) unsalted butter, chilled

For the scones, lightly butter an 11-inch circle in the center of a baking sheet. Mix the flour, sugar, baking powder and salt in a bowl. Cut the butter into ½-inch cubes. Add to the flour mixture and cut with a pastry blender or 2 knives to resemble coarse crumbs. Combine the eggs, milk, vanilla and lemon zest in a small bowl and stir to mix well. Stir into the crumbly mixture. (The dough will be extremely sticky. Add a small amount of flour if needed to make the dough workable.) Knead in the blueberries until evenly distributed. Shape the dough into a 9- or 11-inch circle on the prepared baking sheet.

For the topping, mix the flour, brown sugar and cinnamon in a bowl. Cut the butter into ½-inch cubes. Add to the flour mixture and cut with a pastry blender or 2 knives to resemble coarse crumbs.

To assemble, sprinkle the topping evenly over the dough to cover the whole surface. Press the topping lightly into the dough. Cut the circle into 8 wedges using a serrated knife. Bake at 375 degrees for 30 to 35 minutes or until a wooden pick inserted in the center comes out clean and the top is light brown. Cool on the baking sheet on a wire rack for 15 to 20 minutes. Serve warm, recutting the wedges if necessary, or cool completely and store in an airtight container.

Makes 8

Cranberry Oatmeal Scones

1½ cups flour
¼ cup sugar
1 tablespoon baking powder
½ teaspoon salt
1¼ cups quick-cooking oats
½ cup dried cranberries
1 egg
1 cup (2 sticks) butter, melted
⅓ cup milk

Mix the flour, sugar, baking powder, salt, oats and cranberries in a large bowl. Combine the egg, butter and milk in a bowl and mix well. Add to the flour mixture and mix until moistened. Do not overmix. (Add a small amount of additional flour if the mixture is too thin.) Drop by spoonfuls onto an ungreased baking sheet. Bake at 450 degrees for 10 to 12 minutes or until light brown. Serve warm.

Makes 8

NOTE: You may prepare the dough in advance and chill in the refrigerator for 8 to 12 hours.

Chocolate Banana Bread

1¼ cups flour
1 teaspoon baking soda
¼ cup baking cocoa
½ cup (1 stick) unsalted butter, softened
1 cup sugar
2 eggs
3 bananas, mashed
1 teaspoon vanilla extract
½ cup sour cream
6 ounces bittersweet chocolate, finely chopped

Mix the flour, baking soda and baking cocoa in a medium bowl. Beat the butter and sugar at medium-high speed in a mixing bowl for 2 minutes or until light and fluffy. Add the eggs 1 at a time, beating well after each addition. Add the bananas and vanilla. Beat at low speed until combined. Add the flour mixture ⅓ at a time, alternating with the sour cream ½ at a time and beating well after each addition. Add the chocolate and mix for a few seconds. Spoon into a buttered 5×9-inch loaf pan and smooth the top. Bake at 350 degrees for 55 to 60 minutes or until a wooden pick inserted in the center comes out clean. Cool in the pan for 15 minutes. Invert onto a wire rack to cool completely.

Serves 12

NOTE: This bread freezes well.

Roux Do: When removing the butter from the refrigerator for softening, also remove the eggs and milk. The dough or batter consistency will be better when all ingredients are at room temperature.

Blueberry Banana Bread

½ cup shortening
1 cup sugar
2 eggs
1 cup mashed bananas
½ cup quick-cooking oats
½ cup chopped pecans
1½ cups flour
1 teaspoon baking soda
¼ teaspoon salt
½ cup fresh blueberries

Cream the shortening in a mixing bowl. Add the sugar gradually, beating until light and fluffy. Add the eggs 1 at a time, beating well after each addition. Stir in the bananas.

Mix the oats, pecans, flour, baking soda, salt and blueberries in a bowl. Add to the banana mixture, stirring gently just until moistened. Spoon into a greased and floured 5×9-inch loaf pan.

Bake at 350 degrees for 50 to 55 minutes or until light brown. Cool in the pan for 10 minutes. Remove to a wire rack to cool completely.

Serves 12

My grandmother, Mama Ruth, made everything from scratch and always had food for anyone who dropped by. She didn't worry about flour spills or fingers in the bowl. Mama Ruth made biscuits every morning, and I used to eat the dough. I also got to cut the biscuits and supervise. My granddad's favorite thing on them—besides lots of butter—was a thick slice of Cheddar cheese cut from the big wheel at the local store. The cheese melted between the biscuit halves—uhm, I can still taste that today. I don't make biscuits, but I do make Blueberry Banana Bread. I know Mama Ruth would be proud.

—Phoebe Faggard Whealdon

Cheddar Pepper Quick Bread

5 cups flour
2 tablespoons sugar
2 teaspoons baking powder
1½ teaspoons salt
1½ teaspoons coarsely ground pepper
1 teaspoon baking soda
2 cups (8 ounces) shredded extra-sharp Cheddar cheese
4 eggs
4 scallions, thinly sliced
2 cups plain low-fat yogurt
⅔ cup olive oil
2 tablespoons Dijon mustard
½ cup (2 ounces) shredded extra-sharp Cheddar cheese

Mix the flour, sugar, baking powder, salt, pepper and baking soda in a large bowl. Stir in 2 cups cheese. Whisk the eggs, scallions, yogurt, olive oil and Dijon mustard in a medium bowl. Add to the flour mixture and mix just until combined. (The batter will be stiff.) Spoon into 2 greased 5×9-inch loaf pans, spreading evenly and smoothing the tops.

Bake at 350 degrees for 40 to 45 minutes or until the tops are brown and a wooden pick inserted in the centers comes out clean. Remove the pans to wire racks. Sprinkle the loaves with ½ cup cheese. Cool in the pans.

Makes 2 loaves

Southern Hospitality Cranberry Bread

Juice and zest of 1 orange
2 tablespoons shortening
Boiling water
2 cups flour
1/2 teaspoon baking soda
1/2 teaspoon salt
1 1/2 teaspoons baking powder
1 cup sugar
1 egg, beaten
1 cup cranberry halves
1 cup nuts

Place the orange juice, orange zest and shortening in a 1-cup measure. Add enough boiling water to measure 3/4 cup. Let stand until cool.

Mix the flour, baking soda, salt, baking powder and sugar in a bowl. Add the orange juice mixture and egg and mix well. Fold in the cranberries and nuts. Spoon into a nonstick 5×9-inch loaf pan.

Bake at 350 degrees for 45 to 60 minutes or until golden brown. Serve with butter.

Serves 12

Key Lime Muffins

2 cups flour
1 tablespoon baking powder
1/2 teaspoon salt
1 cup sugar
1/3 cup milk
2 eggs, lightly beaten
1/4 cup vegetable oil
1/3 cup Key lime juice
1 teaspoon lime zest

Mix the flour, baking powder, salt and sugar in a large bowl. Make a well in the center. Combine the milk, eggs, oil, lime juice and lime zest in a bowl and mix well. Add to the well in the center of the flour mixture and stir just until moistened. Spoon into lightly greased muffin cups, filling 3/4 full.

Bake at 400 degrees for 28 minutes or until light brown. Remove immediately from the muffin cups.

Makes 1 dozen

Roux Do: Place hot muffin pans on a wet towel for no-stick removal.

Pistachio Bread

BATTER
1 cup (2 sticks) butter, softened
8 ounces cream cheese, softened
1¼ cups sugar
4 eggs
½ teaspoon vanilla extract
2 cups flour
1½ teaspoons baking soda
1 (4-ounce) package pistachio pudding mix

FILLING
½ cup packed brown sugar
½ cup chopped pistachios
1 tablespoon cinnamon

For the batter, beat the butter, cream cheese and sugar in a mixing bowl until smooth. Add the eggs 1 at a time, beating well after each addition. Stir in the vanilla. Add the flour, baking soda and pudding mix and mix well.

For the filling, mix the brown sugar, pistachios and cinnamon in a bowl.

To assemble, divide ½ of the batter between 2 greased 5×9-inch loaf pans. Divide the filling between each pan, spreading evenly. Pour the remaining batter over the top of each, spreading evenly.

Bake at 325 degrees for 50 to 60 minutes or until golden brown.

Makes 2 loaves

Old-Fashioned Pumpkin Bread

1⅔ cups flour
¼ teaspoon baking powder
1 teaspoon baking soda
¾ teaspoon salt
½ teaspoon cinnamon
½ teaspoon nutmeg
1⅓ cups sugar
⅓ cup shortening
2 eggs
1 cup cooked fresh or canned pumpkin
⅓ cup water
½ teaspoon vanilla extract
½ cup pecans, chopped

Sift the flour, baking powder, baking soda, salt, cinnamon and nutmeg together. Cream the sugar and shortening in a mixing bowl. Add the eggs, pumpkin, water and vanilla and mix well. Add the flour mixture and pecans and mix just until moistened. Do not overmix. Pour into a greased 5×9-inch loaf pan.

Bake at 350 degrees for 50 minutes or until a wooden pick inserted in the center comes out clean.

Serves 12

ROUX DO: Do store eggs in their original carton in the coldest part of the refrigerator, discarding cracked, broken, or leaking eggs.

ROUX DON'T: Don't store eggs in one of the door compartments of the refrigerator, even if the manufacturer has provided a space for them. Storing eggs in the door will expose them to fluctuating temperatures every time you open your refrigerator door.

Strawberry Bread

3 cups flour
1 teaspoon salt
1 teaspoon baking soda
1 tablespoon cinnamon
2 cups sugar
3 eggs, beaten
1¼ cups vegetable oil
2 (10-ounce) packages frozen sliced
strawberries, thawed
1¼ cups chopped pecans

Mix the flour, salt, baking soda, cinnamon and sugar in a large bowl. Make a well in the center. Add the eggs and oil to the well and mix until moistened. Stir in the strawberries and pecans. Pour into 2 greased 5×9-inch loaf pans.

Bake at 350 degrees for 1 hour or until the loaves test done.

Makes 2 loaves

Louisiana Seasons: The Art of Laissez les Bon Temps Rouler!

It is a popular Southeast Louisiana joke that we have three seasons: hot, humid, and rainy! In reality, however, we have more seasons than the rest of the states—we have crawfish season, crab season, oyster season, shrimp season, duck season, fishing season, Mardi Gras season, horse racing season, LSU football season, LSU basketball season, LSU baseball season, and of course—it's all flavored with cayenne seasoning!

—St. Tammany Parish President Kevin Davis

Overnight Banana French Toast

3 medium bananas, cut into slices
¼ inch thick
1 tablespoon lemon juice
12 (½-inch-thick) slices French bread,
untrimmed
2 eggs, beaten
¾ cup milk
2 tablespoons honey
½ teaspoon vanilla extract
¼ teaspoon cinnamon
¼ cup sliced almonds
1 teaspoon sugar
Maple syrup or confectioners' sugar (optional)

Toss the bananas with the lemon juice in a bowl. Arrange ½ of the bread slices in a greased 2-quart square baking dish. Layer the banana slices over the bread. Top with the remaining bread.

Beat the eggs, milk, honey, vanilla and cinnamon in a bowl. Pour gradually over the bread to coat evenly. Chill, covered, for 6 to 24 hours.

Uncover the baking dish. Sprinkle with the almonds and sugar. Bake at 425 degrees for 5 minutes. Reduce the oven temperature to 325 degrees. Bake for 20 to 25 minutes longer or until a knife inserted in the center comes out clean and the top is light brown. Let stand for 10 minutes before slicing to serve. Serve with maple syrup or sprinkle with confectioners' sugar if desired.

Serves 4 to 6

French Toast Custard

8 to 10 (1-inch-thick) slices dry
French bread
5 tablespoons butter, melted
4 eggs
2 egg yolks
3 cups milk
1 cup heavy cream
1/2 cup sugar
1 teaspoon vanilla extract
1/4 teaspoon nutmeg
Confectioners' sugar for sprinkling (optional)

Brush both sides of the bread slices with the butter. Place in a greased 9×13-inch baking dish. Beat the eggs and egg yolks in a large mixing bowl. Add the milk, heavy cream, sugar, vanilla and nutmeg and mix well. Pour over the bread. Chill, covered, for 8 to 12 hours. Remove from the refrigerator 30 minutes before baking.

Bake, uncovered, at 350 degrees for 55 to 60 minutes or until a knife inserted near the center comes out clean. Cool for 10 minutes before serving. Sprinkle with confectioners' sugar if desired.

Serves 8 to 10

Make-Ahead Praline French Toast

THIS IS SO GOOD. IT'S NICE BECAUSE
YOU CAN PREPARE THE NIGHT BEFORE AND BAKE
THE NEXT MORNING.

1/2 cup (1 stick) butter
1 cup packed brown sugar
2 tablespoons light corn syrup
1 loaf French bread, or 2 baguettes,
sliced 2 inches thick
5 eggs
1 1/2 cups cream or milk
1 teaspoon vanilla extract
1/2 teaspoon cinnamon
1/4 teaspoon nutmeg

Heat the butter, brown sugar and corn syrup in a saucepan until the butter melts, stirring constantly. Pour into a 9×13-inch baking dish. Arrange the bread in the mixture. Combine the eggs, cream, vanilla, cinnamon and nutmeg in a bowl and mix well. Pour over the bread, soaking each slice. Chill, covered, for 8 to 12 hours.

Bake, uncovered, at 350 degrees for 30 minutes. Remove from the oven. Flip the bread slices onto each serving plate. You already have the syrup on your toast.

Serves 4 to 6

Roux Do: To differentiate between a hard-cooked and uncooked egg, carefully spin the egg on a countertop. The hard-cooked egg will spin because it's solid, so everything will spin in one direction. The uncooked egg, however, will not spin, as the white and yolk will slosh around in different directions, preventing the egg from spinning.

Stuffed French Toast

FILLING
8 ounces cream cheese, softened
1 teaspoon vanilla extract
½ cup chopped pecans

FRENCH TOAST
1 loaf French bread
4 eggs
1 cup heavy cream
½ teaspoon vanilla extract
½ teaspoon grated nutmeg
½ teaspoon grated cinnamon

TOPPING
1 (12-ounce) jar strawberry preserves
½ cup orange juice

For the filling, beat the cream cheese and vanilla in a mixing bowl until fluffy. Stir in the pecans.

For the French toast, cut the bread into 12 slices 1½ inches thick. Cut a pocket in the top of each. Fill each with 1½ tablespoons of the cream cheese mixture. Beat the eggs, heavy cream, vanilla, nutmeg and cinnamon in a medium bowl. Dip the filled bread slices in the egg mixture, being careful not to squeeze out the filling.

Cook on a lightly greased griddle until both sides are golden brown. Keep warm on a baking sheet in a 200-degree oven until ready to serve.

For the topping, heat the strawberry preserves and orange juice in a saucepan, stirring constantly.

To serve, place the filled French toast on individual serving plates. Drizzle the topping over the top.

Serves 12

NOTE: You may also top with maple syrup or puréed fresh strawberries.

Magnificent Morning Breakfast Pie

1 pound uncooked shrimp, peeled, deveined and chopped
2 tablespoons butter
1½ cups (6 ounces) shredded Swiss cheese
1 unbaked (10-inch) deep-dish pie shell
4 eggs
1 cup light cream
2 teaspoons chopped onion
¼ cup chopped red bell pepper
¼ cup chopped green bell pepper
¼ cup chopped yellow bell pepper (optional)

Sauté the shrimp in the butter in a skillet for 2 minutes. Remove the shrimp to a bowl with a slotted spoon. Add the cheese and toss to mix well. Prick the pie shell with a fork. Spoon the shrimp mixture into the pie shell. Beat the eggs, cream, onion and bell peppers in a bowl. Pour over the shrimp mixture.

Bake at 375 degrees for 40 to 45 minutes or until set.

Serves 6 to 8

"Louisiana may be, as is rumored, the end of the earth. But along with the humid crevices where the swamp rats breed and thrive, Louisiana has got the sweet old places such as Mandeville and Covington. Mandeville is green and sadly glamorous in spots, owing to a proximity to the lake, but Covington, to the north, has the dark surging rivers, the Tchefuncte, the Pearl, the Bogue Falaya, that put you in mind of unstoppable urges and the allurement of carnal promises."

—Excerpt from *Slow Poison* was used with the permission of the author, Sheila Bosworth. Publisher: Alfred A. Knopf.

Chile Egg Puff

10 eggs
½ cup flour
1 teaspoon baking powder
½ teaspoon salt
16 ounces small curd cottage cheese
1 pound Monterey Jack cheese, shredded
½ cup (1 stick) butter, melted
2 (4-ounce) cans chopped green chiles

Beat the eggs in a mixing bowl until light and pale yellow. Add the flour, baking powder, salt, cottage cheese, Monterey Jack cheese and butter and beat well. Stir in the green chiles. Pour into a well-greased 9×13-inch baking dish.

Bake at 350 degrees for 35 to 40 minutes or until the top is brown and the center appears firm. Serve hot.

Serves 10 to 12

Breakfast Treat

2 cups cubed ham
1 cup fresh or thawed frozen hash browns
1 cup (4 ounces) shredded sharp
Cheddar cheese
5 eggs
¼ cup milk
⅛ teaspoon pepper
2 tablespoons grated Parmesan cheese

Sprinkle the ham in a greased 10-inch pie plate. Cover with the hash browns. Sprinkle with the Cheddar cheese. Beat the eggs, milk and pepper in a mixing bowl. Pour over the Cheddar cheese. Sprinkle with the Parmesan cheese.

Bake at 375 degrees for 30 to 35 minutes or until the top is slightly puffed and a knife inserted in the center comes out clean.

Serves 6 to 8

Time Line for Storing Eggs

- *Fresh eggs in the shell will keep for 3 to 4 weeks in the coldest part of your refrigerator.*

- *Fresh egg whites, covered, will keep for 2 to 4 days in your refrigerator.*

- *Fresh, unbroken egg yolks, covered with cold water, will keep for 2 to 4 days in your refrigerator.*

- *Hard-cooked eggs will keep for 1 week in your refrigerator.*

- *Deviled eggs will keep for 2 to 3 days in your refrigerator.*

- *Leftover egg dishes, such as quiches or breakfast casseroles, will keep for 3 to 4 days in your refrigerator.*

- *How can you tell a good egg from a bad egg? Place the egg in a bowl of heavily salted cold water. If it sinks, it's a good egg. If it floats, it's a bad egg—throw it away.*

Breakfast Quesadilla

TOO GOOD JUST FOR BREAKFAST.

8 eggs
Salt and pepper to taste
7 tablespoons butter
8 whole wheat or flour tortillas
16 thick slices bacon, cooked
1 cup guacamole
2 cups salsa or pico de gallo

GARNISH
Sprigs of cilantro or flat-leaf parsley

Whisk the eggs, salt and pepper in a bowl. Heat 4 tablespoons of the butter in a nonstick skillet or sauté pan over medium heat until melted and sizzling. Add the eggs. Reduce the heat. Cook to the desired degree of doneness, stirring constantly. Remove from the heat and keep warm in a 250-degree oven.

Heat the remaining 3 tablespoons butter in a skillet or on a griddle over medium-high heat until melted and sizzling. Add 1 tortilla. Cook for 2 minutes. Turn the tortilla. Place 1/8 of the scrambled eggs, 2 slices of the bacon and 2 tablespoons of the guacamole in the middle of the tortilla. Fold the tortilla in half to form a quesadilla. Cook for 1 minute longer or until crisp. Remove from the heat and keep warm in a 250-degree oven. Repeat the process with the remaining tortillas, scrambled eggs, bacon and guacamole.

To serve, place 2 quesadillas on each serving plate. Top with salsa. Garnish with cilantro or flat-leaf parsley.

Serves 4

Shahreya (Sha-reé-ah)

SHAHREYA IS A TRADITIONAL MIDDLE EASTERN BREAKFAST. INSTEAD OF PANCAKES, MY FATHER ALWAYS MADE SHAHREYA FOR MY BROTHER AND ME ON SUNDAY MORNINGS. NOW MY BROTHER AND I MAKE SHAHREYA FOR OUR CHILDREN. YOUR KIDS WILL LOVE THIS.

1 tablespoon butter
1 package fine vermicelli
Water
1½ cups sugar
Milk

Melt the butter in a 5-quart stockpot over medium-high heat. Break up the vermicelli and add to the butter. Cook until the vermicelli is brown, stirring constantly. Add enough water to just cover the vermicelli. Cover the stockpot and reduce the heat to medium-low. Cook until the vermicelli has absorbed the water. Stir in the sugar. Serve warm with milk in cereal bowls.

Serves 6 to 8

NOTE: Vermicelli is very thin pasta that comes in small bundles resembling birds' nests. It is available on the pasta aisle in most grocery stores.

Baked Garlic Cheese Grits

THESE GRITS ARE TRADITIONALLY SERVED
AT OUR ANNUAL SUSTAINER CHRISTMAS BRUNCH.
EVERYONE LOVES THEM.

4 cups water
1 cup uncooked grits
1/2 teaspoon salt
1/2 cup (1 stick) butter
1 (6-ounce) roll garlic cheese, sliced
8 ounces sharp Cheddar cheese, shredded
2 tablespoons Worcestershire sauce

Bring the water to a boil in a saucepan.
Stir in the grits and salt gradually. Cook
for 4 minutes or until thickened, stirring
occasionally. Add the butter, garlic cheese,
Cheddar cheese and Worcestershire sauce
and stir until the butter and cheese melt.
Pour into a greased baking dish.

Bake at 350 degrees for 20 to 25 minutes
or until brown and bubbly.

Serves 8 to 10

Shrimp and Cheese Grits

6 cups water
1/2 teaspoon salt
2 cups quick-cooking grits
1 cup (4 ounces) shredded sharp
Cheddar cheese
Pinch of ground nutmeg
1 teaspoon Tabasco sauce
12 slices bacon, coarsely chopped
2 pounds uncooked large shrimp,
peeled and deveined
8 ounces mushrooms, sliced
2 cups sliced green onions
2 teaspoons minced garlic
2 1/2 tablespoons fresh lemon juice
Salt and pepper to taste
Tabasco sauce to taste
1/4 cup fresh parsley, chopped

Bring the water and 1/2 teaspoon salt to a boil
in a heavy saucepan. Whisk in the grits. Cover
and reduce the heat. Simmer for 10 minutes or
until thickened and soft, stirring occasionally.
Whisk in the cheese and nutmeg. Season
with 1 teaspoon Tabasco sauce. Cover and
keep warm.

Cook the bacon in a heavy skillet over
medium heat until brown but not crisp.
Remove to a bowl using a slotted spoon. Drain
the skillet, reserving 1/2 of the drippings. Sauté
the shrimp in the reserved drippings in the
skillet for 2 minutes per side or until the
shrimp turn pink. Remove to a platter using a
slotted spoon, reserving the drippings in the
skillet. Add the mushrooms to the reserved
drippings. Sauté for 4 minutes or until tender.
Add the green onions and garlic. Sauté for
3 minutes. Return the shrimp and bacon to
the skillet. Stir in the lemon juice. Season
with salt, pepper and Tabasco sauce to taste.

Return the grits to a simmer, adding water
1 tablespoon at a time if too thick. Spoon the
grits onto serving plates. Spoon the shrimp
mixture over the grits. Sprinkle with parsley.

Serves 4

1999
HARVEST CUP POLO CLASSIC

Supporting Roles...To Serve on the Side

To Serve on the Side

The love of good food is part of your heritage if you are born in the heart of Cajun country in Southwest Louisiana. When I think of home in Church Point, Louisiana, I think of our family in the kitchen seated around the table. Mama would stir the pots and serve what I still believe to be the best food in the world. There was always enough in the pot to feed anyone who showed up at the dinner hour.

I learned my basic cooking skills from watching my mother in the kitchen, just as she had learned from generations before her. After graduating from college and moving to Baton Rouge, I taught classes in Cajun cooking.

In 1975, I was asked to write a weekly gourmet column for *The Baton Rouge Morning Advocate* newspaper. I agreed but wondered how I would come up with enough recipes to get through two months. Today, twenty-eight years later, I'm still writing two weekly columns in *The Advocate*.

I'm a firm believer in the family sitting together for meals. Special rewards come from creating and serving a good meal. I call it "making memories."

The recipe for Ursula's Corn Bread Dressing is from my cookbook *Extra! Extra! Read All About It!* Ursula Beaugh was our neighbor. I cannot imagine a holiday meal without this dressing. We must continue passing on recipes and traditions so lovingly passed on to us.

—Corinne Cook
Food Columnist, *The Advocate*
Cookbook Author

One of the fun things about South Louisiana is that words don't mean what they mean in the dictionary. "She's such a confident girl" really means she's pushy and high-handed. Saying "Your niece is real sweet" means she'll never win Miss Mayhaw Nectar, bless her. And the same euphemisms apply to food.

"Christmas" is really just another word for cream. Christmas Mold is three cranberries trying to fight their way out of six pounds of cream cheese. Christmas Salad is neither Christmas nor salad, more like ambrosia with half-and-half, doubled. And when someone says "Don't cha just love Sissie's Christmas Spinach?" the fitting response is "What's not to like when the ratio of heavy cream to spinach is 4 to 1?" The *proper* response is "Oh I live for it!" In bayou country, if more is better, then a stockpot's worth is just right. Sauces are thicker; étouffées are denser; and stirring a proper gumbo builds muscle. We don't skimp on flavor, portions, passion—much less butter, sugar, or cream. The secret, though, is never to talk about any of this. "Have you tried Sissie's Christmas Spinach? It's sooo good, I don't know what she puts in it…"

—Tim Allis
Senior Editor, *In Style*

Ursula's Corn Bread Dressing

2½ cups cornmeal
¾ cup flour
1½ teaspoons salt
3 tablespoons baking powder
1 tablespoon sugar
3 tablespoons vegetable oil
3 eggs
3 cups milk
2 pounds lean ground beef
2 onions, chopped
1 bell pepper, chopped
3 garlic cloves, chopped
1 cup chopped celery
Salt, black pepper and cayenne pepper to taste
1 (14-ounce) can beef broth
2 (10-ounce) cans cream of mushroom soup
1 teaspoon Kitchen Bouquet
¼ cup chopped fresh parsley
¼ cup chopped green onions
3 eggs, lightly beaten

Mix the cornmeal, flour, salt, baking powder and sugar in a bowl. Add the oil, eggs and milk and mix well. Pour into a greased 11-inch cast-iron skillet. Bake at 425 degrees for 30 to 35 minutes or until golden brown.

Brown the ground beef in a large skillet, stirring until crumbly; drain. Add the onions, bell pepper, garlic and celery. Season with salt, black pepper and cayenne pepper to taste. (This should be relatively spicy since you will be mixing it with the corn bread.) Add the beef broth. Cook slowly, covered, for 45 minutes. Add the soup, Kitchen Bouquet, parsley and green onions and mix well.

Crumble the corn bread. Add to the ground beef mixture and mix well. Adjust the seasonings to taste. Stir in the eggs. Spoon into a large baking dish.

Bake at 350 degrees for 30 to 45 minutes or until set.

Serves 12

Harvest Cup Polo Classic

Imagine a crisp fall Sunday afternoon and a field covered with colorful flying flags and big white tents filled with fun, conversation, and laughter. Sip Mint Juleps and sample gourmet treats from great restaurants while enjoying a polo match that could include Major Ferguson (Fergie's dad) or Tommy Lee Jones. You might meet David Yurman and treat yourself to a new piece of jewelry; or shop for original artwork, spa treatments, and New Orleans weekend packages at a silent auction market; or bid on a Napa Valley trip in the live auction. Peruse the polo match and the sometimes even greater spectacle of the local Who's Who dressed to kill. It's all a part of the Junior League of Greater Covington's Harvest Cup Polo Classic! It may sound a bit indulgent, but it's all for a good cause. All proceeds benefit the many community projects of the Junior League of Greater Covington.

The Harvest Cup Polo Classic is held on the first Sunday in November at Folsom Equestrian Center in Folsom. For more information, call 985-727-4038 or go to www.JLGC.net.

Crawfish Pecan Dressing

1 pound lean ground beef
1 medium onion, chopped
1 rib celery, chopped
1 green bell pepper, chopped
1 red bell pepper, chopped
2 garlic cloves, minced
3 (16-ounce) packages frozen peeled crawfish tails, thawed
2 cups cooked long grain rice
1 cup pecans, chopped
1/4 cup (1/2 stick) butter or margarine, cut into pieces
1 small bunch green onions, chopped
2 tablespoons Creole seasoning
1/2 teaspoon pepper
Chopped fresh parsley

Cook the ground beef, onion, celery, bell peppers and garlic in a Dutch oven over medium-high heat for 10 minutes or until the ground beef is brown and crumbly, stirring constantly. Stir in the crawfish tails, rice, pecans, butter, green onions, Creole seasoning and pepper. Cook until heated through. Spoon into a greased 9×13-inch baking dish.

Bake at 350 degrees for 25 to 30 minutes or until light brown. Sprinkle with parsley.

Serves 8 to 10

Corn Bread Soufflé

1/2 cup (1 stick) butter
2 eggs
1/2 cup water
1 package corn bread mix, such as Jiffy
2 (14-ounce) cans cream-style corn
1 onion, chopped

Melt the butter in a 9×12-inch baking dish in a 350-degree oven. Beat the eggs and water in a mixing bowl. Add the corn bread mix, corn and onion and mix well. Pour into the melted butter. Spread the butter that collects in the corners of the dish over the top.

Bake at 350 degrees for 1 hour.

Serves 10 to 12

Perfect Rice

1 cup uncooked long grain rice
1 1/2 cups boiling water

Place the rice in a 2-quart glass baking dish with a lid. Add the boiling water. Cover with the lid. Bake at 350 degrees for 20 to 25 minutes or until you can't see water bubbling through the sides of the dish. This rice comes out perfectly every time.

Serves 4

"Cato's people were natives of Ohio, he didn't know any better than not to stir rice."

—Excerpt from *Slow Poison* used with the permission of the author, Sheila Bosworth. Publisher: Alfred A. Knopf.

Italian Sausage and Wild Mushroom Risotto

1 pound Italian sweet sausage
8 ounces portobello mushrooms
2 tablespoons olive oil
10 ounces fresh shiitake mushrooms,
    stemmed and sliced
1 teaspoon chopped fresh thyme
1 teaspoon chopped fresh oregano
1½ cups madeira
½ cup (1 stick) butter
4 garlic cloves, minced
2 cups arborio rice
4 cups chicken stock
1½ cups (6 ounces) freshly grated
    asiago cheese
Salt and pepper to taste
Freshly grated asiago cheese
    to taste

Remove the casings from the sausage. Crumble the sausage into ½-inch pieces. Remove the stems and dark gills from the portobello mushrooms. Cut the portobello mushrooms into slices.

Heat the olive oil in a large skillet over medium-high heat. Add the sausage. Sauté for 3 minutes or until the sausage begins to brown. Add the portobello mushrooms, shiitake mushrooms, thyme and oregano. Sauté for 10 minutes or until the mushrooms are tender. Add ½ cup of the madeira. Boil for 1 minute or until almost absorbed.

Melt the butter in a 4-quart or larger pressure cooker over medium-high heat. Add the garlic. Sauté until translucent. Add the rice. Cook for 2 minutes or until light brown, stirring frequently. Add the remaining 1 cup madeira. Simmer for 2 minutes or until absorbed. Add the chicken stock. Increase the heat to high. Bring to a boil, stirring constantly. Stir in the sausage mixture; seal. Bring pressure to high heat using the manufacturer's directions. Adjust the heat to stabilize the pressure. Cook for 6 to 7 minutes, reducing the heat to medium. Remove from the heat and release the pressure. Stir in 1½ cups cheese. Season with salt and pepper. Sprinkle with cheese to taste.

Serves 4 to 6

Lemon Florentine Rice

1 bunch fresh spinach (4 ounces)
1/2 small onion, finely chopped
2 tablespoons olive oil
1 cup uncooked brown rice
1/4 teaspoon salt
3 tablespoons lemon juice
1 3/4 cups water

Rinse the spinach and chop medium-fine.
Sauté the onion in the olive oil in a skillet.
Stir in the brown rice, spinach, salt and lemon
juice. Add the water. Bring to a boil and reduce
the heat. Simmer, covered, for 45 minutes or
until the rice is tender.

Serves 4

Roux Do: Do add a tablespoon of lemon
juice to the water for fluffier rice.

Lemon Risotto

LEMON JUICE AND LEMON ZEST OFFER A DOUBLE
PUNCH OF FLAVOR IN THIS DELICIOUS DISH. SERVE
THE RISOTTO ITALIAN-STYLE AS A FIRST COURSE
OR AMERICAN-STYLE AS A MAIN COURSE.

6 cups canned low-sodium chicken broth
1 1/2 tablespoons butter
1 1/2 tablespoons olive oil
2 shallots, chopped
2 cups arborio rice or medium grain white rice
1/4 cup dry white wine
1 cup (4 ounces) freshly grated
Parmesan cheese
2 tablespoons butter
2 tablespoons chopped fresh parsley
2 tablespoons fresh lemon juice
4 teaspoons lemon zest
Salt and pepper to taste

Bring the chicken broth to a simmer in a large
saucepan over medium heat. Reduce the heat
to low. Cover to keep warm.
  Melt 1 1/2 tablespoons butter with the
olive oil in a large heavy saucepan over
medium heat. Add the shallots. Sauté for
6 minutes or until tender. Add the rice. Cook
for 1 minute, stirring constantly. Add the
wine. Cook for 30 seconds or until evaporated,
stirring constantly. Add 1 1/2 cups of the hot
chicken broth. Simmer until absorbed, stirring
frequently. Repeat with the remaining broth
1/2 cup at a time until all of the broth has been
absorbed and the rice is creamy and tender.
(The process should take about 35 minutes.)
Stir in the cheese and 2 tablespoons butter.
Stir in the parsley, lemon juice and lemon zest.
Season with salt and pepper.

Serves 4 to 6

NOTE: Serve with Marinated Tuna with
Vinaigrette Niçoise (page 104).

Zucchini Lasagna Luzianne

2 pounds Creole-seasoned bulk sausage
1 pound Italian sausage, casings removed
5 garlic cloves, minced
1 pound fresh mushrooms, thinly sliced
1/2 bell pepper, minced
1 medium onion, minced
3 ribs celery, minced
3 tablespoons fresh parsley, minced
1 tablespoon vegetable oil
4 cups whole tomatoes, chopped
1 cup tomato paste
1/2 cup water or dry red wine
2 beef bouillon cubes
1/4 teaspoon cayenne pepper
1 teaspoon basil
1 teaspoon oregano
1 teaspoon salt
1/2 teaspoon allspice
1/2 teaspoon pepper
4 teaspoons sugar
12 medium zucchini (about 5 ounces each)
2 2/3 cups part-skim ricotta cheese, at room temperature
1 1/2 pounds mozzarella cheese, shredded
6 ounces Parmesan cheese, grated

Brown the Creole sausage and Italian sausage in a skillet, stirring until crumbly; drain well. Sauté the garlic, mushrooms, bell pepper, onion, celery and parsley in the oil in a heavy 5-quart stockpot until tender. Add the tomatoes, tomato paste, water, bouillon cubes, cayenne pepper, basil, oregano, salt, allspice, pepper and sugar and mix well. Stir in the sausage mixture. Simmer for 1 hour.

Steam the whole zucchini in a steamer for 5 minutes. Let stand until cool. Cut the zucchini lengthwise into slices about 1/4 inch thick.

Alternate layers of the sauce, zucchini, ricotta cheese, mozzarella cheese and Parmesan cheese in a roasting pan or lasagna pan sprayed with nonstick cooking spray, beginning and ending with the sauce. Bake at 350 degrees for 1 hour. Let stand for 10 minutes before serving.

Serves 8 to 10

Louisiana has a unique culture, and one that has become ingrained in our daughters who have grown up on the Northshore. We cherish the special memories of the food and the festivals, the gumbo, crawfish, and barbecued shrimp, all an integral part of our lives in this area. We proudly share these Louisiana experiences and culinary delights with our out-of-state guests.

We appreciate the supper times in our home, which have been a key to solidifying our family unit. These are the times we share a meal and the activities of the day, with the old pine kitchen table serving as the main gathering place around some of our favorite dishes. As adults, our daughters now display excellent skills in their kitchens, having gleaned the magic of the savory spices that so saturate our wonderful Louisiana culture, and now pass them on to their families.

—JoAnne and Jim Cole

Manicotti

SAUCE
1 onion, chopped
Vegetable oil for sautéing
2 garlic cloves
2 (6-ounce) cans tomato paste
2 (8-ounce) cans tomato sauce
4 tomato sauce cans water
1 tablespoon (heaping) sugar
Basil to taste
Salt and pepper to taste

FILLING
1 pound ricotta cheese
2 tablespoons parsley
2 tablespoons grated Parmesan cheese
4 ounces mozzarella cheese, shredded
2 teaspoons sugar
Salt and pepper to taste

ASSEMBLY
8 to 10 manicotti shells
1/4 cup (1 ounce) shredded mozzarella cheese

For the sauce, sauté the onion in a small amount of oil in a skillet until light brown. Add the garlic, tomato paste, tomato sauce, water, sugar, basil, salt and pepper and mix well. Cook until of the desired consistency, stirring frequently.

For the filling, mix the ricotta cheese, parsley, Parmesan cheese, mozzarella cheese, sugar, salt and pepper in a bowl.

To assemble, stuff the filling into the manicotti shells. Arrange in a nonstick baking dish. Cover with the sauce.

Bake, covered with foil, at 400 degrees for 1 hour. Sprinkle with the cheese. Bake for 10 minutes longer.

Serves 4

Linguini with Asparagus, Garlic and Lemon

6 ounces dried linguini
Salt to taste
1 onion, chopped
2 teaspoons minced garlic
1/4 cup olive oil
2 tablespoons unsalted butter
Pepper to taste
8 ounces asparagus, trimmed and cut
diagonally into thin slices
3 tablespoons dry white wine
1 tablespoon water
2 tablespoons fresh lemon juice, or to taste
3 tablespoons freshly grated Parmesan cheese

Cook the linguini in boiling salted water in a saucepan for 10 minutes or until al dente; drain.

Sauté the onion and garlic in the olive oil and butter in a heavy skillet over medium heat until golden brown. Season with salt and pepper. Add the asparagus. Cook over medium heat for 2 minutes, stirring constantly. Add the wine. Cook for 2 minutes longer, stirring constantly. Remove from the heat. Add 1 tablespoon water, lemon juice, hot linguini, cheese, salt and pepper and toss to mix well.

Serves 2

Shrimp and Spinach Orzo with Fresh Herbs

7 ounces baby spinach leaves,
trimmed and rinsed
5½ ounces arugula, rinsed and
coarsely chopped
¼ cup fresh flat-leaf parsley leaves,
coarsely chopped
¼ cup fresh cilantro leaves, coarsely chopped
5 green onions, coarsely chopped
2 tablespoons extra-virgin olive oil
1 tablespoon garlic olive oil
9 ounces orzo
1 pound cooked spicy shrimp, peeled and
deveined (optional)
Crumbled feta cheese to taste

GARNISH
Lemon slices

Blanch the spinach, arugula, parsley, cilantro and green onions in boiling water in a saucepan for 15 seconds; drain. Immerse in ice water to stop the cooking process; drain. Squeeze out the excess moisture. Process in a small food processor. Add the extra-virgin olive oil and garlic olive oil in a fine stream, processing constantly until well blended.

Cook the orzo using the package directions; drain. Combine the orzo, spinach mixture and shrimp in a large bowl and toss to mix well. Adjust the seasonings to taste. Sprinkle with cheese. Garnish with lemon slices. Serve hot, at room temperature or cold.

Serves 4

Pasta with Brie Cheese

1 wheel Brie cheese
1 tomato, chopped
½ cup fresh basil, chopped
1 garlic clove, minced
16 ounces pasta
Shredded Parmesan cheese to taste

Remove the rind from the Brie cheese and place the cheese in a large bowl. Let stand until room temperature. Add the tomato, basil and garlic and mix well. Let stand to come to room temperature.

Cook the pasta using the package directions; drain. Add to the Brie cheese mixture and toss until the Brie cheese is completely melted. Sprinkle with Parmesan cheese. Serve hot or cold.

Serves 6 to 8

Roux Don't: Don't overcook shrimp, it will ruin the delicate flavor of the shrimp. To properly boil shrimp, place a pound of shrimp in a quart of rapidly boiling highly seasoned water. Cover and return to a boil. Reduce the heat and simmer until the shrimp loses its glossy appearance and is opaque in the center. Jumbo shrimp will cook in about 7 to 8 minutes, and medum shrimp in about 3 to 4 minutes.

Penne
à la Vodka

1 pound penne
3 tablespoons olive oil
¼ cup chopped onion
1 teaspoon crushed red pepper
2 garlic cloves, crushed
4 ounces prosciutto, chopped
1 (28-ounce) can whole tomatoes
¼ cup chopped parsley
3 tablespoons fresh basil, chopped
Salt to taste
½ cup vodka
1 cup heavy cream
1 cup (4 ounces) grated Parmesan cheese

GARNISH
Fresh basil leaves

Cook the pasta in a saucepan using the package directions until al dente. Heat the olive oil in a skillet. Add the onion and red pepper. Sauté until tender. Stir in the garlic and prosciutto. Sauté for 2 minutes.

Drain the tomatoes, reserving ¼ cup juice. Add the tomatoes, reserved tomato juice, parsley, basil, salt and vodka to the prosciutto mixture. Simmer until the sauce is thickened and reduced, stirring to break up the tomatoes. Simmer for 15 minutes. Stir in the heavy cream. Simmer for 5 minutes.

Drain the pasta. Add the sauce and cheese and toss to coat. Spoon into a large serving bowl. Garnish with fresh basil.

Serves 6 to 8

Muffuletta Pasta

24 ounces penne
4 (10-ounce) cans seasoned chicken broth
¼ cup minced garlic
Olive oil for sautéing
12 ounces Genoa salami, finely chopped
12 ounces ham, finely chopped
1 pound provolone cheese
1 large jar olive salad, slightly drained
1 (4-ounce) can sliced black olives
12 ounces Romano cheese, shredded

Boil the pasta in the chicken broth in a large saucepan until al dente; drain. Sauté the garlic in olive oil in a skillet. Add the sautéed garlic, salami, ham, provolone cheese, olive salad, black olives and Romano cheese to the pasta and mix well, adding additional olive oil if necessary. Spoon into a large baking pan. Bake at 350 degrees for 30 to 40 minutes or until all of the cheese melts.

Serves 6 to 8

Summertime Spaghetti

Make this spaghetti in the summer so you can use fresh tomatoes. Creole tomatoes from Plaquemines or St. Bernard Parish are the best.

6 fresh tomatoes, peeled, seeded and chopped
4 sweet basil leaves, chopped
2 garlic cloves, minced
1/4 cup extra-virgin olive oil
Salt and white pepper to taste
12 ounces spaghetti
8 ounces tomato-basil feta cheese or
plain feta cheese
6 to 8 kalamata olives, sliced
Freshly grated Parmesan cheese

Mix the tomatoes, basil, garlic, olive oil, salt and white pepper in a saucepan. Let stand at room temperature for 1 hour to allow the flavors to blend. Heat the sauce gently, but do not cook.

Cook the pasta using the package directions; drain. Add the heated sauce, feta cheese and olives and toss to coat. Spoon into a pasta bowl. Sprinkle with Parmesan cheese.

Serves 4

NOTE: You may add 2 cups chopped cooked chicken to serve as an entrée.

Holiday Baked Fruit

This is a great side dish for any type of pork. It is great served with ham for Sunday brunch. This is made one day ahead of time and then reheated, so plan accordingly. If you are in a pinch, you can serve it immediately after you have baked it (just increase the baking time by 15 minutes), but it really tastes best when made ahead, allowed to cool, and reheated.

1 (14- to 15-ounce) can apricot
halves, drained
1 (14- to 15-ounce) can cling peaches, drained
1 (14- to 15-ounce) can pineapple
slices, drained
1 (14- to 15-ounce) can pear halves, drained
2 bananas, sliced
1/2 cup pitted black cherries, drained
1/3 cup butter, melted
3/4 cup packed light brown sugar
4 teaspoons curry powder

Cut the apricot halves, peaches, pineapple slices and pear halves into bite-size pieces. Pat dry with paper towels. Place the apricots, peaches, pineapple, pears, bananas and cherries in a 1 1/2-quart baking dish. Mix the melted butter, brown sugar and curry powder in a small bowl. Spoon over the fruit.

Bake, uncovered, at 325 degrees for 1 hour. Remove from the oven to cool. Chill, covered, for 8 to 12 hours.

To serve, bake the fruit mixture at 350 degrees for 30 minutes. Serve with Coca-Cola Ham (page 130) and Moggie's Angel Biscuits (page 67).

Serves 8 to 10

Stuffed Artichokes

4 large artichokes
3 cups Italian bread crumbs
3 cups (12 ounces) grated Parmesan cheese
12 to 16 garlic cloves, pressed
6 ounces (3/4 cup) extra-virgin olive oil

Trim off the prickly ends of the artichokes. Rinse the trimmed artichokes well with water; drain.

Mix the bread crumbs, cheese and garlic in a bowl. Drizzle about 2 to 3 ounces of the olive oil over the mixture to moisten. (This process is done so that after the artichoke is stuffed, the added olive oil will not run off but will be absorbed into the mixture.)

Starting at the bottom of each artichoke, fill each of the leaves with 1 tablespoon of the bread crumb mixture, working around the artichoke until you reach the top. Drizzle the remaining olive oil around and over the top. Arrange the stuffed artichokes in a steamer. Steam, without letting the artichokes touch the water, for 1 hour or until the leaves pull away easily and are tender. Serve hot or cold.

Serves 4

Roux Do: Do pick artichokes that are deep green with a light leaf formation. To store artichokes, sprinkle with a little water and refrigerate in an airtight container.

Creamy Cabbage Casserole

1 head cabbage, chopped
1 teaspoon salt
1/4 teaspoon black pepper
1 onion, chopped
1 (8-ounce) block Velveeta cheese, sliced
1 (10-ounce) can cream of mushroom soup
1 tablespoon parsley
1/8 teaspoon red pepper (optional)
1/2 cup bread crumbs

Cook the cabbage in a small amount of water seasoned with the salt and black pepper in a saucepan for 10 to 12 minutes or until tender; drain.

Place the onion in a 2-quart microwave-safe ovenproof baking dish. Microwave on High for 3 to 4 minutes or until translucent. Add the cheese. Microwave on High until melted. Stir in the soup and parsley. Season with the red pepper. Add the cabbage and toss to mix well. Sprinkle with the bread crumbs. Bake at 325 degrees for 25 minutes or until bubbly.

Serves 6 to 8

Sweet and Spicy Baby Carrots

1 1/2 pounds baby carrots
2 tablespoons brown sugar
1 teaspoon soy sauce
1 tablespoon vegetable oil or canola oil
1 tablespoon mustard

Cook the carrots in water to cover in a saucepan or steam until tender; drain. Do not overcook.

Combine the brown sugar, soy sauce, oil and mustard in a large bowl and mix well. Add the carrots and toss to coat.

Arrange the carrots in a single layer on a baking sheet.

Broil for 8 to 10 minutes or until brown.

Serves 8 to 10

The Art of Horse Country

Heading north out of Covington, you're not immediately struck by the change of terrain— it sneaks up on you. By the time you come to the first of many horse farms, you realize that the land is no longer flat. It undulates gently now, slowly, shimmering into the haze. Thick stands of pine trees and hedgerows brimming with azaleas have given way to the sweep of lush pastures and majestic oaks. State-of-the-art stud farms, polo barns, equestrian centers, and backyard boarding enterprises stand shoulder to shoulder for mile after rolling mile. Folsom is the village heart of this horse country.

—Judi Sinclair Dauterive

Sponsored by Bank One

Eight-Goal Eggplant

1 large eggplant, peeled and thinly sliced
Salt to taste
2 cups cornflake crumbs
1 teaspoon garlic salt
1 teaspoon pepper
2 eggs, beaten
1/2 to 1 cup olive oil
1 (8-ounce) can tomato sauce
2 (10-ounce) cans tomatoes with
green chiles, drained
2 tablespoons minced onion
Oregano, basil and Creole seasoning to taste
1/3 to 1/2 cup (1 1/3 to 2 ounces) freshly grated
Parmesan cheese

Soak the eggplant in salted water to cover in a bowl for 30 minutes. Drain and pat dry. Mix the cornflake crumbs with the garlic salt and pepper in a shallow dish. Dip the eggplant in the eggs. Dredge in the cornflake mixture. Fry in the olive oil in a skillet until golden brown. Drain on paper towels.

Process the tomato sauce, tomatoes with green chiles, onion, oregano, basil and Creole seasoning in a blender. Layer the eggplant, tomato sauce mixture and cheese 1/3 at a time in a deep baking dish. Bake at 350 degrees for 35 to 45 minutes or until bubbly.

Serves 6 to 8

Horseradish Green Beans

THESE ARE EXCELLENT AND DIFFERENT—SO MUCH BETTER THAN THE SAME OLD GREEN BEANS. YOUR GUESTS AND FAMILY WILL LOVE THEM.

GREEN BEANS
2 pounds fresh green beans, trimmed
1 onion, sliced
3 garlic cloves, minced
1 ham hock, or several pieces of
ham and bacon

HORSERADISH SAUCE
1 cup light mayonnaise
2 hard-cooked eggs, chopped
1 tablespoon horseradish, or to taste
1 teaspoon Worcestershire sauce
Juice of 1 lemon
2 teaspoons parsley flakes

For the green beans, cook the green beans, onion, garlic and ham hock in water to cover in a saucepan for 1 hour or longer.

For the horseradish sauce, blend the mayonnaise, hard-cooked eggs, horseradish, Worcestershire sauce, lemon juice and parsley flakes in a bowl. Let stand to come to room temperature.

To assemble and serve, drain the green beans. Spoon the horseradish sauce over the green beans and toss to coat, being careful to not break the green beans.

Serves 6 to 8

NOTE: The horseradish sauce may be stored in the refrigerator for up to 2 weeks. If you are in a hurry, you may use two 14-ounce cans whole green beans, but fresh is best.

Variation: Serve chilled green beans with the horseradish sauce in a bowl for a cocktail party, or you can use as a dip with other vegetables.

Roasted Portobello Mushrooms

THIS IS A GREAT SIDE FOR GRILLED MEAT OR MAKES A DELICIOUS MEATLESS SANDWICH.

1/2 cup balsamic vinegar
1 1/2 cups olive oil
2 or 3 garlic cloves, finely minced
1 teaspoon salt
1 teaspoon pepper
4 large whole portobello mushrooms
4 medium shallots, minced, or 1 small bunch green onions, minced

GARNISHES
Crumbled feta cheese
Chopped fresh chives

Blend the balsamic vinegar, olive oil, garlic, salt and pepper in a bowl. Clean the mushrooms thoroughly with a soft cloth. Trim the stems. Place the mushroom caps upside down in a shallow baking dish lined with waxed paper. Sprinkle with the shallots. Pour the marinade over the mushroom caps, being sure to coat each one thoroughly. Marinate at room temperature for 20 minutes or longer. Bake, uncovered, at 350 degrees for 20 minutes. To serve, carefully lift the mushrooms from the marinade using a large slotted spatula. Serve garnished with cheese and chopped chives.

Serves 4

How Much Garlic to Use?

One clove = 1/2 teaspoon minced garlic = 1/8 teaspoon garlic powder = 1/4 teaspoon garlic juice = 1/2 teaspoon garlic salt.

Pick cloves that are firm, with tight skins and paper-like covering intact. Unbroken bulbs can last up to 4 months, but individual cloves only last up to 10 days. Store in a cool, dark, dry place.

Baked Potato Casserole

6 white potatoes
1 cup sour cream
1 cup (4 ounces) shredded Cheddar cheese
1/2 cup (1 stick) butter, melted
1 cup crumbled crisp-cooked bacon
1 cup chopped green onions
Salt and pepper to taste

Rinse and scrub the potatoes well. Boil the unpeeled potatoes in water to cover in a saucepan until tender; drain. Chill in the refrigerator.

Grate, mash or chop the unpeeled potatoes in a large bowl. Add the sour cream, cheese, butter, bacon and green onions and mix well. Season with salt and pepper. Spoon into a large baking dish.

Bake at 350 degrees for 25 minutes or until bubbly.

Serves 10

NOTE: Cutting the potatoes into large chunks prior to boiling will cut down on the cooking time. Cutting the potatoes into cubes will cut even more boiling time.

Cajun Mashed Potatoes

2 pounds white potatoes, peeled and chopped
Salt to taste
1 pound crawfish tails with fat, cooked
2 teaspoons Creole seasoning
1/8 teaspoon cayenne pepper
2 tablespoons butter
1 teaspoon minced garlic
2 tablespoons thinly sliced green onions
2 tablespoons butter
1/2 to 1 cup heavy cream
White pepper to taste

Bring the potatoes to a boil in salted water to cover in a saucepan and reduce the heat. Simmer for 8 to 10 minutes or until fork-tender. Remove from the heat and drain. Return the potatoes to the saucepan. Cook for 2 minutes or until the potatoes are dehydrated, stirring constantly.

Season the crawfish with Creole seasoning and cayenne pepper.

Melt 2 tablespoons butter in a sauté pan. Add the potatoes. Sauté for 2 minutes. Stir in the garlic and green onions. Mash the potatoes with 2 tablespoons butter in a bowl. Fold in the crawfish and continue mashing. Add enough heavy cream to make of the desired consistency. Season with salt and white pepper to taste.

Serves 4

Treasured Potatoes

8 to 10 medium potatoes
1 cup (4 ounces) shredded provolone cheese
1 tablespoon finely chopped onion
1 teaspoon Creole seasoning
1/2 teaspoon salt
1/2 teaspoon black pepper
Cayenne pepper to taste
1/4 cup (1/2 stick) butter
1 cup half-and-half

Boil the potatoes in water to cover in a saucepan just until tender. Drain and cool completely. Peel the potatoes and grate into a large bowl using the large side of a food grater. Add the cheese, onion, Creole seasoning, salt, black pepper and cayenne pepper and mix well. Adjust the seasonings to taste. Spoon into a 9×13-inch baking dish. Dot with the butter. Pour the half-and-half over the potatoes just before baking.

Bake at 375 degrees for 30 minutes or until bubbly.

Serves 6 to 8

Truck Stop Potatoes

5 pounds small red potatoes
2 large onions, chopped
3/4 cup (1 1/2 sticks) butter
2 cups sour cream
8 ounces Monterey Jack cheese, shredded
8 ounces Cheddar cheese, shredded
Salt and cayenne pepper to taste

GARNISHES
2 tomatoes, chopped
1 avocado, sliced
Chopped green onions
1 cup sour cream

Boil the potatoes in water to cover in a saucepan until tender; drain. Finely chop the unpeeled potatoes. Combine the potatoes, onions and butter in a bowl and mix well. Spoon into a baking dish.

Bake at 350 degrees until the top is brown, stirring occasionally. Remove from the oven and cool slightly.

Combine the potatoes, sour cream, Monterey Jack cheese and Cheddar cheese in a bowl and mix well. Season with salt and cayenne pepper. Return to the oven. Bake until heated through. Garnish with the chopped tomatoes, avocado, green onions and sour cream.

Serves 6 to 8

Spectacular Spinach

2 pounds fresh spinach, or 2 (10-ounce)
packages frozen chopped spinach
1 teaspoon salt
1/4 cup olive oil, or 2 tablespoons olive oil and 2
tablespoons vegetable oil
3 tablespoons sliced almonds or pine nuts
1/4 cup sliced pimento-stuffed green olives
1/4 cup sliced black olives
1 tablespoon capers, drained
3 tablespoons raisins

Rinse the spinach and drain. Place in a skillet
and sprinkle with the salt. Cook, covered, for
5 minutes or until the spinach wilts. (If using
frozen spinach, cook 1 minute less than
the package instructs.) Drain and chop
if necessary.

Heat the olive oil in a skillet. Stir in the
almonds. Sauté until golden brown. Add the
olives, capers and raisins. Sauté until heated
through. Add the spinach. Cook until heated
through, stirring constantly. Serve warm.

Serves 6

Sausage and Squash Casserole

2 pounds yellow squash,
cut into slices 1/2 inch thick
2 medium onions
1 garlic clove
1/4 cup (1/2 stick) butter
1 cup bread crumbs
1 pound bulk pork sausage,
cooked and drained
4 eggs, lightly beaten
1 1/2 cups (6 ounces) grated Parmesan cheese
1 cup chopped pecans
1 cup milk, warmed
1 tablespoon salt
Pepper to taste
1/4 cup (1/2 stick) butter, melted
1 1/2 cups bread crumbs
1 1/2 cups chopped pecans

Boil the squash in water to cover in a saucepan
for 30 minutes; drain. Mash the squash. Sauté
the onions and garlic in 1/4 cup butter in a
skillet until the onions are translucent. Add
to the squash. Stir in 1 cup bread crumbs, the
sausage, eggs, cheese, 1 cup pecans and the
milk. Season with the salt and pepper. Spoon
into a greased 2-quart baking dish.

Mix 1/4 cup butter, 1 1/2 cups bread crumbs
and 1 1/2 cups pecans in a bowl. Sprinkle over
the squash mixture.

Bake at 350 degrees for 30 minutes.

Serves 8 to 10

Gruyère Cheese, Artichoke and Tomato Pie

1 medium onion, sliced
2 tablespoons unsalted butter
1 unbaked (9-inch) pie shell
8 ounces Gruyère cheese,
cut into slices 1/4 inch thick
4 medium tomatoes, sliced
1/2 cup chopped fresh basil
Salt and pepper to taste
1 (14-ounce) can artichoke hearts,
cut into quarters
1/2 cup (2 ounces) thinly sliced
mozzarella cheese

Sauté the onion in the butter in a skillet until the onion is translucent. Cover the bottom of the pie shell completely with the Gruyère cheese. Cover the Gruyère cheese with the tomato slices. Sprinkle with 1/2 of the basil. Season with salt and pepper. Layer with the sautéed onion, artichoke hearts and remaining basil. Top with a layer of the mozzarella cheese.

Bake at 325 degrees for 1 hour or until golden brown.

Serves 6 to 8

Opelousas Yams Supreme

8 medium sweet potatoes
2 tablespoons orange juice
1/2 teaspoon cinnamon
1/4 teaspoon nutmeg
1 cup milk
1/4 cup (1/2 stick) butter
3 tablespoons sugar
2 teaspoons vanilla extract
3/4 cup flour
1/2 cup (1 stick) butter, melted
1 cup packed brown sugar
1 cup chopped pecans

Bake the sweet potatoes at 350 degrees until cooked through. Peel the sweet potatoes and place in a bowl. Mash the sweet potatoes. Add the orange juice, cinnamon and nutmeg and mix well.

Scald the milk in a saucepan. Stir in 1/4 cup butter, the sugar and vanilla. Add to the sweet potato mixture and mix well. Spoon into a baking dish.

Mix the flour, 1/2 cup butter, brown sugar and pecans in a bowl. Spread over the sweet potato mixture.

Bake at 350 degrees for 30 to 40 minutes, covering with foil if the topping begins to brown too quickly.

Serves 10 to 12

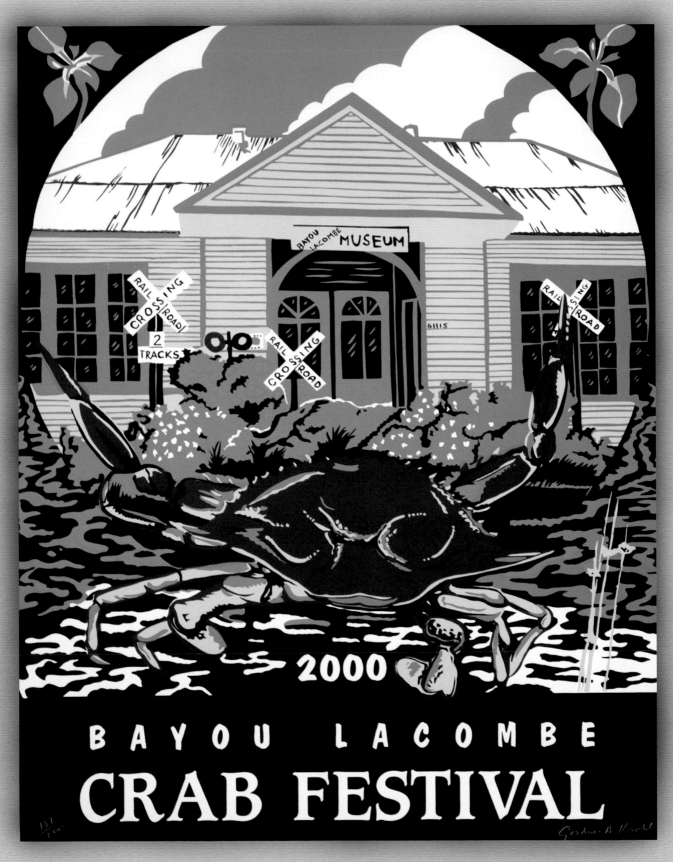

Les Fruits de Mer…A Seafood Spectacular

A Seafood Spectacular

Walker Percy is the writer who put Covington on the map. Percy was reported to have said that when he first started writing, he liked to write in motels at many various locations because the different locales gave him inspiration and perspective.

However, Percy spent the last few years of his career writing in his loft in his daughter Ann's Kumquat Bookstore in Covington.

While Percy and his wife, Bunt, could have lived in any exotic or expensive place in the world, Percy chose Covington. He reportedly said he lived in an ordinary house in an ordinary place on an ordinary tree-lined bayou.

But Percy, himself, was anything but ordinary. Among other honors too numerous to list, he won the National Book Award in 1992 for *The Moviegoer*. Pope John Paul II invited him to Rome for an audience. Every college student in the world who has taken a course in American literature is familiar with the Percy legend.

Percy's wit and wisdom was at its best when describing his life in the small town of Covington. He said the town Budweiser distributor had more name recognition than he. When asked about the role of a famous writer in a small community, Percy chuckled.

"People ask me what I do, and I say I write books. Then they ask me what I REALLY do, and I say 'nothing.' They look at me blankly. I go to the barber shop and the barber says, 'How you doin', Doc?' or I go to the post office and the clerk says, 'What's up, Doc?' or I go to my favorite restaurant on Lake Pontchartrain and the waitress says, 'What you want, Honey?' I then order some cold beer and crawfish that are very good."

Percy's gift was his ability to read and appreciate the nuances of human nature, and to write about it. He is truly an American legend.

Reprinted with the permission of
"West St. Tammany: A Pictorial History Book...Then and Now,"
The News Banner, Covington, Louisiana, 1994

Northshore Seafood Gumbo

SHRIMP STOCK

3 pounds uncooked medium shrimp
12 cups (3 quarts) water
1 tablespoon liquid shrimp boil
2 onions, sliced
10 peppercorns
1 lemon, sliced
4 garlic cloves, crushed
3 ribs celery, cut into quarters

GUMBO

8 ounces okra, thinly sliced
2 tablespoons vegetable oil
1½ cups flour
1 cup vegetable oil
2 onions, finely chopped
½ cup thinly sliced celery
1 cup chopped red bell pepper
6 garlic cloves, minced
4 ounces ham, cut into cubes
Salt to taste
3 bay leaves
½ teaspoon white pepper
½ teaspoon black pepper
¼ teaspoon cayenne pepper
½ teaspoon oregano
½ teaspoon thyme
1 (16-ounce) can tomatoes, crushed
1 (8-ounce) can tomato paste
3 tablespoons Worcestershire sauce
4 gumbo crabs
1 pound lump crab meat, shells removed
1 pint oysters
Hot cooked rice

For the shrimp stock, peel and devein the shrimp, reserving the shells. Chill the shrimp in a bowl in the refrigerator until ready to add to the gumbo. Combine the reserved shrimp shells, water, liquid shrimp boil, onions, peppercorns, lemon, garlic and celery in a large stockpot and mix well. Bring to a boil over high heat and reduce the heat. Simmer for 30 to 45 minutes. Strain the stock, discarding the solid ingredients. Return the strained stock to the stockpot. Simmer over medium-low heat.

For the gumbo, sauté the okra in 2 tablespoons oil in a skillet for 10 to 15 minutes or until tender.

Cook the flour and 1 cup oil in a skillet to make a dark rich roux, stirring constantly. Add the onions, celery and bell pepper. Sauté for 4 minutes. Add the sautéed okra, garlic, ham, salt, bay leaves, white pepper, black pepper, cayenne pepper, oregano and thyme. Sauté for 2 minutes. Spoon gradually into the heated stock and stir to mix well. Add the undrained crushed tomatoes, tomato paste and Worcestershire sauce. Bring to a boil over medium heat and reduce the heat, stirring constantly. Simmer for 30 minutes, stirring occasionally. Add the gumbo crabs and crab meat. Cook for 15 minutes.

Drain the oysters, reserving 2 tablespoons liquor. Add the oysters, reserved liquor and chilled shrimp to the gumbo. Cook for 5 to 10 minutes or until the shrimp turn pink and the oysters curl. Discard the bay leaves. Serve over hot fluffy rice.

Serves 8 to 10

Bayou Lacombe Crab Festival

Under the majestic live oak trees of John Davis Park, the Bayou Lacombe Crab Festival has been a Louisiana summer favorite since 1977. Each year, about 2,000 blue crabs, a Louisiana specialty from the waters of Lake Pontchartrain, are boiled at the festival. Another favorite is the fried soft-shell crab po-boys, but there are many wonderful crab and seafood specialties to tempt your taste buds. New Orleans' Gambit Weekly voted it "The Best Festival You Might Not Have Heard Of." The Bayou Lacombe Crab Festival is held on the last weekend in June at John Davis Park in Lacombe. For more information, please call 1-985-882-3010 or go to www.bayoulacombecrabfestival.com.

Grilled Fish with Mango and Avocado Salsa

FISH
3/4 cup dry white wine
1/4 cup orange juice
2 tablespoons fresh lemon juice
1 tablespoon chopped fresh basil
1 tablespoon vegetable oil
1 tablespoon cracked black peppercorns
1 sprig of fresh rosemary
2 small bay leaves
4 fresh fish fillets, such as grouper, wahoo, amberjack or red snapper

MANGO AND AVOCADO SALSA
1 large mango, peeled, pitted and chopped
1 tablespoon minced onion
3 tablespoons chopped green bell pepper
3 tablespoons chopped red bell pepper
1 1/2 tablespoons white wine vinegar
1 tablespoon chopped fresh cilantro
1 tablespoon minced fresh chives
1 large avocado, peeled, pitted and chopped

For the fish, combine the wine, orange juice, lemon juice, basil, oil, cracked peppercorns, rosemary and bay leaves in a large bowl and mix well. Add the fish. Marinate, covered, in the refrigerator for at least 4 hours. Drain the fish, discarding the marinade. Place on a grill rack. Grill until the fish flakes easily.

For the salsa, combine the mango, onion, bell peppers, vinegar, cilantro and chives in a bowl and mix well. Chill, covered, for up to 3 hours. Stir in the avocado just before serving.

To serve, arrange the fish on a serving platter and serve with the salsa.

Serves 4

Never-Fail Fish

THIS RECIPE HAS BEEN USED WITH ALL KINDS OF FISH FILLETS, AND IT HASN'T FAILED YET.

6 firm white fish fillets, such as trout, snapper or catfish
Salt and pepper to taste
6 tablespoons butter
2 garlic cloves, minced
1 1/2 tablespoons Worcestershire sauce
1/2 cup Italian bread crumbs or crushed potato chips
1/3 cup white wine

GARNISH
Lemon slices

Season the fish with salt and pepper to taste. Melt the butter in a 9×13-inch glass baking dish in a 400-degree oven. Stir in the garlic and Worcestershire sauce. Coat both sides of the fish with the butter mixture and place in the dish.

Bake at 400 degrees for 20 minutes or until the fish flakes easily. Do not overcook. Remove from the oven. Sprinkle with the bread crumbs. Add the wine to the pan juices. Broil until the fish are brown and crispy. (This does not take long, so watch carefully to prevent burning.) Garnish with lemon slices. Serve immediately.

Serves 6

Baked Salmon with Sassy Satsuma Sauce

SALMON
1 (3- to 4-pound) fillet of salmon with skin
Salt and pepper to taste
½ cup water

SAUCE
5 satsumas or tangerines, peeled
¾ cup balsamic vinegar
¾ cup orange juice
½ cup minced red onion
8 ounces spicy sweet red pepper jelly

For the salmon, run your fingers over the salmon to make sure all of the bones are removed. Score the skin side of the salmon. Place skin side down in a baking pan sprayed with nonstick cooking spray. Season with salt and pepper to taste. Pour the water into the pan. Cover with foil. Bake at 350 degrees on the middle oven rack for 13 to 15 minutes or until the salmon flakes easily. Remove from the oven. Place the salmon on a serving platter. Cover and keep warm.

For the sauce, separate the satsumas into sections and discard the seeds. Bring the balsamic vinegar and orange juice to a boil in a saucepan. Add the onion and satsuma sections. Return to a boil. Reduce the heat to medium. Cook for 7 minutes or until the mixture is reduced by ⅓, popping the satsumas with a cooking spoon or spatula as they soften. Increase the heat to medium-high. Add the pepper jelly. Simmer until the jelly is completely melted, stirring constantly.

To serve, spoon the sauce over the salmon.

Serves 4

NOTE: The sauce is also good served over pork roast.

In southeast Louisiana, food is our life. Growing up, I watched my family cook like no one else in the world. We made gallons of gumbo at a time at our Grand Isle camp. Mom tested recipes for her Auxiliary cookbook. Daddy would make enough rabbit sauce piquante for his annual wild game dinner for 500 men. I remember spaghetti and meatballs every Sunday at Grandma's house in Des Allemands. Now, we have our own Covington crawfish boils and Northshore supper club dinners. Our three boys grab their chef hats to help my husband and me; they watch and learn. I know their lives will be full of memories of family, friends, and, of course, all that glorious food.

—Lisa Zaccaria Barnett

Stuffed Whole Red Snapper

SNAPPER

1 onion, cut into slices ¼ inch thick
1 (4- to 5-pound) cleaned deboned whole red
    snapper, head and tail intact
1 tablespoon kosher salt
¾ tablespoon white pepper
¾ tablespoon black pepper
¼ cup (½ stick) butter
¾ cup minced green onions
1 medium red bell pepper, chopped
2 garlic cloves, minced
3 slices white bread, trimmed
1 cup milk
¼ cup finely chopped parsley
8 ounces lump crab meat, shells removed
8 ounces cooked shrimp tails,
    peeled and deveined
8 ounces crawfish tails with fat
1 tablespoon Worcestershire sauce
1 teaspoon Louisiana hot sauce
1 teaspoon fresh thyme, or
½ teaspoon dried thyme
Butter for topping
2 large lemons, thinly sliced
½ cup (1 stick) butter, melted
Juice of 1 large lemon
⅓ cup dry white wine
⅓ cup butter, melted

SAUCE

¾ cup sliced green onions
10 fresh mushrooms, sliced
½ cup (1 stick) butter, melted
4 ounces white wine
Juice of 1 large lemon
4 ounces lump crab meat, shells removed
4 ounces cooked medium
    shrimp tails, deveined
4 ounces crawfish tails
Salt and white pepper to taste

For the snapper, cover the bottom of a shallow roasting pan with the onion slices, adding additional onion slices if needed. Score both sides of the snapper with deep cuts approximately 2 inches apart, being careful not to cut through the fish. Rub the kosher salt, white pepper and black pepper on the outside and in the cavity of the fish.

Melt ¼ cup butter in a large skillet. Add the green onions, bell pepper and garlic. Sauté until the green onions are tender but not brown. Soak the bread in the milk in a bowl. Squeeze the milk from the bread and tear into small pieces. Add the parsley, crab meat, shrimp, crawfish and bread pieces to the sautéed vegetables. Cook for 5 minutes or just until the seafood is heated through. Remove from the heat. Stir in the Worcestershire sauce, hot sauce and thyme. Stuff the cavity of the fish with the seafood stuffing. Place carefully in the prepared roasting pan. Spoon the remaining stuffing into a baking dish and dot with butter. Cover the side of the fish facing up from gills to tail with overlapping lemon slices. Place a slice of lemon over the eye.

Mix ½ cup butter and the lemon juice in a bowl. Mix the wine and ⅓ cup butter in a bowl. Pour the wine mixture over the fish. Bake at 350 degrees for 45 minutes or until the fish flakes easily, basting frequently with the lemon mixture. Bake the extra stuffing with the fish for 30 to 40 minutes.

For the sauce, sauté the green onions and mushrooms in the melted butter in a skillet for 5 minutes. Add the wine and lemon juice. Cook for 3 minutes. Add the seafood. Cook for 5 minutes longer. Season with salt and white pepper to taste.

To serve, spoon the sauce into a gravy boat and serve alongside the stuffed fish and extra stuffing.

Serves 4 to 6

Sea Bass Baked in Parchment

2 to 3 tablespoons extra-virgin olive oil
4 sea bass fillets (about 2 pounds)
Salt and pepper to taste
Juice of 1 lemon
4 medium tomatoes, cut into 1/4-inch slices
3 scallion bulbs or green onion bulbs, chopped
2 tablespoons drained capers
6 to 8 fresh basil leaves, thinly shredded, or
1 tablespoon chopped fresh parsley
Crumbled feta cheese

Cut 4 sheets of parchment paper or foil into 12×16-inch rectangles. Brush lightly with some of the olive oil. Place 1 fish fillet in the center of the top half of each parchment sheet. Season with salt and pepper. Sprinkle with some of the lemon juice. Top each fillet with the tomatoes, scallions, capers, basil and cheese. Drizzle with the remaining olive oil. Fold the other half of the parchment over the fish and tightly fold the edges to form a 1-inch border. Place the fish bundles on a baking sheet.

Bake at 400 degrees for 15 to 20 minutes or until brown and puffed.

Serves 4

Grilled Tuna with Honeydew Salsa

HONEYDEW SALSA
2 cups finely chopped honeydew melon
2 tablespoons fresh lime juice
3 tablespoons finely minced red onion
1 mild jalapeño chile, seeded and minced
2 tablespoons minced fresh mint leaves
1 teaspoon grated fresh gingerroot
1/8 teaspoon white pepper

TUNA
1/3 cup soy sauce
2 tablespoons olive oil
1 tablespoon freshly grated gingerroot
1 tablespoon minced garlic
1 1/2 to 2 pounds tuna, preferably in 1 steak or cut into 1-inch-thick steaks

For the salsa, combine the honeydew melon, lime juice, onion, jalapeño chile, mint, gingerroot and white pepper in a bowl and mix well. Chill, covered, for 30 to 90 minutes. (Serve the salsa within 2 hours of preparing for the best flavor and texture.)

For the tuna, combine the soy sauce, olive oil, gingerroot and garlic in a bowl and mix well. Add the tuna. Marinate, covered, in the refrigerator for 30 to 60 minutes.

Drain the tuna, discarding the marinade. Place on a grill rack. Grill over high heat for 5 minutes for slightly rare steak or for 7 to 8 minutes for desired doneness, turning once. (Do not overcook as the tuna will continue to cook after being removed from the grill.)

To serve, spoon the salsa over the tuna.

Serves 2 to 4

Marinated Tuna with Vinaigrette Niçoise

Vinaigrette Niçoise
2 tablespoons lemon juice
6 tablespoons olive oil
3 tablespoons black olive purée
1 teaspoon chopped anchovies
1 teaspoon chopped green onions
1 teaspoon coarsely chopped capers
1 teaspoon minced garlic
1/4 teaspoon salt
1/8 teaspoon pepper

Tuna
1 pound tuna
Salt and pepper to taste
2 tablespoons olive oil

Garnishes
Haricots verts (green beans), trimmed and blanched
Grape tomatoes

For the vinaigrette niçoise, place the lemon juice in a small bowl. Whisk in the olive oil, olive purée, anchovies, green onions, capers and garlic. Season with the salt and pepper.

For the tuna, sprinkle the tuna with salt and pepper. Rub with the olive oil. Heat a heavy skillet over high heat. Add the tuna. Cook for 10 minutes or until brown, turning occasionally. Remove from the heat. Chill for 30 minutes.

To serve, spoon 1 tablespoon of the vinaigrette niçoise onto each of 6 serving plates. Thinly slice the tuna and arrange slightly overlapping on the plates. Spoon the remaining vinaigrette niçoise over the tuna. Garnish with haricots verts and grape tomatoes. Serve with Lemon Risotto (page 84).

Serves 6

Tuna Burgers with Wasabi Mustard

1 to 2 tablespoons prepared wasabi
1 cup sour cream
2 teaspoons Dijon mustard
2 teaspoons sugar
6 tuna steaks, cut into large chunks (about 3 pounds)
1 egg, lightly beaten
2 tablespoons soy sauce
1 tablespoon sesame seeds
Sesame oil for coating
12 sourdough buns or buns of choice
Shredded green cabbage

Mix the prepared wasabi, sour cream, Dijon mustard and sugar in a small bowl. Cover and let stand at room temperature.

Pulse the tuna in a food processor just until coarsely ground. Combine the ground tuna, egg, soy sauce and sesame seeds in a large bowl and mix well. Spray hands with nonstick cooking spray. Shape the tuna mixture into 12 patties. Brush both sides with sesame oil. Place on a grill rack or a rack in a broiler pan sprayed with nonstick cooking spray. Grill over medium-high heat or broil 4 inches from the heat source for 2 to 3 minutes on each side or until cooked through. Serve on split buns with the wasabi mustard and shredded green cabbage.

Serves 12

NOTE: You can find tubes of prepared wasabi on the Asian aisle of most major supermarkets or in Asian specialty markets. If you can't find prepared wasabi, you can purchase the powdered form. Mix 1 tablespoon wasabi powder with 1 tablespoon water to make prepared wasabi.

Very "Crabby" Crab Cakes with Dijon Sauce

CRAB CAKES
1 egg, beaten
1 teaspoon kosher salt
½ teaspoon pepper
½ teaspoon paprika
1 tablespoon Dijon mustard
1 teaspoon Worcestershire sauce
1 tablespoon mayonnaise
1 tablespoon chopped parsley
½ cup minced green onions
¼ cup minced seeded red bell pepper
1 tablespoon butter, melted
1 pound jumbo lump crab meat,
shells removed
2 tablespoons bread crumbs or as needed for
coating
Butter or olive oil for frying

DIJON SAUCE
½ cup olive oil
½ cup plain yogurt
2 tablespoons (rounded) Dijon mustard
2 tablespoons red wine vinegar
1 tablespoon fresh lemon juice
Salt and pepper to taste

ASSEMBLY
Mango and Avocado Salsa (page 102)

GARNISHES
Sprigs of fresh parsley
Lemon wedges

For the crab cakes, combine the egg, kosher salt, pepper, paprika, Dijon mustard, Worcestershire sauce, mayonnaise, parsley, green onions, bell pepper and 1 tablespoon butter in a large bowl and mix lightly. Fold in the crab meat. Add enough bread crumbs gradually so the mixture will stick together. Shape into 3-inch crab cakes. Coat lightly with the bread crumbs. Chill, covered, for 2 to 3 hours.

Heat a nonstick 12-inch skillet over medium heat. Place enough butter or olive oil in the hot skillet for frying. Add the crab cakes. Fry for 10 minutes or until brown on both sides and cooked through, adjusting the heat as needed.

For the Dijon sauce, process the olive oil, yogurt, Dijon mustard, vinegar, lemon juice, salt and pepper in a food processor until well blended. Chill, covered, until ready to serve.

To serve, spoon some of the Dijon sauce onto each individual serving plate. Top with 1 or 2 crab cakes. Spoon Mango and Avocado Salsa over the crab cakes. Garnish with sprigs of fresh parsley and lemon wedges.

Serves 4

NOTE: You may substitute Caper Rémoulade Sauce (page 191) for the Mango and Avocado Salsa.

The Art of Festivals

In the state of Louisiana, we love festivals so much that we have made it into an art form. In fact, although there are only 365 days in the year, annually there are over 450 festivals in Louisiana! Festivals are such an essential part of our lifestyle because they combine all of our favorite pastimes: music, food, dance, community, art, creativity, and family!

Marinated Crabs

1½ to 2 dozen crabs, cleaned, cooked and cut
into quarters, or cooked crab claws
1 onion, thinly sliced and separated into rings
2 ribs celery, chopped
1 green bell pepper, sliced into rings
1 cucumber, sliced
1 or 2 lemons, thinly sliced
1 cup extra-virgin olive oil
1 cup vinegar
½ cup lemon juice
1 (16-ounce) bottle Italian salad dressing
1 bunch parsley, finely chopped
4 or 5 garlic cloves, finely chopped
Creole seasoning to taste
Salt and pepper to taste

Layer the crabs in a large container. Arrange the onion, celery, bell pepper, cucumber and lemons around the crabs. Pour the olive oil, vinegar, lemon juice and salad dressing over the top. Sprinkle with the parsley, garlic, Creole seasoning, salt and pepper. Marinate, covered, in the refrigerator for 2 days, turning 3 or 4 times each day.

Break out the newspaper tablecloths, have plenty of ice cold Abita beer and enjoy!

Serves 4 to 6

NOTE: You may add any other favorite fresh vegetables, such as broccoli, carrots, or cauliflower.

Once when my husband and I were traveling through rural coastal Maryland, we decided to stop and sample some Maryland steamed crabs. We ordered and tasted the crabs and found them to be tasty but a little bland. My husband commented that the crabs looked very similar to Lake Pontchartrain crabs. I assured him these were Chesapeake Bay crabs, not Lake Pontchartrain crabs. To satisfy his curiosity, he asked the waitress whether the crabs they served were caught in the Chesapeake Bay. The waitress quickly answered, "No, they were caught someplace you probably never heard of—Lake Pontchartrain." My husband just responded, "You're right. I never heard of it." Of course he never let me forget how little I know about crabs and still reminds me that the sweetest crab meat in the world comes from Lake Pontchartrain crabs.

—Paula Kelly Meiners

Crab Napoleon

2½ tablespoons mayonnaise
3 tablespoons chopped red bell pepper
1½ teaspoons Dijon mustard
½ teaspoon fresh lime juice
2 avocados, chopped
1 teaspoon lime zest
Salt and pepper to taste
½ to 1 teaspoon Creole seasoning
1 pound jumbo lump crab meat,
shells removed
12 grape tomatoes, cut into halves
½ small European cucumber, thinly sliced
2 teaspoons extra-virgin olive oil
1 teaspoon fresh lime juice
12 whole plain bagel chips
Extra-virgin olive oil for drizzling
1 teaspoon balsamic vinegar

GARNISH
Sprigs of fresh flat-leaf parsley

Combine the mayonnaise, bell pepper, Dijon mustard, ½ teaspoon lime juice, 1 of the avocados and lime zest in a medium bowl and mix well. Season with salt, pepper and Creole seasoning. Fold in the crab meat, being careful to not break up the lumps.

Combine the remaining avocado, tomato halves and cucumber in a small bowl and mix well. Add 2 teaspoons olive oil and 1 teaspoon lime juice and toss to coat.

Place 1 bagel chip on each of 4 plates. Divide ½ of the crab mixture evenly among the 4 bagel chips. Layer ½ of the remaining bagel chips, the remaining crab mixture and the remaining bagel chips on top of each. Place the avocado mixture in mounds of equal portions on top of each. Drizzle olive oil and balsamic vinegar on each plate. Garnish with parsley.

Serves 4

Grilled Soft-Shell Crabs with Avocado Oil

DELICATE EXTRA-VIRGIN AVOCADO OIL FLAVORS BOTH THE CRABS AND SALAD IN THIS DISH. IF YOU CAN'T LOCATE THIS PARTICULAR OIL, USE A GOOD QUALITY EXTRA-VIRGIN OLIVE OIL INSTEAD.

SALAD
2 avocados
4 ounces jicama, peeled and thinly sliced
(about 1 cup)
2 oranges, peeled and cut into sections
2 ounces watercress (about 2 cups)
Extra-virgin avocado oil for drizzling
Salt and freshly ground pepper to taste

CRABS
9 soft-shell crabs, cleaned
¼ cup extra-virgin avocado oil for brushing
Salt and pepper to taste

For the salad, peel and chop the avocados. Combine the avocados, jicama, oranges and watercress in a large bowl and toss to mix well. Drizzle with avocado oil. Season with salt and pepper.

For the crabs, brush the crabs with the avocado oil. Season with salt and pepper. Place on a grill rack. Grill over high heat for 2 to 3 minutes per side or until the crabs turn bright orange, turning occasionally.

Serve the crabs with the salad.

Serves 4

Soft-Shell Crabs with Creole Mustard Sauce

CRABS
4 soft-shell crabs
6 eggs, beaten
1/2 cup all-purpose flour
1/2 cup milk
1/4 to 1/2 cup hot sauce
2 cups corn flour
2 tablespoons Creole seasoning
4 cups (1 quart) peanut oil
4 cups (1 quart) vegetable oil

CREOLE MUSTARD SAUCE
1/2 cup mayonnaise
1/2 cup Creole mustard or
country-style Dijon mustard
1/2 teaspoon prepared horseradish
1 teaspoon Worcestershire sauce
Juice of 1 lemon

For the crabs, rinse the crabs gently and pat dry with paper towels. Whisk the eggs, all-purpose flour, milk and hot sauce in a bowl until smooth. Mix the corn flour and Creole seasoning together. Dip the crabs in the batter and then in the corn flour mixture. Heat the peanut oil and vegetable oil to 350 degrees in a large deep skillet. Add the crabs. Deep-fry for 3 to 4 minutes or until golden brown on each side.

For the mustard sauce, whisk the mayonnaise, Creole mustard, horseradish, Worcestershire sauce and lemon juice in a bowl until smooth.

Serve the mustard sauce with the warm crabs.

Serves 4

Variation: For Soft-Shell Crab Po-Boys, serve the soft-shell crab and sauce, dressed, between slices of hot crusty French bread. "Dressed" is a term used in Louisiana to request that lettuce, tomato and mayonnaise be added to a sandwich or po-boy.

Fontainebleau State Park and Fairview-Riverside State Park: The Art of Relaxing

West St. Tammany Parish is lucky to have two state parks. Originally a nineteenth-century sugar plantation, Mandeville's Fontainebleau State Park offers 2,800 acres of gorgeous oak trees on the shores of Lake Pontchartrain. Recreation activities include fishing, crabbing, camping, hiking, and exploring the ruins of the old sugar mill. Other park features include a sandy beach, swimming pools, picnic spots, playground, camping areas, and over 400 different species of animals and birds.

Another beautiful state park is Fairview-Riverside State Park, located on the Tchefuncte River near Madisonville. The late nineteenth-century Otis House, a recent addition to the National Registry of Historic Places, adds charm and history to the beautiful setting. Picnic tables, playgrounds, and group shelters make the park family-friendly. Bass, bluegill, perch, bream, white perch, speckled catfish, and redfish make this the perfect spot for fishing!

Sponsored by St. Tammany Parish Hospital

Crawfish Catahoula over Fried Green Tomatoes

OUT-OF-TOWN GUESTS REALLY ENJOY THIS. IT IS A DELICIOUS RECIPE AND VERY YA-YA.

CRAWFISH SAUCE
2 shallots
2 tablespoons olive oil
1 cup chopped seeded peeled tomato
12 ounces Louisiana crawfish tails
3 tablespoons fresh basil, chopped
1/2 cup white wine
1 1/2 teaspoons salt
1/4 teaspoon cayenne pepper
2 cups cream
1/4 cup sliced green onions

FRIED GREEN TOMATOES
1 egg
1/2 cup milk
2 or 3 large green Creole tomatoes, sliced
Creole seasoning to taste
1 cup flour
2 cups bread crumbs
Vegetable oil for frying

For the crawfish sauce, sauté the shallots in the olive oil in a large saucepan for 2 minutes. Add the tomato. Sauté for 4 minutes. Add the crawfish tails and basil. Sauté for 2 minutes. Add the wine. Cook until the liquid is reduced by 1/2. Add the salt, cayenne pepper and cream. Stir in the green onions. Remove from the heat.

For the tomatoes, beat the egg and milk in a bowl. Season the tomatoes with Creole seasoning. Dredge in the flour. Dip in the egg mixture. Coat with the bread crumbs. Heat oil to 350 degrees in a large deep skillet. Add the tomatoes. Fry for 4 minutes or until golden brown.

To serve, place 1 or 2 fried tomato slices on each serving plate. Pour the crawfish sauce over the tomatoes. Serve with a green salad and French bread.

Serves 4 to 6

A Crawfish Boil

THE BEST WAY TO SERVE CRAWFISH—BOILED IN THEIR SHELLS AND PERFECTLY SEASONED. BE SURE TO HAVE PLENTY OF BEER, PREFERABLY FROM ABITA BREWERY, ON HAND.

2 cups salt
20 pounds live crawfish
12 gallons water
4 to 5 cups Creole seasoning
1/2 to 1 cup cayenne pepper, or to taste
1 cup whole black peppercorns
8 bay leaves
4 artichokes
12 lemons, cut into halves
6 garlic bulbs, cut into halves
8 yellow onions, cut into quarters
2 pounds small new red potatoes, scrubbed
6 ears of corn, shucked and halved
16 ounces whole large mushrooms

Purging the crawfish is highly recommended as it gets rid of any impurities in the crawfish and cleans their outer shells. To purge crawfish, fill an ice chest with water; add the salt and stir. Add the crawfish. Let stand for 10 minutes. Drain and rinse with fresh water.

Place a 20-gallon pot on a gas burner. Pour 12 gallons of water into the pot. (Do not add the water before you place the pot on the burner because it will be too heavy to lift.) Place the basket in the pot. Add the Creole seasoning, cayenne pepper, peppercorns, bay leaves, artichokes and lemons. Bring to a boil. Boil for 15 minutes to increase the flavor. Add the garlic, onions, unpeeled potatoes, corn and mushrooms. Return to a boil. Add the crawfish. (Make sure the crawfish are covered with 3 to 5 inches of water. If not, add additional water.) Return to a boil. Boil for 10 to 15 minutes. (To add flavor, you can turn off the flame and allow the crawfish mixture to steep in the water for 15 minutes longer, but this is not necessary.) Remove the basket and drain. Discard the bay leaves. Pour onto a picnic table covered with newspapers and enjoy.

Serves 40

NOTE: Most sacks of live crawfish weigh about 40 pounds. If you can't get 1/2 of a sack in the pot, just make the crawfish in 2 batches, being sure to double the ingredients.

My husband, Mike, tells me only poor people ate crawfish when he was growing up in Mandeville in the 1950s. His family may have been poor, but they ate well off the abundant crabs, shrimp, and crawfish from Lake Pontchartrain and the surrounding creeks and swamps. His family boiled crawfish but seasoned theirs with only black pepper, salt, and bay leaves from the tree in their yard. In later years, Mike and his daughters, Teri and Lorraine, caught crawfish at the edge of the lawn at what is now our home at the head of Chinchuba Creek. He tells me crawfish are best caught in the brackish water of the marsh and that crawfish caught in fresh water require too much purging. Sadly, we buy our crawfish at the seafood market these days.

—Paula Kelly Meiners

Crawfish Champagne

¼ cup (½ stick) butter
1 pound blanched crawfish tails
½ cup chopped shallots
1 cup Champagne
2 cups heavy cream
¼ cup (½ stick) butter
4 medium puff pastry shells, baked

Melt ¼ cup butter in a sauté pan over high heat. Add the crawfish and shallots. Sauté for 5 minutes. Add the Champagne. Cook until the liquid is reduced by ½. Stir in the heavy cream. Reduce the heat to medium. Cook until the sauce is thickened, stirring constantly. Add ¼ cup butter. Heat until melted. Spoon into the warm pastry shells and serve.

Serves 4

"We hike on through the woods and it's an easy hike if you stay out of the palmetto brakes . . . It's mostly live oak with Spanish moss and ash and hackberry and palmetto and jack vine and some muscadine, with Tupelo gum and cypress where the land gits low. It's beautiful in here—Daddy thinks so, too—though I've never been in woods, 'cept maybe scrub willow, that I didn't think wasn't.

We git to the crawfish spot where the ridge gives up to water. The swamp's shallow here and there's woods irises bloomin' deep blue along the bank and cypress knees pokin' up everywhere. A fox squirrel goes skitterin' up an oak and is gone as quick as we saw him and a woodpecker knocks loud on a cypress in the near distance and it echoes between the trees.

Then woods gets quiet still. Not a breath of wind."

—Excerpt from *Meely LaBauve* reprinted with the permission of the author, Ken Wells.
Publisher: Random House, Inc.

Crawfish Enchiladas

1 cup chopped onion
¾ cup chopped green bell pepper
¼ cup (½ stick) butter
3 pounds crawfish tails
3 (10-ounce) cans cream of shrimp soup
2 cups (1 pint) heavy cream
1 pound Monterey Jack cheese, shredded
8 ounces Colby cheese, shredded
1 tablespoon chili powder
1 tablespoon cumin
50 flour tortillas

GARNISH
1 cup chopped green onions

Sauté the onion and bell pepper in the butter in a skillet until the onion is translucent. Add the crawfish. Simmer over medium-low heat. Add the soup, heavy cream, ½ of the Monterey Jack cheese, the Colby cheese, chili powder and cumin. Simmer for 10 minutes. Do not boil. Remove from the heat to cool.

Fill each tortilla with the crawfish mixture and roll up. Place seam side down in a single layer in a 9×12-inch baking pan. (You may need to use another baking pan.) Spoon the remaining crawfish mixture over the tortillas. Sprinkle with the remaining Monterey Jack cheese.

Bake at 350 degrees for 30 to 40 minutes or until bubbly. Garnish with the green onions.

Serves 25

NOTE: This recipe may be halved.

Seafood and Andouille Cajun Pasta

1/2 cup (1 stick) butter
1/4 cup chopped green onions
1 garlic clove, minced
1/2 cup chopped mushrooms
1/2 cup chopped andouille
1 pound fresh crawfish tails with fat, and/or deveined small (50-count) shrimp
2 ounces Cognac, dry white wine or sherry
1 tablespoon lemon juice
1 (10-ounce) can tomatoes with green chiles and/or chopped tomatoes, drained
2 cups heavy cream
1/2 cup chopped red and/or green bell peppers
1 teaspoon nutmeg
4 ounces cream cheese, cut into cubes
1/2 cup (2 ounces) grated Parmesan cheese and/or Romano cheese
1/4 cup chopped fresh parsley
Salt and cracked black pepper to taste
24 ounces fresh or dried pasta, such as fettuccini, angel hair, shells, penne or rotini, cooked and drained
Paprika for sprinkling

Melt the butter in a heavy 3-quart skillet over medium-high heat. Add the green onions, garlic, mushrooms and andouille. Sauté for 5 minutes. Add the crawfish. Cook for 3 minutes. Add the Cognac and lemon juice, stirring to deglaze the skillet. Add the tomatoes with green chiles. Cook until the liquid is reduced by 1/2. Reduce the heat to medium. Add the heavy cream, bell peppers and nutmeg. Cook for 5 minutes or until thickened, stirring constantly. Add the cream cheese and Parmesan cheese. Cook for 5 minutes or until the cream cheese melts, stirring frequently. Remove from the heat. Stir in the parsley, salt and black pepper. Fold in the pasta. Sprinkle with paprika.

Serves 6 to 8

Crawfish Étouffée

1/2 cup (1 stick) unsalted butter
2 onions, chopped
2 ribs celery, chopped
3 garlic cloves, minced
1 bell pepper, chopped
2 teaspoons salt
1/4 to 1/2 teaspoon cayenne pepper, or
to taste
1/4 teaspoon white pepper
1/2 teaspoon black pepper
1 teaspoon paprika
2 to 4 dashes of Tabasco sauce to taste
1 to 2 pounds crawfish tails with fat
1/4 cup flour
4 chicken bouillon cubes
2 cups water
1/2 cup chopped green onions
Hot cooked rice

Melt the butter in a large skillet. Add the
onions, celery, garlic and bell pepper. Sauté
over low heat for 30 minutes. Add the salt,
cayenne pepper, white pepper, black pepper,
paprika and Tabasco sauce. Add the crawfish
tails with fat. Cook for 1 minute. Stir in the
flour. Cook for 5 minutes, stirring constantly.
Dissolve the bouillon cubes in the water. Add
the bouillon water and green onions. Cook over
low heat for 10 to 15 minutes. Serve over rice.

Serves 4 to 6

Classic Crawfish Monica

2 cups (1 pint) half-and-half
1 cup (1/2 pint) heavy cream
6 green onions, chopped
1/2 cup (1 stick) butter
1 pound crawfish tails with fat
2 garlic cloves, minced (optional)
Thyme, salt, black pepper, cayenne pepper and
Creole seasoning to taste (optional)
1 pound fresh fettuccini, cooked and drained
3/4 cup (3 ounces) freshly grated
Parmesan cheese

Combine the half-and-half and heavy cream
in a saucepan. Cook for 10 minutes or until
slightly reduced. Sauté the green onions in
the butter in a skillet. Add the crawfish, garlic,
thyme, salt, black pepper, cayenne pepper and
Creole seasoning to taste. Stir in the cream
mixture. Cook until creamy and reduced
slightly, stirring frequently. Pour over the hot
fettuccini in a large serving bowl. Add the
cheese and toss to mix well.

Serves 6

Crawfish Monica® is proprietary and
trademarked to Kajun Kettle Foods, Inc.
The recipe is not official nor endorsed
by Kajun Kettle Foods, Inc.

Chili-Crusted Sea Scallops with Honey-Roasted Jalapeño and Corn Aïoli and Grilled Pineapple Relish

Courtesy of Chef Kim Kringlie, The Dakota Restaurant and Restaurant Cuvée

CHILI-CRUSTED SEA SCALLOPS
¼ cup chili powder
1 teaspoon black pepper
1 teaspoon paprika
1 teaspoon salt
18 (U-12 size) fresh sea scallops
¼ cup (2 ounces) olive oil

HONEY-ROASTED JALAPEÑO AND CORN AÏOLI
1 ear of fresh corn, shucked
2 fresh jalapeño chiles
2 tablespoons honey
1 egg yolk
¼ cup lime juice
1 tablespoon honey
1 cup olive oil
1 teaspoon salt
1 teaspoon cracked black pepper

GRILLED PINEAPPLE RELISH
½ fresh pineapple
1 red bell pepper
1 medium red onion, cut into ¼-inch slices
¼ cup olive oil
¼ cup red wine vinegar
3 tablespoons cilantro
1 teaspoon salt
1 teaspoon black pepper

For the scallops, mix the chili powder, black pepper, paprika and salt in a bowl. Dust the scallops lightly with the chili powder mixture. Heat the olive oil in a skillet until hot. Add the scallops. Sear on both sides until tender.

For the aïoli, rub the corn and jalapeño chiles with 2 tablespoons honey. Place on a grill rack. Grill over low heat until brown and toasted on all sides. Cut the corn away from the cob. Remove the skin from the jalapeño chiles and discard the seeds. Process the corn, jalapeño chiles, egg yolk, lime juice and 1 tablespoon honey in a food processor until puréed. Add the olive oil in a fine stream, processing constantly. Season with the salt and black pepper.

For the relish, cut the skin from the pineapple. Slice the pineapple into ½-inch circles. Remove the stem and skin from the bell pepper and cut into 4 pieces. Brush the pineapple, bell pepper and onion with ½ of the olive oil. Place in a grill basket. Grill until brown on all sides. Cut the grilled pineapple and vegetables into ¼-inch pieces and place in a bowl. Add the remaining olive oil, vinegar, cilantro, salt and black pepper and mix well.

Serve the scallops with the aïoli and relish.

Serves 6

NOTE: To avoid raw eggs that may carry salmonella, we suggest using an equivalent amount of pasteurized egg substitute.

Grilled Oysters with Ginger Lime Butter

3 dozen unshucked oysters
1 cup (2 sticks) unsalted butter
3 quarter-size pieces of fresh gingerroot, crushed
1/4 cup lime juice
Salt and cayenne pepper to taste

Scrub the oyster shells with a stiff brush. Arrange in a single layer on a grill rack. Grill about 4 inches from the hot coals for 10 to 15 minutes or just until the shells begin to open.

Melt the butter with the ginger pieces and lime juice in a small saucepan. Season with salt and cayenne pepper. Remove from the heat. Discard the ginger pieces. Serve with the oysters.

Serves 6

Oysters Louisiana

Courtesy of Chef Raymond "Pops" Thomas, Acme Oyster House

1/2 cup (1 stick) butter
1 1/2 pints oysters, drained
4 green onions, finely chopped
3 garlic cloves, minced
8 ounces fresh lump crab meat, shells removed
1/2 cup bread crumbs
Salt and pepper to taste

Melt the butter in a skillet. Add the oysters. Cook until the edges curl. Add the green onions and garlic. Cook over low heat for 10 minutes. Fold in the crab meat and bread crumbs. Simmer for 5 minutes. Season with salt and pepper.

Serves 4

ROUX DO: Do chop the root of the onion last or freeze the onion for 5 minutes before cutting to prevent tears; also, a wet onion is easier to peel than a dry one.

Seviche

THIS IS A TRADITIONAL SALAD THAT IS STRANGELY FILLING AND VERY, VERY GOOD. YOU MIGHT WANT TO DOUBLE THE RECIPE.

1 pound scallops or fresh firm white fish, such as flounder, red snapper or catfish
3/4 cup fresh lime juice or lemon juice
2 tablespoons grated lime zest or lemon zest
1/4 cup fresh lime juice or lemon juice
4 serrano chiles or jalapeño chiles, minced
6 ounces finely chopped red onion
1 red bell pepper, finely chopped
1 small tomato, peeled, seeded and finely chopped
1 avocado, finely minced
1/4 cup cilantro, chopped
2 tablespoons olive oil
2 teaspoons minced garlic
1 teaspoon salt
1/2 teaspoon Louisiana hot sauce or pepper

Chop the scallops coarsely but evenly. Place in a nonreactive container made of glass, plastic or wood. Stir in 3/4 cup lime juice and the lime zest. Marinate, covered, in the refrigerator for 4 hours for scallops or 6 to 8 hours if using fish. Add 1/4 cup lime juice, the serrano chiles, onion, bell pepper, tomato, avocado, cilantro, olive oil and garlic and toss to mix well. Season with the salt and hot sauce. Chill until ready to serve. Serve as a salad with tortilla chips.

Serves 4

NOTE: If the seviche is to be held for more than 2 hours, the liquid should be drained and chilled separately. Add the liquid back to the seviche just before serving.

Barbecued Shrimp Orleans

TEXANS BEWARE! BARBECUED SHRIMP IS NOT BARBECUED. IT'S SHRIMP THAT HAS BEEN WELL SEASONED, SAUTÉED IN BUTTER, AND SERVED WITH FRENCH BREAD FOR SOPPING UP THE SAUCE. IT'S DELICIOUS.

4 to 6 pounds large shrimp
2 cups (4 sticks) butter or margarine
1/3 cup Worcestershire sauce
1 tablespoon cayenne pepper
1 teaspoon MSG
1/2 teaspoon paprika
1/8 teaspoon rosemary
1/8 teaspoon thyme
1/8 teaspoon oregano
Pinch of cinnamon
2 tablespoons (heaping) salt

Rinse the unpeeled shrimp and drain well. Place in a 12×16-inch baking pan. Combine the butter, Worcestershire sauce, cayenne pepper, MSG, paprika, rosemary, thyme, oregano and cinnamon in a 4-cup glass measure. Microwave on High until the butter melts. Pour over the shrimp.

Bake at 350 degrees for 15 minutes. Turn the shrimp. Bake for 25 minutes longer, turning the shrimp every 5 minutes. Remove the shrimp from the oven. (The shrimp should be slightly underbaked.) Drain the shrimp, reserving the sauce. Reserve 1/2 of the sauce in a bowl for dipping. Mix the remaining sauce and the salt in a bowl. Baste the shrimp with the salted sauce for 3 to 5 minutes. Discard any remaining salted sauce.

Serve the warm shrimp with a generous supply of French bread or any available coarse bread. Dip the peeled shrimp and bread into the reserved sauce, and don't even stop until all have been devoured.

Serves 8 to 10

NOTE: You may use 1 cup (2 sticks) to 1 1/2 cups (3 sticks) butter with an equal amount of olive oil.

Seafood Manicotti

PASTA
16 ounces manicotti shells
(about 20 to 24 shells)
1 to 2 tablespoons olive oil or
softened butter

FILLING
8 ounces Brie cheese
16 ounces cream cheese
1/2 cup (1 stick) unsalted butter
5 to 8 dashes of Tabasco sauce or
hot red pepper sauce
2 teaspoons Worcestershire sauce
2 pounds lump crab meat, shells removed

ASSEMBLY
1 pound uncooked medium shrimp,
peeled and deveined
1/3 cup finely chopped red bell pepper
10 slices bacon, crisp-cooked and crumbled
Creole seasoning to taste
Salt and white pepper to taste
3/4 cup (3 ounces) freshly grated
Parmesan cheese
1 1/2 cups (6 ounces) shredded
mozzarella cheese

NOTE: You may use light cream cheese if desired, but do not use fat-free cream cheese.

For the pasta, cook the pasta in a saucepan using the package directions until al dente, omitting the oil. Do not overcook the pasta; drain. Add the olive oil and toss gently to prevent the pasta from sticking together. Let stand until cool.

For the filling, remove the rind from the Brie cheese. Cut the Brie cheese into cubes. Place the Brie cheese, cream cheese and butter in a microwave-safe container. Microwave on 50% power until melted and smooth, stopping and stirring a few times. Add the Tabasco sauce and Worcestershire sauce and mix well. Reserve 1/2 cup of the cheese mixture. Fold the crab meat into the remaining cheese mixture.

To assemble, stuff each manicotti shell with about 2 tablespoons of the filling. Place in a greased 9×13-inch baking dish. Combine the shrimp, bell pepper, bacon, Creole seasoning, salt and white pepper in a bowl and toss to mix well. Spread over the stuffed manicotti. Spread the reserved cheese mixture and any remaining filling over the shrimp mixture. Sprinkle the Parmesan cheese and mozzarella cheese evenly over the top.

Bake, covered, at 350 degrees for 20 to 30 minutes or until the shrimp turn pink and the mixture is hot and bubbly.

Serves 10 to 12

Fais Do-Do
Drunken Shrimp

FAIS DO-DO (FAY-DŌ-DŌ) IS A LOUISIANA TERM FOR DANCE. IT LITERALLY MEANS "GO TO SLEEP"—THE PHRASE WHISPERED BY FRENCH-SPEAKING CREOLE MOTHERS TO THEIR CHILDREN SO THE PARENTS COULD JOIN IN THE DANCING.

1/4 cup olive oil
1/4 cup minced onion
5 garlic cloves, minced
2 pounds shrimp, peeled and deveined
with tails left on
1/4 cup tequila
1/4 cup lime juice
Salt and Creole seasoning to taste
2 tablespoons chopped cilantro

Heat the olive oil in a large skillet. Add the onion and garlic. Cook over medium heat for 3 minutes or until tender. Add the shrimp and tequila. Simmer for 3 to 5 minutes or until the shrimp turn pink. Spoon into a nonreactive bowl. Add the lime juice and toss to coat. Season with salt, Creole seasoning and cilantro. Chill, covered, in the refrigerator.

Serves 4

ROUX DO: Do devein shrimp before cooking them. To devein shrimp, run a deveiner or the tip of a small sharp knife down the back of the shrimp to expose the black vein running down the back. You can remove the vein by slipping the tip of the knife underneath it or by rinsing the back of the shrimp under a stream of cold water.

Fried Shrimp
Pontchartrain

THESE ARE GREAT FOR FRIED SHRIMP PO-BOYS.

5 pounds shrimp, peeled and deveined
with tails left on
Creole seasoning and cayenne pepper to taste
2 eggs
1 (5-ounce) can evaporated milk
2 tablespoons vinegar
1 tablespoon baking powder
4 cups flour
Vegetable oil for frying

Rinse the shrimp. Season with Creole seasoning and cayenne pepper. Mix the eggs, evaporated milk, vinegar and baking powder in a bowl. Season with Creole seasoning and cayenne pepper. Add the shrimp and stir to coat. Chill, covered, for 1 hour.

Place the flour and Creole seasoning to taste in a sealable plastic bag. Add the shrimp and shake well to coat. Heat oil to 400 degrees in a skillet. Add the shrimp in batches. Fry each batch for 2 1/2 minutes or until golden brown. Drain on paper towels.

Serves 8 to 10

The Art of Commuting

The Northshore has so much to offer that literally thousands of people choose to live here although it means a daily commute over the Causeway Bridge, which spans Lake Pontchartrain. At 23.75 miles, the Causeway is the longest bridge in the world, and it is estimated that approximately 30,000 vehicles cross Lake Pontchartrain every weekday. Northshore commuters, however, are fortunate that instead of miles of concrete jungle, we catch glimpses of pelicans and seagulls swooping down into the waters of Lake Pontchartrain for their daily meals; we are able to watch majestic and smaller sailboats skim across the water on beautiful spring days, and then after a long day at work, we are greeted by the breathtaking sight of the sun setting over Lake Pontchartrain.

Grilled Vegetable and Shrimp Salad with Warm Andouille Dressing

Courtesy of Pat's Seafood Market and Cajun Deli

SALAD

4 cups (1 quart) chicken stock
3 cups pasta shells
3 tablespoons olive oil
4½ ears of fresh corn, shucked
8 ounces mushrooms, sliced
1 pound peeled shrimp, rinsed
1 teaspoon Cajun seasoning
2 tablespoons olive oil
1 avocado, chopped
16 ounces snow peas
1 tablespoon parsley

ANDOUILLE DRESSING

1 tablespoon olive oil
6 ounces andouille, chopped
¼ cup chopped green onions
2 tablespoons minced garlic
1½ cups olive oil
¼ cup balsamic vinegar
2 tablespoons honey
1½ tablespoons salt
½ teaspoon pepper

NOTE: You may add cherry tomatoes or sliced plum tomatoes.

For the salad, bring the chicken stock to a boil in a 3-quart stockpot. Add the pasta. Cook until al dente; drain.

Heat 3 tablespoons olive oil in a skillet over medium-high heat. Add the corn. Cook for 8 minutes, turning frequently. Remove the corn from the skillet, reserving the drippings. Cut the corn from the cob into a large bowl. Add the mushrooms to the drippings in the skillet. Sauté for 4 minutes. Season the shrimp with Cajun seasoning. Sauté in 2 tablespoons olive oil in a skillet over medium-high heat for 6 minutes or until the shrimp turn pink.

Add the pasta, sautéed mushrooms, shrimp, avocado, snow peas and parsley to the corn and toss lightly.

For the dressing, heat 1 tablespoon olive oil in a skillet over medium-high heat. Add the sausage. Sauté for 2 minutes. Add the green onions and garlic. Sauté for 1½ minutes or until the sausage is cooked through. Add 1½ cups olive oil, the balsamic vinegar and honey. Cook until heated through, stirring frequently. Reduce the heat. Stir in the salt and pepper. Remove from the heat.

To serve, spoon the salad into 6 to 8 bowls. Drizzle with the warm dressing.

Serves 6 to 8

Stir-Fried Satsuma Shrimp

Courtesy of Tom Fitzmorris, Food Critic and Radio Show Host, WSMB-New Orleans

WHEN SATSUMAS START COMING IN FROM PLAQUEMINES PARISH, WE EAT THEM BY THE SACK. BUT I NEVER COOKED WITH THEM UNTIL MY CUB SCOUTS PICKED A SHORT TON OF THEM, AND I HAD ENOUGH THAT I LOOKED FOR NOVEL WAYS TO USE THEM. STIR-FRY DISHES, IN ORDER TO COME OUT RIGHT, REQUIRE A GREAT DEAL OF HEAT AND EITHER A WOK OR ONE OF THOSE WOK-LIKE SKILLETS. FLAT-BOTTOMED WOKS ARE BETTER FOR MOST HOME COOKS, AND ESSENTIAL IF YOU HAVE AN ELECTRIC STOVE. YOU HAVE TO PREHEAT THE WOK FOR ABOUT 10 MINUTES BEFORE YOU START COOKING. AND THE PIECES OF FOOD, PARTICULARLY MEATS, NEED TO BE CUT UP SMALLER THAN YOUR INSTINCTS TELL YOU.

1/3 cup chopped pecans
1 pound medium shrimp, peeled and deveined
1 red bell pepper
3 green onions
1/2 cup satsuma juice, strained
1 1/2 tablespoons Vietnamese fish sauce
(nuoc mam)
1 tablespoon hoisin sauce
1 teaspoon Asian hot sauce
2 teaspoons cornstarch
1/4 cup chopped cilantro or parsley
3 tablespoons canola oil
1 tablespoon chopped garlic
Zest of 1 satsuma
Salt to taste

Spread the pecans on a pizza pan. Bake at 350 degrees for 5 minutes or until toasted, shaking the pan once or twice. Remove from the oven to cool.

Cut the shrimp crosswise into 4 or 5 slices. Remove the stem and seeds from the bell pepper. Chop the bell pepper finely. Cut the green onions into 1/4-inch-long strips. Mix the satsuma juice, fish sauce, hoisin sauce, hot sauce, cornstarch and cilantro in a bowl and stir to blend well.

Preheat the wok on the highest heat setting for 10 minutes. Add the canola oil and tilt to coat the side of the wok. Add the garlic and satsuma zest. Cook for a few seconds. Add the shrimp. Stir-fry for 30 seconds or until the shrimp turn white on the outside. Add the bell pepper and green onions. Stir-fry for 15 seconds or until the vegetables are tender-crisp. Add the satsuma juice mixture. Cook for 15 to 30 seconds or until thickened, stirring constantly. Add the toasted pecans. Season with salt to taste. Spoon onto a warm platter.

NOTE: This recipe is best served in the center of a salad of some kind. Hugh Carpenter recommends Belgian endive and radicchio, which is a beautiful thing. But a spring mix salad with sesame oil dressing would also be nice.

Serves 2

Zesty Shrimp and Rice Casserole

1 medium bell pepper, chopped
1 medium onion, chopped
½ cup (1 stick) butter
2 to 3 pounds shrimp, peeled and deveined
1 (10-ounce) can tomatoes with green chiles
1 (10-ounce) can cream of mushroom soup
2 (10-ounce) packages Mahatma
yellow rice, cooked

Sauté the bell pepper and onion in the butter in a stockpot. Add the shrimp. Sauté until the shrimp turn pink. Add the tomatoes with green chiles, soup and rice and mix well. Spoon into a baking dish. Bake at 350 degrees for 30 minutes.

Serves 4

Roux Don't: Don't defrost shrimp in a warm place or in the microwave. Do defrost shrimp in the refrigerator or in cold water.

Shrimp Rosemary

1½ pounds shrimp
2 tablespoons butter
2 tablespoons olive oil
Salt and pepper to taste
6 green onions, thinly sliced
2 teaspoons fresh rosemary, chopped
3 garlic cloves, minced
2 tablespoons sherry (optional)
Dash of lemon juice
Hot cooked rice

Peel the shrimp and rinse under cold water. Heat the butter and olive oil in a skillet until the butter foams. Add the shrimp. Season with salt and pepper. Sauté for 2 minutes. Add the green onions, rosemary, garlic and sherry. Simmer for a few minutes or until the shrimp turn pink and the sauce is reduced slightly. Stir in the lemon juice. Serve over hot cooked rice.

Serves 6

Roux Do: Do cook shrimp quickly to preserve flavor and prevent toughness. Remember 1 pound of uncooked shrimp in shells equals about 8 ounces peeled cooked shrimp tails.

Barbecued Shrimp Pie

Courtesy of Chef Greg Sonnier, Gabrielle Restaurant

SWEET POTATO FILLING
2 pounds sweet potatoes, roasted and peeled
Zest and juice of 2 oranges
1/2 cup packed light brown sugar
Pinch of ground cloves
1 teaspoon vanilla extract
1 teaspoon cinnamon
Pinch of salt

BARBECUED SHRIMP
Butter for sautéing
1 teaspoon cracked black peppercorns
1 teaspoon finely chopped rosemary
16 jumbo shrimp, peeled in center with head
and tail intact (about 2 pounds)
2 teaspoons Creole seasoning
1 tablespoon finely chopped garlic
1 tablespoon Worcestershire sauce
Juice of 2 lemons
1/4 cup beer
1/2 cup seafood stock
4 to 6 tablespoons butter

ASSEMBLY
4 baked (4- to 5-inch) tart shells

GARNISH
4 sprigs of fresh rosemary

For the filling, process the sweet potatoes, orange zest, orange juice, brown sugar, cloves, vanilla, cinnamon and salt in a food processor until smooth. Adjust the salt and brown sugar to taste. Keep warm until ready to serve.

For the shrimp, brown a small amount of butter in a skillet. Add the pepper, rosemary, shrimp, Creole seasoning and garlic. Sauté over high heat until the shrimp turn pink. Add the Worcestershire sauce, lemon juice, beer and seafood stock. Bring to a boil. Boil until the liquid is reduced. Finish the sauce by emulsifying with 4 to 6 tablespoons butter.

To assemble, fill the tart shells with the sweet potato filling. Arrange the shrimp on top. Pour the sauce over and around the tarts. Garnish each with a sprig of fresh rosemary.

Serves 4

Quick Crawfish Tarts

Sauté 8 to 10 green onions, sliced, 3 to 5 ribs celery, chopped, 1 bunch parsley, chopped, 1/2 teaspoon salt, 1 teaspoon Creole seasoning, 1/2 teaspoon pepper and 2 to 4 dashes of Louisiana hot sauce, or to taste, in 1/2 cup (1 stick) butter in a skillet. Add one 10-ounce can cream of celery soup, one 10-ounce can cream of shrimp soup and 2 pounds crawfish or shrimp tails, cooked and peeled. Cook for 10 to 15 minutes over medium-high heat. Pour into 24 small tart shells. Bake at 350 degrees for 30 to 40 minutes or until golden brown. If any of the filling is left over, serve over hot cooked rice or noodles.

Chef Soirée
2 0 0 2

Bogue Falaya Park • Covington, LA • Sunday, March 17, 2002 • 5-9 pm

The Moviegoer Main Attractions…Entrées

Lunch at Bechac's

"I lost my anomie in St. Tammany!" Back in the late '70s, this was a popular bumper sticker that left bewildered travelers scratching their heads. It was really saying, "I've moved to St. Tammany, I've escaped, and I've made it." Living in St. Tammany supposedly meant an angst-free life.

True native New Orleanians, however, know that the best way to relieve angst is through a good meal at a favorite restaurant. It's cheaper than counseling and the conversation is better. Possibly that's what Walker Percy might have had in mind when he organized Thursday lunches at Bechac's restaurant on the Mandeville lakefront. In the late 1970s, I was a young reporter for the New Orleans *States-Item* and later the *Times-Picayune* and a newcomer to Covington when Percy invited me to join the Thursday group.

Bechac's even had a reserved table in a corner overlooking the lake for "Doc" and us. The regulars were mostly local writers, an artist, a bookstore owner, and other celebs passing through New Orleans who stopped by for lunch at Percy's invitation. Outsiders familiar with Percy's novels often thought we must have had the deepest intellectual conversations about literature, philosophy, and the meanings of life. Sometimes that was true. We discussed topics such as the Pulitzer-prize-winning novel *Confederacy of Dunces*, which Percy helped get published, and the tragic life of its author, John Kennedy Toole. Percy once asked us to read and critique an outline for a new book he was writing, *Lost in the Cosmos*. Mainly, conversation centered around what the Saints were up to, Louisiana and local parish politics, food, movies, new books, and anything else that came to mind. The conversations were free-flowing, streams of consciousness fueled by glasses of bourbon, beer, wine, and iced tea over meals of broiled flounder, shrimp salad, and delicious turtle soup with a dash of sherry. Bechac's once had a menu that could hold its own against any in south Louisiana. That soup and the little round table in the corner for "Doc" and the Thursday lunch group are now but a good memory.

—John Kemp
Author and Associate Director,
Louisiana Endowment for the Humanities

Foolproof Filet of Beef

THIS IS SO EASY, AND YOU WON'T BELIEVE HOW GOOD
IT IS. IT IS VERY IMPORTANT TO HAVE THE OVEN AT
500 DEGREES FOR THE FILET TO BAKE PROPERLY.

1 whole filet of beef (about 4 pounds)
Kosher salt and freshly ground pepper to taste
1/4 cup (1/2 stick) butter, softened
3 garlic cloves, crushed

Allow the beef to come to room temperature.
Place on a baking sheet and pat dry with a
paper towel. Season the beef with kosher salt
and pepper. Mix the butter and garlic in a
bowl to form a paste. Spread over the top of
the beef. Bake, uncovered, at 500 degrees
for 22 minutes for rare or for 25 minutes for
medium-rare. Remove the beef from the
oven and cover tightly with foil. Let stand
for 20 minutes. Uncover and slice to serve.

Serves 8 to 10

NOTE: Add 2 minutes of baking time for each
additional pound of beef.

ROUX DO: Wrapping beef in foil after grilling
or cooking and allowing it to rest for 15
minutes will cook the beef further; the internal
temperature will rise by 5 to 10 degrees.

Chef Soirée

*A food lover's delight, the Chef Soirée has
been the primary fund-raiser for the Youth
Service Bureau since 1984. Over 100 top-
notch restaurants participate and provide an
amazing array of food with lots of Louisiana
specialties. Live entertainment is provided
throughout the evening, so you can dance
the night away. Cap off the evening with a
spectacular fireworks display on the banks
of the Bogue Falaya River.*

*The Chef Soirée is held on the third
Sunday evening in March at the Bogue Falaya
Park in Covington. For more information, go
to www.chefsoiree.com.*

Stuffed Beef Tenderloin

1 (4½- to 5-pound) beef tenderloin, slit
Salt and pepper to taste
1 garlic clove, finely chopped
Greek seasoning to taste
4 to 6 tablespoons butter, softened
8 ounces fresh mushrooms, finely chopped
3 green onion tops, finely chopped
1 garlic clove, finely chopped
Bread crumbs

Let the beef stand at room temperature for
30 minutes. Season the beef with salt, pepper,
1 garlic clove and Greek seasoning.

Mix the butter, mushrooms, green onions
and 1 garlic clove in a bowl. Add enough bread
crumbs to bind the mixture. Stuff into the
beef and enclose with wooden picks. Place on
a rack in a broiler pan. Bake, uncovered, at
500 degrees for 15 minutes for rare, for
20 minutes for medium, or for 25 minutes for
medium-well. Turn off the oven. Cover the beef
tightly with foil. Return to the oven for about
1 hour. Unwrap and serve.

Serves 8 to 10

ROUX DO: Marbled beef, which has
intermingling fat and lean, indicates tenderness
and rich flavor.

Beef with Broccoli

Courtesy of Trey Yuen

1 tablespoon water
1 tablespoon soy sauce
1 teaspoon cornstarch
1 egg white
8 ounces flank steak, cut into
2- to 3-inch strips
1 tablespoon vegetable oil
1 bunch broccoli (3 or 4 stalks)
4 cups water
1/2 cup chicken broth
2 teaspoons oyster sauce
1 1/2 teaspoons cornstarch
1 tablespoon soy sauce
1/2 teaspoon sesame seed oil
1 tablespoon vegetable oil
Salt and pepper to taste
2 tablespoons vegetable oil
1/2 teaspoon minced garlic
1 tablespoon sherry

Combine 1 tablespoon water, 1 tablespoon soy sauce, 1 teaspoon cornstarch and the egg white in a bowl and mix well. Add the beef and stir to coat well. Marinate, covered, in the refrigerator for 30 minutes. Stir in 1 tablespoon vegetable oil. Marinate at room temperature for 30 minutes.

Cut the broccoli into individual florets, trimming the excess stems. Bring 4 cups water to a boil in a saucepan. Add the broccoli. Boil for 2 minutes or until tender-crisp; drain. Rinse in cold water to stop the cooking process.

Mix the chicken broth, oyster sauce, 1 1/2 teaspoons cornstarch, 1 tablespoon soy sauce, the sesame seed oil, 1 tablespoon vegetable oil, salt and pepper in a bowl and mix well.

Heat a wok over high heat until hot. Add 2 tablespoons vegetable oil. Add the garlic and the beef mixture. Stir-fry until the beef is 75% cooked through. Add the broccoli and sherry. Stir-fry for a few minutes longer. Stir in the broth mixture. Cook until thickened, stirring constantly.

Serves 1 to 2

Covington and Coordinated Art Openings: The Art of Appreciation

Born on the Fourth of July in 1813, the town of Covington was founded by New Orleans merchant John Wharton Collins. Collins designed the town by using "ox lots," a unique grid of streets and squares with central lots and alleys. Collins then named the town "Wharton," which was changed three years later to "Covington," when the legislature chartered the town in honor of General Leonard Covington of Natchez, a hero in the War of 1812. In 1819, Covington became the parish seat.

In the late 1800s, Covington enjoyed much popularity as a summer destination for picnicking, dancing, and swimming. With its winding river, shady oak trees, and grand pavilion, Covington's Bogue Falaya Park became a social center for locals and New Orleanians who came for the summer climate.

Modern-day Covington is known for its celebration of the arts. Historic downtown Covington is rich with art galleries, antique stores, restaurants, coffeehouses, and boutiques. The live oaks and riverbank at the Columbia Street Landing are transformed into a natural arena from March to October, when the town sponsors free outdoor entertainment ranging from concerts to Shakespearian plays. Downtown Covington plays host to the Final Friday Block Parties, the Three Rivers Art Festival, and the Coordinated Art Openings when stores, restaurants, and galleries open their doors to exhibit the works of regional artists. Other Covington treasures include St. Joseph's Abbey, Symphony Swing in the Pines, Christ Episcopal Church's "Third Sunday Concert Series," and the Farmer's Market, which is held every Wednesday and Saturday at City Hall.

Courtesy of Brenchley Shoes and Accessories

Covington Cannelloni

TOMATO SAUCE
1 small onion
2 tablespoons olive oil
2 (16-ounce) cans whole tomatoes, chopped
3 tablespoons tomato paste
1 teaspoon basil
1 teaspoon sugar
1 teaspoon salt
Black pepper to taste

CREAM SAUCE
¼ cup (½ stick) butter
¼ cup flour
1 cup milk
1 cup heavy cream
1 teaspoon salt
White pepper to taste

CANNELLONI
4 garlic cloves
1 medium onion
2 tablespoons butter
2 tablespoons olive oil
1 pound ground round
1 (10-ounce) package frozen chopped
spinach, thawed
5 tablespoons grated Parmesan cheese
½ teaspoon oregano
Salt and black pepper to taste
2 eggs
2 tablespoons cream
14 cannelloni, cooked and drained

ASSEMBLY
Grated Parmesan cheese for sprinkling
Butter for topping

For the tomato sauce, process the onion in a blender. Heat the olive oil in a skillet. Add the onion. Process the undrained tomatoes in a blender. Add to the onion mixture. Stir in the tomato paste, basil, sugar, salt and black pepper. Simmer for 30 minutes.

For the cream sauce, melt the butter in a skillet. Stir in the flour. Cook for 2 minutes, stirring constantly. Add the milk and heavy cream. Cook until thickened, stirring constantly. Season with salt and white pepper.

For the cannelloni, process the garlic and onion in a blender. Melt the butter with the olive oil in a skillet. Add the onion mixture. Sauté for 5 minutes. Add the ground round. Cook until the ground round is brown, stirring until crumbly. Add the spinach. Cook until the moisture evaporates. Add the cheese, oregano, salt and black pepper. Remove from the heat to cool. Beat the eggs and cream in a bowl. Stir into the ground round mixture. Stuff into the cannelloni.

To assemble, layer ⅔ of the tomato sauce, the stuffed cannelloni, cream sauce and remaining tomato sauce in a 9×13-inch baking dish. Sprinkle with Parmesan cheese and dot with butter. Bake at 350 degrees for 30 to 40 minutes or until bubbly.

Serves 6 to 8

NOTE: For 28 cannelloni, triple the ground round filling and double the cream sauce and tomato sauce. You may also add ½ cup (2 ounces) shredded mozzarella cheese and ¼ cup (1 ounce) grated Parmesan cheese to the thickened cream sauce.

Wild Rice Hot Dish

THIS RECIPE IS FROM THE BIRTHPLACE OF THE MISSISSIPPI RIVER AND HAS FOUND ITS WAY DOWN TO ST. TAMMANY PARISH. IT IS DERIVED FROM A RECIPE FOUND AT A LODGE IN NORTHERN MINNESOTA.

2 pounds ground beef
1 cup chopped celery
1 onion, chopped
1/2 cup uncooked wild rice, rinsed,
soaked and drained
1/2 cup uncooked white rice
1 (10-ounce) can cream of mushroom soup
1 (10-ounce) can cream of rice soup
2 soup cans water
5 tablespoons low-sodium soy sauce
1 (6-ounce) can sliced mushrooms,
drained (optional)
1 (8-ounce) can water chestnuts,
drained (optional)
Salt and pepper to taste

Brown the ground beef with the celery and onion in a skillet, stirring until the ground beef is crumbly; drain. Add the wild rice, white rice, mushroom soup, rice soup, water, soy sauce, mushrooms and water chestnuts and mix well. Season with salt and pepper. Spoon into a baking dish. Bake at 350 degrees for 1 1/4 hours or until the rice is tender.

Serves 6 to 8

Roux Do: For juicier burgers, add a stiffly beaten egg white to each pound of ground beef or make patties with 1 tablespoon cottage cheese in the center.

Crescent City Meat Loaf

1/2 cup sun-dried tomatoes,
reconstituted and chopped
1 1/2 pounds ground chuck
8 ounces ground pork or ground chuck
1 cup finely chopped onion
4 garlic cloves, finely chopped
1 cup (4 ounces) shredded Swiss cheese
2 eggs
1/2 cup spicy steak sauce
1/2 cup milk
1 teaspoon salt
1 cup seasoned bread crumbs
1/4 cup spicy steak sauce

Mix the sun-dried tomatoes, ground chuck, ground pork, onion, garlic and cheese in a bowl and mix well. Beat the eggs in a small bowl. Stir in 1/2 cup steak sauce, the milk and salt. Add to the ground chuck mixture and mix well. Add the bread crumbs a small amount at a time, stirring well after each addition. Shape into a 5×9-inch loaf. Place in a 9×13-inch baking pan. Spread 1/4 cup steak sauce over the loaf. Bake at 350 degrees for 1 hour and 10 minutes.

Serves 6

Rosemary Rack of Lamb

2 tablespoons fresh rosemary
1 tablespoon kosher salt
1 tablespoon freshly ground pepper
2 tablespoons honey
3 garlic cloves, minced
1/2 cup Dijon mustard
1 tablespoon balsamic vinegar
2 racks of lamb

Process the rosemary, kosher salt, pepper, honey and garlic in a food processor until minced. Add the Dijon mustard and balsamic vinegar and process for 1 minute. Place the racks of lamb with the ribs curving down in a roasting pan. Coat the tops with the Dijon mustard mixture. Let stand at room temperature for 1 hour.

Roast at 450 degrees for 20 minutes for rare or 25 minutes for medium-rare. Remove from the oven. Cover with foil. Let stand for 15 minutes. Cut into individual ribs to serve.

Serves 4

Marinated Pork Roast

AN EXCELLENT SUNDAY FAMILY RECIPE.

PORK
½ cup soy sauce
½ cup sherry
2 garlic cloves, minced
1 tablespoon dry mustard
1 teaspoon ginger
1 teaspoon thyme, crushed
1 (4- to 5-pound) pork loin roast, boned,
rolled and tied

CURRANT SAUCE
1 (10-ounce) jar currant jelly
2 tablespoons sherry
1 tablespoon soy sauce

For the pork, blend the soy sauce, sherry, garlic, dry mustard, ginger and thyme in a bowl. Place the pork in a sealable plastic bag. Pour the marinade over the pork and seal the bag. Marinate in the refrigerator for 2 to 12 hours, occasionally pressing and turning the bag to evenly distribute the marinade. Drain the pork, reserving the marinade.

Boil the reserved marinade in a saucepan for 3 minutes. Place the pork on a rack in a shallow roasting pan. Bake, uncovered, at 325 degrees for 2½ to 3 hours or until a meat thermometer inserted in the thickest portion registers 170 degrees, basting with the cooked marinade during the final hour.

For the sauce, heat the jelly in a small saucepan until melted. Add the sherry and soy sauce. Simmer for 2 minutes, stirring constantly.

To serve, carve the pork and serve with the sauce.

Serves 10 to 12

The Art of Theatre in St. Tammany Parish

Since 1991, the North Star Theatre has served as a cultural center in Old Mandeville, functioning as a theatre, center for the arts, and children's drama camp. As a member of Theatre Communications Group in New York, the North Star is one of 253 professional nonprofit theatres in the United States that hires professional actors, directors, and designers who work with volunteers in the community onstage and backstage.

Playmakers, Inc., a nonprofit, voluntary, amateur theatre located in the piney woods of Covington, has been bringing theatre to locals since 1955, as well as developing local talent through its drama camps.

A new jewel in historic downtown Covington's art district is the Skyfire Theatre. A renovated classic movie theatre, the Skyfire Theatre presents musicals, drama, live bands, art showings, and new and classic cinema.

There are several opportunities to appreciate Shakespeare Under the Stars in Southeast Louisiana. The Bard comes to the Northshore twice in the spring and twice in the fall with Shakespeare at the Landing in Covington and Shakespeare at the Mandeville Trailhead.

The Northlake Performing Arts Society Chorale and Chamber Singers is another nonprofit St. Tammany treasure that produces musicals and concerts three times a year. Its goal is "to enrich the cultural life of the Northshore by using choral music as a catalyst to embrace and promote other art forms."

Sponsored by Catherine Brown

Crown Roast of Pork

1 (6- to 10-pound) crown roast of pork
2 tablespoons olive oil
2 tablespoons minced garlic
2 teaspoons Creole seasoning
Salt and freshly ground pepper to taste
1/4 cup chopped sage
2 tablespoons chopped thyme
1 1/4 cups dry white wine

Place the roast on a rack in a shallow roasting pan. Mix the olive oil, garlic and Creole seasoning in a small bowl. Rub over the roast. Season generously with salt and pepper. Sprinkle with the sage and thyme. Bake at 350 degrees for 1 1/2 to 2 hours or until a meat thermometer registers 160 degrees, basting frequently with the wine. Remove from the oven. Let stand for at least 10 minutes before carving. Serve with Crawfish Pecan Dressing (page 82) and Spectacular Spinach (page 95).

Serves 10 to 12

Coca-Cola Ham

1 ham
1 (10-ounce) can sliced pineapple or crushed pineapple
6 ounces Coca-Cola
1/2 to 3/4 cup packed dark brown sugar
Whole cloves
Cherries (optional)

Score the ham in a diamond pattern about 1/4 inch deep. Place in a baking pan. Bake at 350 degrees for 18 minutes per pound.

Drain the pineapple, reserving the juice. Mix the reserved pineapple juice, Coca-Cola and brown sugar in a small bowl. Remove the ham from the oven prior to the last 45 minutes of baking time. Arrange the pineapple rings over the ham, securing with whole cloves or wooden picks. Secure cherries in the center of the pineapple rings. Pour the Coca-Cola mixture over the ham. Bake for 45 minutes, basting with the sauce every 10 minutes. Remove from the oven. Let stand for 5 to 10 minutes. Cut into slices and serve.

Serves 8 to 10

Pork St. Tammany

1/2 cup boiling water
1/2 cup chopped dried apricots
2 green onions, finely chopped
1/2 cup chopped fresh mushrooms
1/4 cup chopped green bell pepper
2 tablespoons butter or margarine, melted
1 (6-ounce) package long grain and wild rice mix, cooked
3 tablespoons chopped pecans
1 tablespoon chopped parsley
1/8 teaspoon salt
1/8 teaspoon black pepper
Dash of red pepper
Dash of garlic powder
4 (1 1/2-pound) boneless pork tenderloins
Salt and pepper to taste
4 slices bacon

GARNISHES
Canned apricot halves
Sprigs of fresh parsley

Pour the water over the apricots in a bowl. Let stand for 20 minutes or until softened; drain. Sauté the green onions, mushrooms and bell pepper in the butter in a skillet until tender. Add the cooked rice, apricots, pecans, parsley, 1/8 teaspoon salt, 1/8 teaspoon black pepper, red pepper and garlic powder and mix well.

Cut a slit lengthwise on the top of each tenderloin, being careful not to cut through the bottom and sides. Season with salt and pepper to taste. Spoon 1/2 of the rice mixture into the opening of 1 tenderloin. Place the cut side of another tenderloin over the rice mixture. Tie the tenderloins together securely with kitchen string. Place on a rack in a roasting pan. Top with 2 bacon slices. Repeat the procedure with the remaining tenderloins. Cover with foil.

Roast at 325 degrees for 1 1/2 to 2 hours or until a meat thermometer inserted in the thickest portion registers 170 degrees, removing the foil during the last 30 to 40 minutes of roasting. Remove and let stand for 5 minutes. Remove the strings and cut the tenderloins into slices. Garnish with apricot halves and parsley.

Serves 8 to 10

Roux Do: For maximum moisture and flavor, cook meat fat side up.

Chile and Citrus Crusted Pork Tenderloin with Roasted Vegetable Mole Sauce

Courtesy of Chef Kim Kringlie, Dakota Restaurant and Restaurant Cuvée

PORK
36 ounces pork tenderloin, cleaned
2 tablespoons Worcestershire sauce
Zest of 1 lime
Zest of 1 orange
Zest of 1 lemon
1 tablespoon paprika
1 teaspoon chili powder
1 teaspoon cumin
1 teaspoon cinnamon
1 teaspoon crushed red chiles
1 teaspoon cracked black pepper
1 teaspoon salt
2 tablespoons vegetable oil

MOLE SAUCE
2 Roma tomatoes
6 garlic cloves
1 red bell pepper
2 ancho chiles
1 medium yellow onion
1 cup chicken stock
1/4 cup raisins
1 tablespoon honey
Juice of 1 orange
Juice of 1 lime
Juice of 1 lemon
1/4 cup sliced almonds
1 dry flour tortilla, torn
1 slice dry white bread, torn
2 tablespoons chocolate sauce
1 teaspoon salt

For the pork, rub the pork with the Worcestershire sauce and citrus zest. Mix the paprika, chili powder, cumin, cinnamon, red chiles, black pepper and salt together. Sprinkle over the pork. Heat the oil in a skillet. Add the pork. Sear on all sides until a meat thermometer inserted in the thickest portion registers 160 degrees. Remove the pork and keep warm, reserving the pan drippings for the mole sauce.

For the mole sauce, place the tomatoes, garlic, bell pepper, ancho chiles and onion in the reserved pan drippings in the skillet. Sear until brown and wilted. Add the chicken stock, stirring to deglaze the skillet. Pour into a blender. Add the raisins, honey, orange juice, lime juice, lemon juice, almonds, tortilla, white bread, chocolate sauce and salt and process until puréed. Return to the skillet. Cook for 10 minutes or until reduced.

Cut the pork into slices and serve with the mole sauce.

Serves 6

Louisiana Red Beans and Rice

1 pound dried red beans
2 onions, chopped
1 bell pepper, chopped
1 pound sausage or ham, sliced
Vegetable oil for sautéing
2 garlic cloves, chopped
1 bay leaf
Salt and pepper to taste
Tabasco sauce to taste
1 (8-ounce) can tomato paste

Rinse the beans thoroughly. Soak the beans in water to cover in a bowl for 8 to 12 hours; drain. Sauté the onions, bell pepper and sausage in a small amount of oil in a stockpot until the onions are translucent. Add the garlic. Sauté for 1 minute. Add the drained beans, bay leaf, salt, pepper and Tabasco sauce. Cover with water. Bring to a boil over high heat, stirring constantly to prevent the beans from sticking. Stir in the tomato paste. Cover and reduce the heat to low. Cook for 5 to 6 hours or until the beans are tender and the mixture is the desired consistency, adding additional water as needed. Remove the bay leaf. Serve over Perfect Rice (page 82).

Serves 8 to 10

Roux Do: Bay leaves are a standard in Louisiana cooking—getting a bay leaf in your serving is believed to be good luck.

Cajun Grilled Veal Chops

¼ cup Dijon mustard
¼ cup red wine vinegar
1 teaspoon cayenne pepper
½ teaspoon salt
2 teaspoons fresh thyme leaves, chopped, or
1 teaspoon dried thyme, crushed
¾ cup canola oil
4 (7-ounce) veal chops or pork chops

Whisk the Dijon mustard, vinegar, cayenne pepper, salt, thyme and canola oil in a bowl until blended. Place the veal in a sealable plastic bag. Add the marinade and seal the bag. Turn the bag a number of times to coat the veal. Marinate in the refrigerator for 12 hours, turning the bag occasionally. Drain the veal, discarding the marinade. Place on a grill rack. Grill over hot coals for 3 minutes per side to sear. Move to a cooler spot on the grill. Grill for 6 to 8 minutes for medium-rare or to the desired degree of doneness.

Serves 4

NOTE: For pork chops, grill until a meat thermometer registers 160 degrees.

Roux Do: To add flavor to grilled meats and vegetables, dampen fresh herbs, such as rosemary, with water and add to the coals.

Veal Marcelle

Courtesy of Emeril Lagasse, Emeril's Delmonico Restaurant and Bar

3 tablespoons butter
4 cups sliced exotic mushrooms
Salt and freshly ground black pepper to taste
1 tablespoon minced garlic
8 ounces lump crab meat, shells removed
¼ cup chopped green onions
4 egg yolks
Juice of 1 lemon
1 tablespoon water
1 tablespoon Creole mustard
Cayenne pepper to taste
1 cup (2 sticks) butter, melted
1 tablespoon butter
16 spears of fresh pencil asparagus, blanched
8 (2½-ounce) veal loin cutlets
1 cup flour
2 tablespoons butter

GARNISHES
4 thin slices lemon
1 tablespoon finely chopped fresh
parsley leaves

Melt 3 tablespoons butter in a large sauté pan over medium heat. Add the mushrooms and season with salt and black pepper. Sauté for 2 to 3 minutes. Add the garlic and crab meat. Season with salt and black pepper. Sauté for 2 minutes. Remove from the heat. Stir in the green onions and keep warm.

Whisk the egg yolks, lemon juice, water and Creole mustard in a stainless steel bowl. Set over simmering water in a saucepan over medium heat. Season with salt and cayenne pepper. Cook until thickened and pale yellow, whisking constantly and being careful not to let the bowl touch the water. Remove the bowl from the saucepan. Add 1 cup melted butter 1 teaspoon at a time, whisking vigorously and constantly until incorporated. Keep warm.

Melt 1 tablespoon butter in a large sauté pan. Add the asparagus. Season with salt and black pepper. Sauté for 2 minutes. Remove from the heat and keep warm.

Place each piece of veal between sheets of plastic wrap. Pound thin using a meat mallet. Season both sides with salt and black pepper. Season the flour with salt and black pepper. Dredge the veal in the flour mixture, coating completely.

Melt 2 tablespoons butter in a large sauté pan over medium heat. Add the veal. Fry for 1 minute on each side. Remove from the heat.

To serve, place 2 pieces of veal in the center of each individual serving plate. Spoon the sauce over the veal. Place 4 asparagus spears over the veal. Place a spoonful of the crab mixture in the center of the asparagus. Garnish with the lemon slices and parsley.

Serves 4

Grilled Stuffed Venison Backstrap

VENISON
2 cups red wine
1½ cups vegetable oil
½ cup soy sauce
¼ cup Worcestershire sauce
1 onion, chopped
6 garlic cloves, minced
2 tablespoons dry mustard
1 tablespoon chopped parsley leaves
½ teaspoon Creole seasoning
1 tablespoon cracked black pepper
Juice of ½ lemon
1 (1½- to 2-pound) venison backstrap

STUFFING
3 tablespoons butter
3 green onions, finely chopped
1 (3-ounce) jar mushrooms,
drained and chopped
2 garlic cloves, crushed
2 tablespoons chopped fresh parsley leaves
1 small jalapeño chile, seeded and
finely chopped

For the venison, combine the wine, oil, soy sauce, Worcestershire sauce, onion, garlic, dry mustard, parsley, Creole seasoning, pepper and lemon juice in a large sealable plastic bag and shake to mix well. Slit the venison lengthwise, being careful not to cut all the way through and leaving the ends and 1 side intact. Add the venison to the marinade and seal the bag. Marinate in the refrigerator for 8 to 24 hours, turning once.

For the stuffing, melt the butter in a skillet. Add the green onions, mushrooms, garlic, parsley and jalapeño chile. Sauté for 5 minutes. Remove from the heat.

To assemble, remove the venison from the marinade, being careful to keep in 1 piece. Pour the marinade into a saucepan. Cook over medium-high heat until reduced by ½. Remove from the heat. Stuff the venison with the mushroom mixture and enclose tightly with wooden picks. Place on a grill rack.

Grill, covered, over medium-hot to hot coals for 15 to 20 minutes or to the desired degree of doneness, basting frequently with the cooked marinade and turning once.

Serves 4 to 6

Venison Chili

¼ cup vegetable oil
2 pounds ground venison
2 medium onions, chopped
1 beef bouillon cube
2 cups water
1 (14-ounce) can chopped tomatoes
¾ cup red wine
¼ cup Worcestershire sauce
2 large green chiles, seeded and chopped
1 garlic clove, minced
¾ teaspoon oregano
1 teaspoon cumin
1 tablespoon chili powder
1 teaspoon salt
2 (15-ounce) cans red kidney beans, rinsed
and drained

Heat the oil in a large Dutch oven or stockpot with a heavy metal bottom. Add the venison and onions. Cook over medium-high heat until the venison is brown, stirring until crumbly. Dissolve the bouillon cube in the water. Add the bouillon, undrained tomatoes, wine, Worcestershire sauce, green chiles, garlic, oregano, cumin, chili powder, salt and beans to the venison mixture and stir to mix well. Bring to a boil and reduce the heat. Simmer for 1 to 2 hours, stirring occasionally to prevent sticking. Serve with corn bread.

Serves 6 to 8

NOTE: This is even better if made 1 day ahead, refrigerated, and then reheated to serve.

Venison is lower in fat and a healthier alternative to beef. It can be easily substituted for beef in recipes like lasagna, tacos, and roasts. Because it is leaner, a little more oil may be necessary when browning because it will be drier.

Kentucky Burgoo

STANDARD FARE IN THE SOUTH, THIS
KENTUCKY STEW IS OFTEN MADE IN LARGE BATCHES
AND SERVED AT CHURCH SUPPERS, TAILGATE PARTIES,
AND POLITICAL RALLIES. OF COURSE, IT IS A
FAVORITE ON DERBY DAY.

4 cups water
1 (16-ounce) can tomatoes, cut up
12 ounces boneless beef chuck roast,
cut into 3/4-inch pieces
2 teaspoons instant chicken bouillon granules
1 pound chicken pieces, such as breasts, thighs
or drumsticks
2 cups chopped peeled potatoes
1 (10-ounce) package frozen succotash
1 (10-ounce) package frozen okra
1 cup sliced carrots
1/2 cup chopped onion
1 teaspoon sugar

Combine the water, undrained tomatoes, beef
and chicken bouillon granules in a 4 1/2-quart
Dutch oven. Bring to a boil and reduce the
heat. Simmer, covered, for 30 minutes. Add the
chicken. Return to a boil and reduce the heat.
Simmer, covered, for 45 minutes or until the
beef and chicken are cooked through. Remove
the chicken to a platter. Stir the potatoes,
succotash, okra, carrots, onion and sugar into
the mixture in the Dutch oven. Return to a boil
and reduce the heat. Simmer, covered, for
20 minutes or until the vegetables are tender.

Cut the chicken into bite-size pieces,
discarding the skin and bones. Stir into the
mixture in the Dutch oven. Cook for 5 minutes
or until the chicken is heated through.

Serves 5 to 6

Cha-Cha Chicken

1 chicken, cut up
1 onion, thinly sliced
1 bell pepper, thinly sliced
1 (15-ounce) can tomato sauce
1 tomato sauce can water
3/4 teaspoon garlic powder
1 bay leaf
3/4 teaspoon oregano
2 tablespoons brown sugar
2 tablespoons prepared mustard
2 tablespoons Worcestershire sauce
1 teaspoon salt
1/2 teaspoon pepper
1/4 cup vinegar

Rinse the chicken pieces and pat dry. Place
side by side in a 9×13-inch baking dish.
Layer the onion and bell pepper evenly over
the chicken.

Combine the tomato sauce, water, garlic
powder, bay leaf, oregano, brown sugar,
mustard, Worcestershire sauce, salt, pepper
and vinegar in a bowl and mix well. Pour
evenly over the chicken.

Bake at 350 degrees for 1 1/2 hours or until
the chicken is cooked through, turning after
45 minutes.

Serves 4 to 6

*Like Kentucky, Louisiana is home to a
thriving racehorse industry. Risen Star, the
first Louisiana Derby winner to capture two
jewels of the Triple Crown, is probably the
most famous Louisiana-owned racehorse.
Following in daddy's hoofbeats, this son of
Triple Crown winner Secretariat captured
the imagination of America's racing public
with his brilliant three-year-old campaign.
He placed third in the Kentucky Derby before
capturing the Preakness and then the Belmont,
by an astounding fifteen lengths.*

*Sponsored by Wilhelmina H. Fulgenzi,
Private Care, Inc.*

Private Care

"For All Your Private Duty Needs"

Citrus Grilled Chicken Breasts

1 cup orange juice
1/2 cup tomato purée
3 tablespoons honey
2 teaspoons orange zest
1 teaspoon minced lemon zest
1/2 teaspoon minced lime zest
1/4 cup fresh lemon juice
1/4 cup fresh lime juice
1 tablespoon minced garlic
1 teaspoon thyme
1/2 teaspoon cayenne pepper
3/4 teaspoon black pepper
1/2 teaspoon salt
4 chicken breasts, skinned

Combine the orange juice, tomato purée, honey, orange zest, lemon zest, lime zest, lemon juice, lime juice, garlic, thyme, cayenne pepper, black pepper and salt in a large sealable plastic bag and shake to mix well. Place the chicken in the bag and seal. Marinate in the refrigerator for 8 to 12 hours.

Let the chicken stand at room temperature for 30 minutes before grilling. Drain the chicken, reserving the marinade. Strain the marinade into a small saucepan, discarding the solids. Bring to a boil. Boil for 3 minutes.

Place the chicken on a grill rack. Grill for 20 minutes or until the juices run clear, basting with the cooked marinade every 5 minutes. Serve immediately.

Serves 4

The Art of the Marinade

- *Marinate meat in the refrigerator to prevent any unsafe bacteria growth.*

- *Set aside any marinade you want to use for basting before adding the meat. Toss out any marinade that comes in contact with uncooked meat or boil the used marinade for 3 minutes to eliminate any unsafe bacteria.*

- *Marinate vegetables separately from meat.*

Crawfish-Stuffed Chicken Breasts

8 boneless chicken breasts
Creole seasoning, salt and pepper to taste
1/2 cup (1 stick) margarine
1 onion, chopped
1 bell pepper, chopped
1/2 cup chopped celery
1 1/2 pounds crawfish tails
3 tablespoons Italian bread crumbs
5 tablespoons parsley

Season the chicken with Creole seasoning, salt and pepper. Melt the margarine in a skillet. Add the onion, bell pepper and celery. Sauté for 10 minutes or until the onion is translucent. Add the crawfish. Sauté for 10 minutes over medium heat. Season with Creole seasoning, salt and pepper. Stir in enough bread crumbs to make of the consistency of stuffing. Stir in the parsley. Fill each chicken breast with the stuffing and fold over, fastening the edges with wooden picks or kitchen string to enclose the stuffing. Place in a single layer in a baking dish and cover with foil.

Bake at 375 degrees for 45 minutes. Remove the foil. Bake for 15 minutes longer or until brown and cooked through. Remove all wooden picks and string before serving.

Serves 8

Gris-Gris Chicken

GRIS-GRIS (GREE-GREE) MEANS GOOD LUCK CHARM.

4 boneless skinless chicken breasts
4 tablespoons cream cheese
1/2 cup Dijon mustard
1/2 cup packed dark brown sugar
1/4 cup chopped pecans

Pound each chicken breast 1/2 inch thick. Spread each with 1 tablespoon of the cream cheese. Roll up and secure each with 2 wooden picks. Dip in the Dijon mustard and roll in the dark brown sugar. Place in a baking dish sprayed with nonstick cooking spray. Sprinkle with the pecans. Bake at 300 degrees for 45 to 60 minutes or until the chicken is cooked through.

Serves 4

Dr. Capps' Eye-Opening Enchiladas

Steve Capps moved to Louisiana from Arizona, hence this recipe. Dr. Capps' mother made this recipe for him as a child, and now he prepares it.

Mix 2 cups sour cream, two 10-ounce cans cream of chicken soup, two 4-ounce cans chopped green chiles, 1 bunch green onions, finely chopped, ½ cup (2 ounces) shredded Cheddar cheese and ½ cup (2 ounces) shredded Monterey Jack cheese in a bowl. Soften 6 of the 18 corn tortillas at a time. Spoon about 2 tablespoons of the cheese mixture onto each softened tortilla and roll up to enclose the filling. Arrange the roll-ups side by side in a 9×13-inch baking pan sprayed with nonstick cooking spray. Repeat the batches with the remaining tortillas and cheese mixture. Pour two 10-ounce cans green enchilada sauce over the roll-ups. Sprinkle with ½ cup (2 ounces) shredded Cheddar cheese and ½ cup (2 ounces) shredded Monterey Jack cheese. Bake at 325 degrees for 25 to 35 minutes or until heated through. Let stand for a few minutes before serving. Serve with your favorite salsa.

Chicken Cakes with Sherry Sauce

CHICKEN CAKES
2 tablespoons butter or margarine
1 small red bell pepper, seeded and chopped
8 green onion tops, sliced
3 garlic cloves, pressed
4 cups chopped cooked chicken
(4 chicken breasts)
1 cup soft bread crumbs
2 tablespoons mayonnaise
2 tablespoons sherry
1 tablespoon Creole seasoning
2 eggs, lightly beaten
¼ cup vegetable oil

SHERRY SAUCE
1 cup mayonnaise
1 garlic clove, pressed
2 tablespoons sherry
2 tablespoons ketchup
2 teaspoons Creole seasoning
5 green onion tops, sliced

For the chicken cakes, melt the butter in a large nonstick skillet over medium heat. Add the bell pepper, green onion tops and garlic. Sauté until the vegetables are tender. Process the cooked chicken in a food processor until coarsely ground. Combine the sautéed mixture, chicken, bread crumbs, mayonnaise, sherry, Creole seasoning and eggs in a bowl and mix well. Chill for 10 minutes so the ingredients will bind.

Shape the chicken mixture into eight 3½-inch patties. Fry 4 of the patties in 2 tablespoons of the oil in a large skillet over medium heat for 3 minutes on each side or until golden brown. Drain on paper towels. Repeat with the remaining oil and patties.

For the sherry sauce, combine the mayonnaise, garlic, sherry, ketchup, Creole seasoning and green onion tops in a bowl and mix well.

To serve, spoon the sherry sauce over the patties and serve immediately.

Serves 8

Cajun Fried Turkey

THANKSGIVING WITH A CAJUN FLAIR.

1 jar minced garlic
1 cup (2 sticks) butter
2 bottles garlic juice
2 bottles onion juice
1 3/4 bottles Louisiana hot sauce
2 tablespoons Worcestershire sauce
1 tablespoon (heaping) cayenne pepper
2 teaspoons Creole seasoning
1 (12-pound) fresh turkey
Creole seasoning for rubbing
Black pepper for rubbing
Peanut oil for deep-frying

Process the garlic in a food processor. Melt the butter in a saucepan. Add the processed garlic, garlic juice, onion juice, hot sauce, Worcestershire sauce, cayenne pepper and 2 teaspoons Creole seasoning and mix well to form a liquid that will be easy to inject. Place the turkey in a large aluminum baking pan. Use a marinade needle injector to inject the marinade into the entire turkey, including the wings, legs and underneath the turkey. Rub the entire turkey with Creole seasoning and black pepper. Marinate, covered, in the refrigerator for 24 hours.

Preheat the peanut oil to 350 degrees in an outdoor deep fryer. Remove the metal clip from the turkey that holds the legs together. Lower the turkey slowly into the preheated peanut oil. The temperature of the peanut oil will drop. Maintain the temperature of the peanut oil between 325 and 350 degrees while deep-frying. Deep-fry the turkey for 3 minutes per pound. Remove the turkey and cut both legs at the base of the body about 2 inches deep. Deep-fry for 5 minutes longer. Remove the turkey and let stand for 20 minutes before carving.

Serves 16 to 20

Roux Do: Peanut and canola oils are both good choices for frying because they have a high smoke point. Peanut oil is the best choice for frying turkeys, a South Louisiana favorite.

Turkey Andouille and Corn Gumbo

3 smoked turkey legs
2 pounds andouille, cut into slices 1 to 2 inches thick
10 cups rich chicken stock
2 cups water
2 onions, cut into quarters
6 garlic cloves, minced
3 bay leaves
1/2 bunch parsley, chopped
1 1/2 teaspoons black pepper
3 tablespoons vegetable oil
3 tablespoons flour
2 onions, chopped
1 medium bell pepper, finely chopped
8 ounces cooked turkey, chopped
1 (8-ounce) can tomato sauce
2 (14-ounce) cans whole tomatoes
2 (15-ounce) cans corn, drained
1 tablespoon salt
1 tablespoon black pepper
1/8 to 1/4 teaspoon cayenne pepper
1/2 teaspoon Creole seasoning
1/2 teaspoon each oregano and thyme
Hot cooked rice
Filé powder (optional)

Combine the turkey legs, sausage, chicken stock and water in a large 8- to 10-quart stockpot, adding additional water if needed to cover the turkey and sausage. Add the onion quarters, garlic, bay leaves, parsley and 1 1/2 teaspoons black pepper. Bring to a boil over medium heat. Cook for 2 hours, adding additional water or stock if needed. Reduce the heat to low. Remove the turkey legs to a platter. Let stand until cool enough to handle. Chop the turkey legs, discarding the skin and bones. Return the chopped turkey legs to the stockpot. Remove and discard the onion quarters.

Cook the oil and flour in a skillet to form a dark roux, stirring constantly. Add the chopped onions and bell pepper. Sauté for 3 minutes. Add to the mixture in the stockpot and stir to mix well. Add the chopped turkey, tomato sauce, undrained whole tomatoes, corn, salt, 1 tablespoon black pepper, cayenne pepper, Creole seasoning, oregano and thyme and mix well. Adjust the seasonings to taste. Simmer for 1 hour. Discard the bay leaves. Ladle over hot rice in individual soup bowls. Sprinkle each with filé powder.

Serves 8 to 10

Duck, Chicken and Oyster Gumbo

1½ cups vegetable oil
3 cups flour
7 ribs celery, thinly sliced
4 medium onions, chopped
4 bell peppers, chopped
4 garlic cloves, minced
2 tablespoons paprika
¼ teaspoon allspice
¼ teaspoon nutmeg
¼ teaspoon cinnamon
¼ teaspoon black pepper
¼ teaspoon white pepper
1 tablespoon salt
⅛ teaspoon cayenne pepper
2 teaspoons Creole seasoning
½ teaspoon thyme
½ teaspoon oregano
3 bay leaves
2 mallards, dressed and quartered
6 chicken legs
Salt, black pepper and Creole seasoning
to taste
12 cups (3 quarts) hot chicken stock
3 tablespoons Worcestershire sauce
1 quart oysters, drained
3 cups cooked rice

Cook the oil and flour in a stockpot to form a dark rich brown roux, stirring constantly. Add the celery, onions, bell peppers, garlic, paprika, allspice, nutmeg, cinnamon, ¼ teaspoon black pepper, white pepper, 1 tablespoon salt, cayenne pepper, 2 teaspoons Creole seasoning, thyme, oregano and bay leaves. Cook, covered, over low heat for 10 minutes, stirring occasionally to make sure the vegetables do not stick to the bottom.

Season the ducks and chicken legs with salt, black pepper and Creole seasoning to taste. Brown the ducks and chicken legs evenly in a cast-iron skillet.

Stir the hot chicken stock into the roux mixture until well combined. Bring to a slow boil. Stir in the Worcestershire sauce. Add the chicken legs and duck quarters. Simmer for 2 hours, skimming the fat off the top regularly. Remove the chicken legs and duck quarters to a platter. Let stand until cool enough to handle. Chop the chicken and duck, discarding the skin and bones. Return the chicken and duck to the gumbo. Adjust the seasonings to taste. Add the oysters. Cook for 5 minutes or until the edges of the oysters curl. Remove the bay leaves. Serve over the rice in individual soup bowls.

Serves 4 to 8

Roux Do: The "Holy Trinity" of Louisiana cooking consists of celery, onions, and green bell peppers.

In 1975, I turned six, and my family moved to Louisiana from the Middle East. I remember that my parents, Sue and Rifat Nawas, always served at least one traditional Middle Eastern dish, such as hummus, moussaka, or stuffed grape leaves, at their dinner parties. Most of my parents' friends were born and raised in Louisiana and had never heard of any of these dishes. Initially, they were hesitant to try them, but once they did, they couldn't get enough, as evidenced by my wedding reception years later. When I married my husband, my mother and my Aunts Baheya and Salwa cooked for two weeks straight, preparing enough Middle Eastern dishes for our reception to satisfy even the most gluttonous of sultans. And although we had everything from a pasta station to a seafood station, and everything in between, the first thing to go was the Middle Eastern food. This is not to say that my parents have not become wonderful Cajun cooks. My father is the best fish and game cook in my hometown, and my mother makes what I, and anyone who has had it, believe to be the best gumbo ever.

—Naz Nawas Butcher

Benedict's Duck with Honey Sauce

Courtesy of Benedict's Restaurant, Mandeville

12 ducks, about 4 pounds each
1/2 cup chopped garlic
3/4 cup lemon juice
1/2 teaspoon saffron threads
1/2 cup hot water
1/3 cup olive oil
3 pounds (1 1/2 quarts) chopped onions
1/3 cup coriander
1/3 cup ginger
1/3 cup cinnamon
3 tablespoons cumin
2 tablespoons salt
2 tablespoons turmeric
1 tablespoon nutmeg
2 tablespoons freshly ground pepper
2 1/4 gallons veal stock or beef stock
3 cups honey
3/4 cup rose flower water, or to taste
48 pitted prunes

GARNISHES
12 sprigs of fresh chervil
36 whole almonds, toasted
1/2 cup sesame seeds, toasted

Cut each duck into 2 legs and 2 boned breasts, trimming the excess skin and fat. Place in a large shallow dish. Sprinkle each with 1/2 of the garlic. Cover with cold water. Add the lemon juice. Chill, covered, for 24 hours.

Soak the saffron in the hot water in a bowl. Drain the duck pieces, discarding the liquid. Pat the duck pieces dry. Heat the olive oil in an ovenproof skillet. Add the duck legs. Sear on all sides for 10 minutes or until brown and crisp. Remove the duck legs to a platter and keep warm. Drain the skillet, reserving 1 tablespoon of the drippings in the skillet. Add the onions. Sauté for 5 minutes or until caramelized. Coat the duck legs with a mixture of the coriander, ginger, cinnamon, cumin, salt, turmeric, nutmeg and pepper, turning to coat well. Return the duck legs to the skillet. Add the veal stock. Bring to a boil and cover. Bake at 350 degrees for 1 hour or until tender. Remove the duck legs to a platter and keep warm. Stir the saffron mixture, honey and rose water into the pan drippings. Cook until thick and rich and reduced by 1/2.

To serve, reheat 1 duck leg and 4 prunes in 1 cup of the sauce in a skillet over low heat. Lightly score the skin on 1 duck breast in a diamond pattern. Sear skin side down in a hot sauté pan for 6 minutes or just until firm to the touch. Remove from the pan and keep warm. Remove the duck leg from the sauce and brush with honey. Place on a rack in a broiler pan. Broil until glazed. Pool about 1/2 cup of the sauce on a serving plate. Place the duck leg in the center and arrange the prunes around the edge. Slice the duck breast thinly on the diagonal. Arrange around the leg. Ladle the remaining sauce over the duck. Garnish with a sprig of fresh chervil, 6 almonds and 1/2 tablespoon sesame seeds. Repeat for remaining servings. Serve with Moroccan or other flat bread.

Serves 12

NOTE: This recipe can be halved.

A Streetcar Named…Desserts

Desserts

Whenever I meet someone new in my travels and they learn that I'm from New Orleans, I invariably hear, "Oh, Louisiana. You have such great food there." It's true. I tell people all the time the reasons I've never considered living anyplace else are my family and the food. But in addition to the fabulous Creole and Cajun dishes, I think one of our best-kept secrets is our desserts.

After all, where else but Louisiana can you find beignets, pralines, king cakes, chocolate turtles, and bananas Foster? Where else but in Louisiana can you celebrate spring and the Easter season by picking fresh strawberries from the garden and whipping up a scrumptious strawberry chiffon pie? New York cheesecake? Not for this Louisiana girl!

I often tease my husband that the Hingle clan has a "sweet tooth gene" because after every holiday feast, regardless of how stuffed everyone is, there seems to always be room for dessert. Apparently that gene's contagious, or maybe it's acquired in marriage because before I can kill off the villain in my current book, I think I'm going to need a little something sweet. Hmm, murder and dessert? That's a thought. Death by chocolate or strawberry shortcake? I bet I could put something in the whipped cream…

—Metsy Hingle
Author

Bananas Foster Bread Pudding with Custard and Banana Rum Sauces

BREAD PUDDING
1 cup raisins
Warm rum for soaking
5 egg yolks
1¾ cups sugar
5½ cups milk
¼ cup dark rum
¼ cup crème de banana liqueur
1 tablespoon vanilla extract
1 teaspoon almond extract
1½ teaspoons cinnamon
2 bananas, mashed
7 egg whites
2 bananas, sliced diagonally
12 cups dry French bread, torn into bite-size
  pieces (about 2 to 3 loaves bread)
2 tablespoons butter, melted

CUSTARD SAUCE
2 egg yolks
¾ cup sugar
1 cup evaporated milk
1 cup milk
3 tablespoons cornstarch
3 tablespoons cold water
½ teaspoon vanilla extract
¼ teaspoon almond extract
¼ cup dark rum
¼ cup crème de banana liqueur

BANANA RUM SAUCE
¼ cup (½ stick) unsalted butter
1 cup packed dark brown sugar
¼ cup dark rum
¼ cup crème de banana liqueur
Few pinches of cinnamon (optional)
⅓ cup Custard Sauce (above)
1 cup chopped pecans

ASSEMBLY
2 bananas, sliced diagonally

GARNISHES
Whipped cream
Sprigs of fresh mint

For the bread pudding, soak the raisins in warm rum for 1 hour; drain. Beat the egg yolks and sugar in a mixing bowl until pale yellow. Add the milk, ¼ cup rum, crème de banana liqueur, vanilla, almond extract, cinnamon and mashed bananas and mix well.

Beat the egg whites in a mixing bowl until stiff peaks form. Fold into the egg yolk mixture. Fold in the drained raisins and sliced bananas gently so as not to flatten the egg whites.

Place the bread in a large bowl. Pour ½ of the egg mixture over the bread. Soak for 10 minutes. Add the remaining egg mixture. Soak for 10 minutes.

Coat a 9×12-inch baking dish with 1 tablespoon of the butter. Pour the bread mixture into the prepared dish. Cover with foil and place the baking dish in a large roasting pan. Add enough water to the larger pan to come ⅔ of the way up the side of the baking dish.

Bake at 350 degrees for 1 hour. Remove the foil. Bake for 15 minutes longer or until the center is set. Glaze the top with the remaining 1 tablespoon butter while hot.

For the custard sauce, beat the egg yolks and sugar in a mixing bowl until pale yellow. Add the evaporated milk and milk and mix well. Dissolve the cornstarch in the cold water in a bowl. Add the cornstarch mixture, vanilla, almond extract, rum and crème de banana liqueur to the egg yolk mixture and mix well. Pour into a double boiler. Cook until the sauce is thickened and coats the back of a spoon, stirring constantly.

For the banana rum sauce, melt the butter in a skillet. Add the brown sugar. Cook over medium heat for 4 to 5 minutes or until the sugar is melted and dissolved, stirring frequently. Add the rum and crème de banana liqueur. Cook until the mixture is warm. Ignite carefully, stirring carefully and tossing a few pinches of cinnamon into the flames. (It will sparkle beautifully.) Stir in ⅓ cup of the Custard Sauce and the pecans. Cook for 1 minute.

To assemble, slice the pudding into individual servings. Place a pool of the remaining Custard Sauce on individual dessert plates. Place a slice of pudding in the middle of the Custard Sauce. Place a few banana slices on top. Drizzle liberally with the Banana Rum Sauce. Garnish with a dollop of fresh whipped cream and a sprig of mint.

Serves 8 to 10

Traditional Bananas Foster

½ cup (1 stick) butter
2 cups packed brown sugar
1 teaspoon cinnamon
8 teaspoons banana liqueur
8 bananas, cut into halves lengthwise
½ cup rum
8 scoops vanilla ice cream

Melt the butter in a skillet. Add the brown sugar, cinnamon and banana liqueur and stir to mix. Cook for a few minutes. Place the banana halves in the sauce. Sauté until soft and light brown. Remove from the heat. Pour the rum over the top and ignite. Let the flame subside. Serve over the ice cream.

Serves 8

Crème de Chambord

½ cup heavy cream
½ cup sugar
1 envelope unflavored gelatin
½ cup Chambord
2 cups sour cream
1 teaspoon vanilla extract
1 (10-ounce) package frozen sweetened
raspberries, thawed
1 tablespoon cornstarch

Heat the heavy cream and sugar in a double boiler until the sugar dissolves, stirring constantly. Soften the gelatin in the liqueur. Stir into the cream mixture. Cook until the gelatin dissolves, stirring constantly. Remove from the heat. Stir in the sour cream and vanilla. Pour into individual molds, such as Champagne glasses or pots de crème molds. Chill until set.

Combine the raspberries and cornstarch in a saucepan and mix well. Cook over medium heat until thickened, stirring constantly. Remove from the heat to cool.

To serve, spoon a little of the raspberry sauce over the Crème de Chambord.

Serves 6 to 8

NOTE: This is a very rich dessert—a small serving is most appropriate.

White Chocolate Bread Pudding

BREAD PUDDING
6 cups heavy cream
2 cups milk
1 cup sugar
20 ounces white chocolate,
broken into small pieces
3 eggs
15 egg yolks
1 (24-inch) loaf dry French bread,
sliced 1 inch thick

SAUCE
1/2 cup heavy cream
7 ounces white chocolate,
broken into small pieces

GARNISH
1 ounce dark chocolate, shaved

For the bread pudding, heat the heavy cream, milk and sugar in a large saucepan over medium heat. Remove from the heat. Add the white chocolate pieces and stir until melted. Combine the eggs and egg yolks in a large mixing bowl. Pour the hot cream mixture into the eggs in a steady stream, whipping constantly.

Place the bread in a 9×12-inch baking pan. Pour 1/2 of the egg mixture over the bread, using your fingers to press the bread into the mixture so the bread will absorb the liquid and become soggy. Add the remaining egg mixture. Cover the pan with foil. Bake at 350 degrees for 1 hour. Remove the foil. Bake for 30 minutes longer or until set and golden brown.

For the sauce, bring the heavy cream to a boil in a saucepan. Remove from the heat. Add the white chocolate pieces and stir until completely melted and smooth.

To assemble, slice the pudding into triangles and place on individual dessert plates. Spoon the sauce over the bread pudding. Garnish with chocolate shavings.

Serves 12

NOTE: To dry the bread, bake at 275 degrees for 5 to 8 minutes.

Chocolate Shavings

To make chocolate shavings, hold a block of good quality chocolate with a paper towel and pass a vegetable peeler over the narrowest part of the chocolate. The chocolate will curl like wood shavings. Store in a covered container in the refrigerator until needed. You may store indefinitely in the refrigerator.

Jamocha Almond Pot de Crème

6 ounces milk chocolate morsels
¼ cup sugar
1 tablespoon instant coffee granules
Pinch of salt
1 egg
1 teaspoon vanilla extract
3 tablespoons coffee liqueur
1½ cups heavy cream, heated
½ cup almonds, roasted and coarsely chopped

GARNISHES
Sliced almonds
1 maraschino cherry, cut into 8 pieces

Blend the chocolate, sugar, coffee granules, salt, egg, vanilla and coffee liqueur in a blender for 30 seconds. Add the hot heavy cream. Blend at high speed for 2 minutes. Sprinkle about 1 tablespoon of the chopped almonds into each of 8 demitasse cups or custard cups. Pour the chocolate mixture into each cup. Chill for 4 hours or until firm, stirring halfway through the chilling process. Garnish each by arranging sliced almonds on top of each dessert to resemble a daisy and placing a piece of the maraschino cherry in the center. Serve with demitasse spoons.

Serves 8

NOTE: To avoid raw eggs that may carry salmonella, we suggest using an equivalent amount of pasteurized egg substitute.

Berries Abita

3 pounds mixed fresh berries or your favorite berry
2 cups pinot noir
2 cups apple juice
1 bay leaf
2 cups sugar
1 teaspoon vanilla extract
2 tablespoons cornstarch

Rinse the berries well and pat dry. Combine the wine, apple juice, bay leaf, sugar and vanilla in a heavy saucepan and mix well. Bring to a boil over medium heat. Remove from the heat. Stir in the cornstarch. Return to the heat. Cook for 2 minutes or until thickened, stirring constantly. Stir in the berries. Remove from the heat to cool. Remove the bay leaf. Serve over ice cream, pound cake or angel food cake.

Serves 8 to 10

ROUX DO: Use your nose when buying berries. Always choose the plumpest and most fragrant berries that are firm, bright, and free of mold.

Strawberry Festival

Sweet, juicy, and delicious Louisiana strawberries are really something to celebrate, and The Strawberry Festival has been doing just that since 1972. This favorite Tangipahoa Parish spring celebration is held in Ponchatoula, a quaint Louisiana town filled with over forty antique shops within the eight-block downtown area. Strawberry shortcake, chocolate-covered strawberries, and strawberry lemonade are just a few of the delicious treats available for our snacking pleasure. Sample crawfish pies and fried alligator, too.

The Strawberry Festival is held the second weekend in April (or the third weekend if Easter occurs on the second weekend) at Ponchatoula Memorial Park in Ponchatoula. For information, go to www.lastrawberryfestival.com.

Blueberry Cheesecake Divine

CRUST
1/4 cup (1/2 stick) unsalted butter, softened
2 tablespoons sugar
1/4 teaspoon vanilla extract
Pinch of salt
3/4 cup flour

FILLING
3/4 cup (1 1/2 sticks) unsalted butter
14 ounces cream cheese, softened
3/4 cup sugar
Juice of 1/2 lemon
Pinch of salt
1/2 teaspoon vanilla extract
1 tablespoon flour
8 egg yolks

TOPPING
1/4 cup (1/2 stick) unsalted butter
1/4 cup sugar
1/2 cup flour
Pinch of baking powder

ASSEMBLY
1/4 cup apricot preserves
1 pint blueberries, rinsed and patted dry

For the crust, beat the butter, sugar, vanilla and salt in a large mixing bowl until light and fluffy. Add the flour gradually, beating well after each addition to form a smooth dough. (Add 2 to 3 teaspoons ice water gradually if more liquid is needed to make a smooth dough.) Shape into a ball. Wrap in plastic wrap. Chill for 20 minutes.

Roll the dough into a circle 1/4 inch thick on a lightly floured surface. Center a 10-inch springform pan on the dough and trim around the edge to form a circle. Place on an ungreased baking sheet and prick with a fork. Bake at 350 degrees for 10 minutes. Remove from the oven to cool.

For the filling, melt the butter in a saucepan over low heat. Beat the cream cheese and sugar in a mixing bowl until smooth. Add the lemon juice, salt and vanilla and mix well. Stir in the flour. Add the egg yolks 1 at a time, beating well after each addition. Add the melted butter in a slow steady stream, beating constantly at low speed.

For the topping, place the butter and sugar in a medium bowl. Cut in the flour and baking powder until crumbly. Do not overmix.

To assemble, place the baked crust in the bottom of a springform pan. Spread the apricot preserves over the crust. Layer the blueberries over the preserves. Spread the filling over the blueberries. Sprinkle the topping over the filling.

Bake at 350 degrees for 30 minutes or until the topping is golden brown. Remove from the oven to cool. Serve at room temperature or chill, covered, in the refrigerator and serve cold.

Serves 10 to 12

Sweet Potato Cheesecake with Praline Sauce

CRUST
³/4 cup pecans, toasted and ground
1¹/2 cups finely ground ginger cookie crumbs
6 tablespoons unsalted butter, melted

FILLING
8 ounces cream cheese or
mascarpone cheese, softened
¹/2 cup sugar
¹/2 cup packed dark brown sugar
1 teaspoon cinnamon
³/4 teaspoon ginger
¹/4 teaspoon cloves
¹/2 teaspoon nutmeg
1 cup puréed sweet potato or
orange yam
5 eggs
¹/2 cup heavy cream

PRALINE SAUCE
1 cup (2 sticks) unsalted butter
1 cup packed dark brown sugar
1 cup heavy cream
¹/2 cup chopped pecans, toasted

ASSEMBLY
Whipped cream

GARNISH
Sprigs of fresh mint

For the crust, mix the ground pecans and cookie crumbs in a large mixing bowl. Add the melted butter and mix well. Press into a 9-inch springform pan. Chill for at least 30 minutes.

For the filling, beat the cream cheese in a mixing bowl until smooth. Add the sugar, brown sugar, cinnamon, ginger, cloves and nutmeg. Beat for 3 to 4 minutes or until light and fluffy. Add the sweet potato purée and mix just until blended. Add the eggs 1 at a time, beating well and scraping the bowl after each addition. Add the heavy cream and beat at low speed until completely blended.

To assemble, pour the filling into the crust. Wrap the bottom and side of the springform pan with foil to prevent water from leaking in. Place in a larger pan. Add enough water to the larger pan to come 1¹/2 inches up the side of the springform pan. Bake at 350 degrees for 50 minutes. Remove from the oven. Cool for 45 minutes. Chill for at least 4 hours before serving.

For the praline sauce, melt the butter in a saucepan. Add the brown sugar, cream and pecans. Bring to a boil over high heat and reduce the heat. Simmer for 5 minutes, stirring frequently. Keep warm.

To serve, place a slice of the cheesecake on each dessert plate. Spoon a pool of warm praline sauce over and around each serving. Top with a dollop of fresh whipped cream. Garnish with a sprig of fresh mint.

Serves 8

Roux Don't: Don't overbeat or overmix ingredients for cheesecake at high speed—it can cause cracks to form in the cheesecake when it bakes. It is best to beat the ingredients at medium speed until smooth.

Figs with Honey Orange Cream

6 ounces mascarpone cheese or
whipped cream cheese, softened
2 tablespoons honey
2 teaspoons Grand Marnier or orange juice
Zest of ½ orange
8 fresh figs
4 large fig leaves, rinsed and dried

GARNISH
Fresh mint leaves

Mix the mascarpone cheese, honey, Grand Marnier and orange zest in a small bowl. Cut off the stems from the figs; do not peel. Stand the figs upright with pointed end upward. Cut each fig into quarters without cutting all the way through and fan out to resemble flowers.

Place 1 fig leaf on each dessert plate. Arrange 2 figs on top of each leaf. Spoon 1 tablespoon of the honey orange cream onto each fig. Garnish with fresh mint leaves.

Serves 4

NOTE: Be sure the fig leaves have not been treated with insecticide.

Fragole e Mascarpone

STRAWBERRIES SHOULD BE PREPARED AT THE LAST MINUTE TO ENSURE THEY MAINTAIN THEIR TEXTURE. THIS IS A WONDERFUL SPRING DISH WHEN PONCHATOULA STRAWBERRIES ARE AT THE HEIGHT OF SEASON.

4 cups fresh Ponchatoula strawberries
6 tablespoons sugar
½ cup red wine
16 ounces mascarpone cheese, softened
5 tablespoons sugar
½ cup cream

Trim the strawberries and cut into halves. Combine the strawberry halves, 6 tablespoons sugar and the wine in a bowl and toss to mix well. Whisk the mascarpone cheese, 5 tablespoons sugar and the cream in a bowl until of a smooth light consistency.

Place a large dollop of the mascarpone mixture in parfait glasses. Cover with the strawberry mixture.

Serves 4

Roux Don't: Don't wash or hull fresh berries until you are ready to use them.

Crème Caramel, or Caramel Custard

THIS LOOKS DAUNTING, BUT IT IS NOT THAT COMPLICATED AND IS WORTH THE EFFORT. THIS IS SO CREAMY AND WONDERFUL, YOUR FRIENDS AND FAMILY WILL THANK YOU FOR IT.

1 cup sugar
6½ cups milk
9 eggs
5 egg yolks
1½ cups sugar
1 teaspoon almond extract
1 teaspoon vanilla extract
¾ teaspoon salt

ASSEMBLY
Fresh berries (optional)
Caramel topping (optional)
¾ cup whipping cream, whipped (optional)

Butter a 2½-quart ovenproof soufflé dish or twelve 6-ounce custard cups. Melt 1 cup sugar in a cast-iron skillet over medium-high to high heat to form a light brown syrup, stirring constantly. (Be careful not to burn the sugar.) Pour into the soufflé dish or custard cups. Place in a large shallow baking pan.

Scald the milk in a large kettle. Beat the eggs, egg yolks and 1½ cups sugar in a large mixing bowl. Add about ½ of the scalded milk and stir. Pour into the remaining milk and mix well. Stir in the almond extract, vanilla and salt. Pour into the prepared dish or cups.

Fill the large baking pan with hot water to within 1 to ½ inch of the top of the soufflé dish or cups. Bake at 325 degrees for 1 hour and 10 minutes or until a knife inserted in the center comes out clean. Remove from the water bath and cool on a wire rack. Chill in the refrigerator.

To assemble and serve, loosen the custard from the dish or cups by running a knife around the edge. Invert onto a platter or individual dessert dishes, allowing the syrup to run down the sides of the custard onto the platter or dishes. Serve with fresh berries or pass the caramel topping for your guests to pour over the custard. You can also spoon off ¼ cup of the syrup from the custard and fold into the whipped cream.

Serves 12

ROUX DO: Have all the ingredients pre-measured and within an arm's length before starting this recipe.

Lemon Biscuits with Strawberry Maple Compote

Courtesy of Sous Chef Kate Applebaum, Bayona Restaurant

BISCUITS
1½ cups flour
3 tablespoons sugar
1½ teaspoons lemon zest
1½ teaspoons baking powder
¼ teaspoon baking soda
¼ teaspoon salt
6 tablespoons butter, chilled
½ cup chilled heavy cream
2 tablespoons fresh lemon juice
1 tablespoon chilled heavy cream
2 tablespoons sugar

COMPOTE
2 pints strawberries, hulled
½ cup maple syrup

ASSEMBLY
1 pint vanilla ice cream

For the biscuits, mix the flour, 3 tablespoons sugar, the lemon zest, baking powder, baking soda and salt in a large bowl. Cut in the butter until the mixture resembles coarse cornmeal. Add ½ cup heavy cream and the lemon juice and mix until soft and moist. Drop by ¼ cupfuls onto a baking sheet. Brush the tops with 1 tablespoon heavy cream and sprinkle with 2 tablespoons sugar.

Bake at 350 degrees for 25 minutes or until golden brown.

For the compote, cut ½ of the strawberries into slices. Mash the remaining strawberries in a bowl. Add the sliced strawberries and maple syrup and stir to mix well.

To assemble and serve, reheat the biscuits in a 350-degree oven. Place the biscuits in individual dessert bowls. Spoon the compote over the biscuits. Top with vanilla ice cream.

Serves 6

Biscuit Tortoni

1½ cups chilled whipping cream
⅓ cup sugar
1 cup almond macaroon crumbs
(about 24 cookies)
½ cup chopped almonds, toasted
¼ cup maraschino cherries,
drained and chopped
2 tablespoons rum or dry sherry
1 teaspoon vanilla extract

Beat the whipping cream and sugar in a chilled mixing bowl until stiff peaks form. Reserve ¼ cup of the macaroon crumbs. Fold the remaining macaroon crumbs, almonds, cherries, rum and vanilla into the whipped cream. Spoon into 12 small dessert dishes or paper-lined medium muffin cups. Sprinkle with the reserved crumbs. Freeze for 4 hours or until firm.

Serves 12

Roux Do: Chill the mixing bowl and beaters in the freezer before whipping heavy cream.

Pastry Balls, or "Awama"

"AWAMA" IS A DELICIOUS MIDDLE EASTERN DESSERT CONSISTING OF FRIED BITE-SIZE BALLS OF PASTRY SOAKED IN A BOWL OF SYRUP, OR "QATER," THEN DRAINED WHEN SERVED. THESE ARE ALWAYS SERVED WARM. THEY LOOK LIKE GLAZED DOUGHNUT HOLES, BUT TASTE EVEN BETTER. ONCE YOU TRY THEM, YOU, YOUR FAMILY, AND FRIENDS WILL BE HOOKED.

SYRUP, OR "QATER"
1 pound (2¼ cups) sugar
1⅓ cups water
½ teaspoon fresh lemon juice
1 to 3 teaspoons rose water (optional)

PASTRY BALLS
1 pound (3½ cups) flour, sifted
½ teaspoon baking soda
1 teaspoon salt
16 ounces (2 cups) yogurt
1 teaspoon lemon juice
Vegetable oil for deep-frying

NOTE: Rose water is available in Mediterranean, Middle Eastern, or Italian specialty stores.

ROUX DO: In a pinch, use a whisk when a recipe calls for sifting flour.

For the syrup, dissolve the sugar in the water in a saucepan. Boil for 5 to 12 minutes or until the syrup is thickened and coats a metal spoon. Add the lemon juice and rose water. Simmer gently for 2 minutes. Remove from the heat to cool. Pour into a jar and cover with the lid. Store in the refrigerator until ready to use.

For the pastry balls, mix the flour, baking soda and salt in a large bowl. Stir in the yogurt and lemon juice gradually to form a dough. Knead the dough well. Heat oil in a deep fryer. Pour the cold syrup into a deep bowl and place near the area where you are frying the pastry balls. Cut out marble-size balls of dough using a spoon. Drop into the hot oil. Deep-fry until golden brown. Remove the balls with a slotted spoon and immerse in the cold syrup. The balls will absorb more syrup if they are hot and the syrup is cold. After the balls have been well coated with the syrup, remove with a slotted spoon to allow the excess syrup to drain from the balls. Serve warm.

Serves 4 to 6

Mango Tango

¾ cup (1½ sticks) butter or margarine
1 (2-layer) package yellow cake mix
1 (20-ounce) can crushed pineapple, drained
1 (26-ounce) jar refrigerated mango spears,
drained and chopped
½ cup dark rum
1 (14-ounce) can sweetened condensed milk
8 ounces cream cheese, softened
2 eggs
1 cup chopped pecans
2 cups whipping cream, whipped

Cut the butter into the cake mix in a bowl with a pastry blender until crumbly. Reserve 1½ cups of the crumb mixture. Press the remaining crumb mixture into a buttered 9×13-inch baking dish. Layer the pineapple and mangoes in the prepared dish. Drizzle with ¼ cup of the rum. Combine the remaining ¼ cup rum, condensed milk, cream cheese and eggs in a mixing bowl and beat at medium speed until smooth. Pour over the fruit layers. Sprinkle evenly with the reserved crumb mixture and pecans.

Bake at 350 degrees for 50 to 55 minutes or until set and light brown. Cool on a wire rack. Chill, covered, for 8 hours. Pipe or dollop with the whipped cream before serving.

Serves 15

Plaquemines Parish Orange Mousse

Courtesy of La Provence Restaurant, Lacombe

3 tablespoons orange juice concentrate
5 tablespoons water
6 egg yolks
Juice of 1 orange
Juice of 1 lemon
1 cup sugar
Grated zest of 1 orange
Grated zest of 1 lemon
2 cups whipping cream
2 tablespoons sugar

Dissolve the orange juice concentrate in the water in a small bowl. Beat the egg yolks in a stainless steel bowl. Place the bowl over simmering water in a saucepan over medium heat, being careful not to let the bowl touch the water throughout the cooking process. Add the orange juice concentrate mixture, fresh orange juice and lemon juice a small amount at a time, whisking constantly and turning the bowl in a circular motion so the eggs will not scramble. Continue to cook until the mixture is slightly thickened, beating and turning the bowl constantly. Beat in 1 cup sugar gradually. Continue to cook for 20 to 30 minutes or until thickened, whisking constantly and turning the bowl. Stir in the orange zest and lemon zest during the last few minutes of cooking. Remove from the heat to cool.

Whip the cream in a mixing bowl until soft peaks form. Add 2 tablespoons sugar gradually, beating constantly. Fold into the cooled custard until blended. Spoon or pipe into dessert glasses. Chill for several hours before serving.

Serves 6

Strawberries in White Chocolate Mousse

MOUSSE
8 ounces good quality white chocolate, chopped
1/4 cup chilled whipping cream
2 tablespoons light corn syrup
3/4 cup chilled whipping cream
1 1/2 cups sliced Louisiana strawberries

CHOCOLATE TOPPING
6 tablespoons chilled whipping cream
2 tablespoons light corn syrup
4 ounces good quality bittersweet or semisweet chocolate, chopped

GARNISH
Strawberries

For the mousse, combine the white chocolate, 1/4 cup whipping cream and the corn syrup in a small heavy saucepan and mix well. Cook over low heat until the white chocolate is melted and smooth, stirring constantly. Pour into a large bowl and cool to barely lukewarm.

Beat 3/4 cup whipping cream in a mixing bowl until medium-firm peaks form. Fold the whipped cream 1/2 at a time into the white chocolate mixture. Fold in the sliced strawberries. Spoon into 6 large crystal martini glasses or 4 custard cups. Chill, covered, for 4 hours or until set.

For the chocolate topping, combine the whipping cream and corn syrup in a small heavy saucepan and mix well. Bring to a simmer over high heat. (Watch carefully because this does not take long.) Reduce the heat to low. Add the bittersweet chocolate. Heat until melted and smooth, stirring constantly. Remove from the heat and cool to barely lukewarm.

To assemble and serve, drizzle the chocolate topping to taste over each mousse. Slice the whole strawberries to the hull, being sure to keep the strawberries intact, and fan out each berry. Garnish each mousse with a strawberry fan.

Serves 4 to 6

Roux Do: Store chocolate in the refrigerator, but it must be brought to room temperature before using.

Puff Pancakes

THIS IS AN ORIGINAL RECIPE CREATED FOR THE FAMOUS *TIMES-PICAYUNE* COOKING CONTEST, NEW ORLEANS, LOUISIANA, A FEW YEARS AGO. IT MADE THE COOK-OFF AND WAS THE FINALIST FOR DESSERTS.

1 cup flour
1 teaspoon salt
6 eggs
1 cup milk
1/4 cup (1/2 stick) butter, melted
1 cup sour cream
1 (10-ounce) package frozen sliced strawberries in syrup

Sift the flour and salt together. Beat the eggs in a mixing bowl until blended. Add the flour mixture 1/4 at a time, beating well after each addition. Add the milk 1/2 at a time, beating well after each addition. Beat in the butter lightly. Pour into a greased cast-iron skillet. (The batter should be a depth of about 1/2 inch in the skillet.)

Bake at 400 degrees for 20 minutes. Reduce the oven temperature to 350 degrees. Bake for 10 minutes longer.

(The pancake bakes into a puff, and when removed from the oven, the center will collapse to form a well.) Spread sour cream quickly in the well. Spoon the strawberries over the sour cream. Cut into wedges and serve.

Serves 4 to 6

NOTE: Individual pie or tart pans may be used, but reduce the baking time.

Roux Don't: Don't use extra-large eggs for baking; they may stop baked goods from rising.

Layered Sherbet Dessert

DESSERT
2²/₃ cups chocolate wafer crumbs
½ cup (1 stick) butter or margarine, melted
1 quart orange sherbet, softened
1 quart rainbow sherbet, softened
1 quart lime sherbet, softened

RASPBERRY ORANGE SAUCE
2 (10-ounce) packages frozen raspberries in
light syrup, thawed
2 tablespoons frozen orange juice
concentrate, thawed
1 tablespoon plus 1 teaspoon cornstarch

GARNISHES
Chocolate curls
Orange rind curls
Sprigs of fresh mint

NOTE: If you are unable to find chocolate wafers, use chocolate sandwich cookies with the filling removed.

For the dessert, combine 1²/₃ cups of the wafer crumbs and the melted butter in a bowl and mix well. Press evenly in a 10-inch springform pan. Freeze until firm.

Spread the orange sherbet evenly over the frozen crust. Sprinkle with ½ cup of the remaining wafer crumbs. Freeze until firm. Repeat layering with the rainbow sherbet and remaining wafer crumbs. Freeze until firm. Spread the lime sherbet over the top. Freeze, covered, for at least 8 hours.

For the sauce, process the raspberries in a blender until smooth. Press through a sieve into a bowl, discarding the seeds. Combine the orange juice concentrate and cornstarch in a saucepan and mix well. Stir in the raspberry purée. Bring to a boil over medium heat, stirring constantly. Boil for 1 minute, stirring constantly. Pour into a bowl. Chill, covered, until ready to serve.

To serve, carefully remove the side of the springform pan and cut into wedges. Garnish with chocolate curls, orange rind curls and fresh mint sprigs. Serve with the sauce.

Serves 12 to 14

"A cricket orchestra out in the woods that closed in fifty feet from the porch struck up a melancholy tune. The sun was starting to slide down among the pine trees like a half-melted butterscotch ball. The sight of Louisiana at certain hours could kill you if you sat still and let it."

—Excerpt from *Slow Poison* was used with
the permission of the author, Sheila Bosworth.
Publisher: Alfred A. Knopf.

Pink Pears with Grated Chocolate

6 medium Bosc pears
3/4 cup sugar
1 1/2 cups water
1 1/2 cups rosé
1/2 cup dry red wine
1 teaspoon lemon juice
4 whole cloves
1 cinnamon stick
Grated semisweet chocolate

Peel the pears and remove the core from the bottom end. Cut to but not through the stem end. Cut a 1/4-inch slice from the bottom of the pears to form a flat base.

Combine the sugar, water, rosé, red wine, lemon juice, cloves and cinnamon stick in a 5-quart Dutch oven. Bring to a boil over medium heat. Boil until the sugar is dissolved, stirring constantly. Place the pears in the Dutch oven in an upright position, spooning the syrup over the pears. Simmer, covered, for 20 minutes.

Remove the pears to a large bowl. Strain the syrup, discarding the solids. Pour the strained syrup over the pears. Chill, covered, for 2 to 3 hours, basting occasionally.

To serve, spoon the pears and syrup into a serving dish. Sprinkle with chocolate.

Serves 6

Roux Do: Use Bosc pears for cooking. They have a firm texture and hold up well. Anjou and Comice pears are not suitable for cooking.

Roux Don't: Don't cook unpeeled pears. The skin will become bitter and tough, so be sure to peel pears before cooking.

Tiramisu

Courtesy of Benedict's Restaurant, Mandeville

1/4 cup Tia Maria
1/2 cup strong brewed black coffee
16 to 20 ladyfingers
14 ounces mascarpone cheese or cream cheese, softened
3 medium eggs, separated
1/4 cup confectioners' sugar
2 tablespoons Tia Maria
Baking cocoa for sprinkling

Blend 1/4 cup Tia Maria and the coffee in a bowl. Dip the ladyfingers in the mixture and arrange in a shallow dish. Beat the cheese, egg yolks, confectioners' sugar and 2 tablespoons Tia Maria in a mixing bowl until smooth. Whisk the egg whites in a mixing bowl until stiff peaks form. Fold into the cheese mixture. Spoon over the ladyfingers. Sprinkle with baking cocoa.

Serves 8 to 10

NOTE: To avoid raw eggs that may carry salmonella, we suggest using an equivalent amount of pasteurized egg substitute.

Louisiana Pecan Ice Cream

2 tablespoons butter
1 cup coarsely chopped pecans
Pinch of salt
1 (14-ounce) can sweetened condensed milk
2 cups half-and-half
1 cup heavy cream
2 teaspoons vanilla extract

Melt the butter in a skillet over medium heat. Add the pecans and salt. Cook for 5 minutes, stirring frequently. Remove from the heat to cool.

Whisk the condensed milk, half-and-half, heavy cream and vanilla in a large bowl. Pour into an ice cream freezer container. Freeze for 20 minutes using the manufacturer's directions. Add the pecan mixture. Freeze for 5 minutes longer. Remove and place in the freezer to harden.

Makes 1 1/2 quarts

Chocolate Doberge Cake

A DOBERGE CAKE IS A QUINTESSENTIAL SOUTHEAST LOUISIANA CAKE. ALTHOUGH NOT AS WELL KNOWN AS THE MORE FAMOUS KING CAKE, MANY LOCALS WILL TELL YOU IT IS BY FAR ONE OF THEIR FAVORITE DESSERTS.

CAKE
2 cups flour, sifted
1 teaspoon baking soda
1 teaspoon salt
10 tablespoons butter, softened
1½ cups sugar
3 egg yolks
1 cup buttermilk
1½ ounces unsweetened chocolate
squares, melted
3 egg whites, stiffly beaten
1¼ teaspoons vanilla extract
1 teaspoon almond extract

CHOCOLATE FILLING
2½ cups evaporated milk
2 ounces semisweet chocolate
1¼ cups sugar
5 tablespoons flour
4 egg yolks
2 tablespoons butter
1¼ teaspoons vanilla extract
¼ teaspoon almond extract

CHOCOLATE FROSTING
1¼ pounds (about 3 cups) sugar
1 cup evaporated milk
2 ounces bittersweet or unsweetened
chocolate, melted
¼ cup (½ stick) butter
1 teaspoon vanilla extract

For the cake, grease and flour two 9-inch round cake pans. Sift the flour, baking soda and salt together into a medium bowl 3 times. Cream the butter and sugar in a large mixing bowl. Add the egg yolks 1 at a time, beating well after each addition. Add the flour mixture and buttermilk alternately, mixing well after each addition. Add the melted chocolate. Beat for 3 minutes. Fold in the beaten egg whites, vanilla and almond extract. Spoon into the prepared pans. Bake at 300 degrees for 45 minutes or until the layers test done. Cool in the pans for 10 minutes. Invert onto wire racks to cool completely.

For the filling, heat the evaporated milk and chocolate in a heavy saucepan over medium-low heat until the chocolate is melted, stirring constantly. Mix the sugar and flour in a large bowl. Add the chocolate mixture 1 tablespoon at a time, mixing well after each addition to form a paste. Return to the saucepan. Cook over medium heat until thickened, stirring constantly. Add the egg yolks and stir rapidly to completely blend. Cook for 2 to 3 minutes, stirring constantly. Remove from the heat. Add the butter, vanilla and almond extract and mix well. Let stand until cool.

For the frosting, bring the sugar and evaporated milk to a boil in a heavy saucepan over medium-low heat, stirring constantly. Reduce the heat. Simmer for 6 minutes. (Do not stir.) Remove from the heat. Stir in the melted chocolate until blended. Add the butter and vanilla. Cook over medium-low heat for 1 to 2 minutes or until smooth. Chill in the refrigerator to cool.

To assemble, cut each cake layer horizontally into 2 or 3 thin layers. Spread the filling between the layers. Beat the frosting well. Spread over the top and side of the cake.

Serves 12

NOTE: You may omit the unsweetened chocolate for a yellow cake. You may also use one 16-ounce jar of seedless raspberry preserves for an optional quick and not-so-rich filling.

ROUX DO: Use unflavored unwaxed dental floss to cut cake horizontally into layers. Wrap the floss evenly around the cake layer at the desired level. Hold one end of floss in each hand and pull. The floss will slice through the cake.

Red Velvet Cocoa Cake

CAKE
1/2 cup shortening
1 1/2 cups sugar
2 eggs
1 teaspoon salt
1 teaspoon baking cocoa
1 teaspoon vanilla extract
2 ounces red food coloring
2 1/4 cups sifted cake flour
1 cup buttermilk
1 teaspoon vinegar
1 teaspoon baking soda

CHALK WHITE FROSTING
1 1/2 cups milk
1/2 cup cake flour
1 1/2 cups (3 sticks) butter, softened
1 1/2 cups sugar
1 tablespoon vanilla extract

NOTE: You may frost with Cream Cheese Frosting instead of the Chalk White Frosting. Beat 8 ounces cream cheese, softened, and 1/2 cup (1 stick) butter, softened, in a mixing bowl until creamy. Add 16 ounces confectioners' sugar and beat until smooth. Beat in 1 teaspoon vanilla. Sprinkle the cake with 1/2 cup chopped pecans after frosting.

ROUX DO: Frosting mistakes are avoidable if you spread in only one direction.

For the cake, beat the shortening, sugar, eggs, salt, baking cocoa and vanilla in a mixing bowl until light. Beat in the food coloring. Add the cake flour alternately with the buttermilk, beating constantly. Mix the vinegar and baking soda together in a small bowl. Fold into the batter. Pour into 2 greased 9-inch round cake pans.

Bake at 350 degrees for 30 to 35 minutes or until the layers test done. Cool for 8 to 12 hours.

For the frosting, mix the milk and cake flour in a saucepan. Cook over medium heat for 7 minutes or until thickened, stirring constantly. Remove from the heat to cool. Beat the butter and sugar in a mixing bowl until fluffy. Add the milk mixture 1 teaspoon at a time, beating at high speed after each addition until smooth. Beat in the vanilla.

To assemble, cut each cake layer horizontally into halves by using a piece of string or unflavored unwaxed dental floss. Spread the frosting between the layers and over the top and side of the cake.

Serves 12

Butterscotch Pound Cake

1 cup (2 sticks) butter, softened
8 ounces cream cheese, softened
2¼ cups sugar
6 eggs
2½ cups flour
½ teaspoon salt
1 tablespoon vanilla extract
1 cup (6 ounces) butterscotch chips
1 cup chopped pecans

Cream the butter, cream cheese and sugar in a mixing bowl. Add the eggs 1 at a time, beating well after each addition. Add the flour and salt gradually, beating constantly. Add the vanilla. Fold in the butterscotch chips and pecans. Spoon into a well-greased tube pan.

Bake at 325 degrees for 20 minutes. Reduce the oven temperature to 300 degrees. Bake for 1¼ hours longer or until a wooden pick inserted in the center comes out clean. Cool in the pan on a wire rack for 10 minutes. Remove from the pan and cool to room temperature.

Serves 16

Roux Do: Do bring all ingredients for cakes to room temperature before mixing.

Rum Cake

CAKE
1 cup chopped pecans or walnuts
1 (2-layer) package yellow cake mix
1 (4-ounce) package vanilla instant pudding mix
4 eggs
½ cup cold water
½ cup vegetable oil
½ cup dark rum (80 proof)

RUM GLAZE
½ cup (1 stick) butter
¼ cup water
1 cup sugar
½ cup dark rum (80 proof)

For the cake, grease and flour a 10-inch bundt pan. Sprinkle with the pecans. Combine the cake mix, pudding mix, eggs, water, oil and rum in a mixing bowl and beat until smooth. Pour into the prepared pan.

Bake at 350 degrees for 1 hour. Cool in the pan. Invert onto a cake plate.

For the glaze, melt the butter in a saucepan. Stir in the water and sugar. Boil for 5 minutes, stirring constantly. Remove from the heat. Stir in the rum.

To assemble, prick the top of the cake. Spoon and brush the glaze evenly over the top and side of the cake, allowing the cake to absorb the glaze.

Serves 16

NOTE: You may use a cake mix with pudding already in the mix. If so, omit the instant pudding mix, reduce the eggs to 3, and reduce the oil to ⅓ cup.

Sour Cream Coconut Cake

2 cups sour cream
2 cups sugar
2 (12-ounce) packages grated coconut
1 (2-layer) package yellow butter cake mix

Mix the sour cream, sugar and coconut in a bowl. Chill, covered, for 8 to 12 hours.

Bake the cake mix using the package directions for a layer cake. Cool in the pans for 10 minutes. Invert onto wire racks to cool completely. Split each cake layer horizontally into halves. Spread the sour cream mixture between the layers and over the top and side of the cake. Chill, covered, for up to 4 days before serving or freeze until ready to serve.

Serves 12

Roux Do: Chill the cake layers before slicing or frosting to prevent them tearing.

Roux Do: When preparing baked goods from a package, separate any eggs called for in the package directions and beat the egg whites before adding to the batter. This will make the finished product lighter, fluffier, and better tasting.

Sallie's Sour Cream Pound Cake

CAKE
1 cup (2 sticks) butter, softened
3 cups sugar
6 egg yolks, beaten
1/4 teaspoon baking soda
1 cup sour cream
3 cups flour
1 teaspoon each vanilla, lemon and almond extract
6 egg whites, stiffly beaten

LEMON GLAZE
1/2 cup lemon juice
1/2 cup confectioners' sugar

For the cake, cream the butter and sugar in a mixing bowl. Beat in the egg yolks. Stir the baking soda into the sour cream in a bowl. Add to the butter mixture alternately with the flour. Stir in the extracts. Fold in the egg whites. Spoon into a well-greased and floured bundt pan. Bake at 350 degrees for 1½ hours. Cool in the pan for 10 minutes. Invert onto a cake plate.

For the glaze, heat the lemon juice and confectioners' sugar in a saucepan over low heat until smooth, stirring frequently. Drizzle the glaze over the warm cake with a teaspoon.

Serves 16

In my lifetime, I have "toured" more grocery stores than I care to remember. Our family vacations often took a strange turn in search of more efficient layouts or any new concept worth exploring. This is a natural curiosity for my father since he was the president of his third-generation grocery business. The fascination with grocery stores was prevalent on both sides of our family because my maternal grandfather owned grocery stores as well. Needless to say, the buying and preparation of food was an important part of our family.

In honor of my grandmothers, who are fantastic cooks, I am sharing two of our favorite recipes—Sallie's Sour Cream Pound Cake (above) and Nell's Pralines (page 164).

*—Happy Shopping and Cooking,
Tricia McLemore Bruno*

Strawberry Cake

CAKE
1 (2-layer) package white cake mix
1 (3-ounce) package strawberry gelatin
1 cup canola or vegetable oil
½ cup strawberry juice
4 eggs, at room temperature
1 to 1½ cups crushed fresh or thawed
frozen strawberries

STRAWBERRY CREAM CHEESE FROSTING
½ cup crushed strawberries, drained
½ cup (1 stick) butter, softened
8 ounces cream cheese, softened
1 (1-pound) package confectioners' sugar
½ teaspoon butter flavoring
½ teaspoon red food coloring

NOTE: The strawberry juice can be drained
from the thawed strawberries, or you can use
½ cup milk instead. If you don't have enough
strawberry juice, you can also add enough milk
to measure ½ cup. Also, do not use low-fat
cream cheese in the frosting.

ROUX DO: Dust cake surface lightly with
cornstarch before frosting for a thicker,
creamier consistency.

For the cake, combine the cake mix, gelatin,
canola oil and strawberry juice in a mixing
bowl and mix well. Add the eggs 1 at a time,
beating lightly after each addition. Add the
strawberries and mix well. Pour into 2 greased
and floured 9- or 10-inch cake pans.

Bake at 350 degrees for 30 minutes or
until a wooden pick inserted in the center
comes out clean. Remove to wire racks to cool.

For the frosting, wrap the crushed
strawberries in a paper towel to soak up any
excess juice. (This is very important or the
frosting will be too thin.) Cream the butter,
cream cheese and confectioners' sugar in a
mixing bowl. Stir in the drained strawberries,
butter flavoring and food coloring. Chill for
1 hour.

To assemble, spread the frosting between
the layers and over the top and side of the
cake.

Serves 12

Ponchatoula Strawberry Shortcake

1 cup (2 sticks) butter, softened
2 cups sugar
2 teaspoons almond extract
2 cups flour
4 eggs
1 pint (2 cups) whipping cream, whipped
Sliced strawberries

Cream the butter and sugar in a mixing bowl. Add the almond extract, flour and eggs and beat well. (The batter will be thick.) Spoon into 2 greased 8-inch cake pans.

Bake at 350 degrees for 30 minutes. Remove to wire racks to cool completely.

To assemble, spread some of the whipped cream on 1 cake layer. Add a layer of strawberries. Top with the remaining cake layer. Spread the remaining whipped cream over the cake. Top with another layer of strawberries.

Serves 12

Chocolate Lovers' Fudge

3/4 cup (1 1/2 sticks) margarine
2 1/2 cups sugar
1 (5-ounce) can evaporated milk
18 ounces dark chocolate, broken into pieces
1 (7-ounce) jar marshmallow creme
1 teaspoon vanilla extract
1 cup chopped pecans, toasted

Mix the margarine, sugar and evaporated milk in a heavy 2 1/2- to 3-quart saucepan. Bring to a full rolling boil over medium heat, stirring constantly. Boil for 5 minutes or to 234 degrees on a candy thermometer, soft-ball stage, stirring constantly to prevent scorching. Remove from the heat. Stir in the chocolate pieces gradually until smooth. Add the marshmallow creme, vanilla and pecans and mix well. Pour into a buttered 9×12-inch dish. Cool at room temperature. Cut into squares.

Makes 3 dozen

Bayou Buckeyes

1/2 cup (1 stick) butter, softened
1 (1-pound) package confectioners' sugar
1 (16-ounce) jar smooth or chunky peanut butter
1 pound semisweet or milk chocolate

Combine the butter, confectioners' sugar and peanut butter in a bowl and mix until smooth. Roll into 1-inch balls.

Melt the chocolate in a double boiler. Insert a wooden pick into each peanut butter ball. Dip into the chocolate, leaving the top uncoated. Place on waxed paper to dry. Freeze for 10 minutes to harden. Store in the refrigerator or in the freezer for up to 3 months.

Makes about 1 3/4 pounds

Roux Do: Do keep everything dry when melting chocolate—just a few drops of water on utensils, hands, or bowls can sabotage your efforts.

Covington: The Art of Hospitality and Celebration of the Arts

In the 1800s, when my ancestors put down roots in the community, Covington enjoyed much popularity as a summer destination for picnicking, swimming, and dancing. With its winding river, shady oak trees, and grand pavilion, Covington's Bogue Falaya Park became a social center for locals and New Orleanians who came for the comfortable summer climate.

Bogue Falaya Park still hosts family picnics as well as popular events such as Chef Soirée, Art at the Park, and Symphony Swing in the Pines. Indeed, modern-day Covington is widely known for its hospitality and celebration of the arts. Historic downtown Covington is rich with art galleries, antique shops, restaurants, and boutiques. The live oaks and riverbank at the Columbia Street Landing are transformed into a natural arena from March to October, when the town sponsors free outdoor entertainment ranging from concerts to Shakespearean drama. Downtown Covington plays host to the Three Rivers Art Festival, Final Friday Block Parties, and the Coordinated Art Openings, when shops, restaurants, and galleries open their doors to exhibit the work of regional artists.

Other Covington treasures include St. Joseph's Abbey, Pontchartrain Vineyard and Winery, Playmaker's Theatre, St. Tammany Art Association and Historical Society, Greater Covington Center Fuhrmann Auditorium for the Performing Arts, Christ Episcopal Church Third Sunday Concert Series, and the weekly Farmer's Market, which brings flowers, herbs, gourmet delicacies, local wines, and entertainment.

—Sue Brunning Osbon, Ph.D.

Peanut Butter Cookie Candy

THESE WERE SERVED AT OUR TASTING PARTY, AND EVERYBODY LOVED THEM.

3½ tablespoons peanut butter
1 cup (6 ounces) butterscotch chips
3 cups crushed cornflakes

Melt the peanut butter and butterscotch chips in a double boiler. Remove from the heat. Add the crushed cornflakes and mix well. Drop by teaspoonfuls onto waxed paper, shaping by hand. Let stand until set. Store in the refrigerator.

Makes about 5 dozen

Pecan Pralines

2 cups sugar
1 teaspoon baking soda
1 cup buttermilk
1/8 teaspoon salt
2 tablespoons butter
2 1/2 cups pecan halves

Combine the sugar, baking soda, buttermilk and salt in a large heavy saucepan and mix well. Cook over high heat for 5 minutes or to 210 degrees on a candy thermometer, stirring frequently and scraping the bottom of the pan. Add the butter and pecans. Cook for 5 minutes or to 234 degrees on a candy thermometer, soft-ball stage, stirring constantly and scraping the bottom and side of the pan. Remove from the heat and cool slightly. Beat until thick and creamy. Drop by tablespoonfuls onto waxed paper and let stand until cool.

Makes 18 (2-inch) pralines

Nell's Pralines

2 cups sugar
1 cup heavy cream
Pinch of salt
1/2 cup white corn syrup
1 lump of butter the size of an egg
(about 1/4 cup, or 1/2 stick)
1 teaspoon vanilla extract
2 cups pecan halves

Bring the sugar, heavy cream, salt, corn syrup and butter to a boil in a heavy saucepan, stirring frequently. Cook to 234 to 240 degrees on a candy thermometer, soft-ball stage, stirring frequently. Remove from the heat. Add the vanilla and pecans. Beat with a spoon until the shine disappears. Drop by teaspoonfuls onto waxed paper, beginning from the edge of the saucepan because it cools first.

Makes about 2 1/2 dozen

Almond Cream Cheese Brownies

BROWNIE
1 cup (2 sticks) butter
9 tablespoons baking cocoa
3 tablespoons vegetable oil
2 cups sugar
3 eggs, beaten
1 cup flour
1 cup chopped pecans
1 teaspoon vanilla extract

CREAM CHEESE FILLING
1/2 cup (1 stick) butter, softened
3 ounces cream cheese, softened
2 tablespoons milk
1 (1-pound) package confectioners' sugar
1 teaspoon almond extract, or to taste

CHOCOLATE ICING
3 ounces semisweet chocolate
3 tablespoons butter
2 tablespoons sugar
1 tablespoon cream sherry

For the brownie, melt the butter in a large saucepan over medium heat or microwave in a 4-quart measure. Add the baking cocoa and oil and mix well. Add the sugar and eggs and mix well. Stir in the flour, pecans and vanilla. Spoon into a nonstick 9×13-inch baking pan. Bake at 300 degrees for 40 to 45 minutes or until the edges pull away from the sides of the pan. Remove from the oven to cool.

For the filling, cream the butter and cream cheese in a mixing bowl. Add the milk, confectioners' sugar and almond extract and beat until smooth.

For the icing, place the chocolate and butter in a microwave-safe bowl. Microwave until the chocolate and butter melt. Stir to mix well. Stir in the sugar and cream sherry.

To assemble, spread the filling over the cooled brownie. Spread the icing lightly over the filling. Chill, covered, for 8 to 12 hours. Cut into 1-inch squares.

Makes 1 dozen

Bodacious Brownies, AKA "Big Booty Brownies"

EASY AND SO GOOD.

1 (2-layer) package chocolate cake mix
2 cups chopped walnuts
1 egg
1/2 cup (1 stick) butter, melted
8 ounces cream cheese, softened
3 eggs
1 (1-pound) package confectioners' sugar

Mix the cake mix, walnuts, 1 egg and butter in a bowl. (The batter will be stiff.) Press into a buttered 9×13-inch baking pan.

Beat the cream cheese, 3 eggs and the confectioners' sugar in a mixing bowl until smooth. Spread in the prepared pan.

Bake at 350 degrees for 45 minutes. Cool in the pan before serving.

Makes 1 dozen

ROUX

Roux Do: Use unsalted butter when baking for best results.

165

Double Chocolate Mint Dessert Bars

BROWNIE
1 cup flour
1 cup sugar
$1/2$ cup (1 stick) butter or margarine, softened
4 eggs
$1^1/2$ cups chocolate syrup

MINT CREAM
2 cups confectioners' sugar
$1/2$ cup (1 stick) butter, softened
1 tablespoon water
$1/2$ teaspoon mint extract
3 drops of green food coloring (optional)

CHOCOLATE TOPPING
6 tablespoons butter
1 cup (6 ounces) semisweet chocolate chips

For the brownie, beat the flour, sugar, butter, eggs and chocolate syrup in a large mixing bowl until smooth. Pour into a greased 9×13-inch baking pan. Bake at 350 degrees for 25 to 30 minutes or until the top springs back when lightly touched. (The top may still appear wet.) Remove from the oven to cool completely.

For the mint cream, combine the confectioners' sugar, butter, water, mint extract and food coloring in a small mixing bowl and beat until smooth.

For the topping, place the butter and chocolate chips in a microwave-safe bowl. Microwave on 50% power for 1 to $1^1/2$ minutes or just until the chocolate chips are melted. Remove from the microwave and stir until smooth.

To assemble, spread the mint cream over the cooled brownie and chill. Pour the topping over the top. Chill, covered, until set. Cut into small pieces with a warm knife.

Makes 2 dozen

Roux Don't: Don't cut brownies or bar cookies until completely cool...feel the bottom of the pan to make sure it has completely cooled.

Chocolate Chunk Cookies

4 cups unbleached flour
2 teaspoons baking soda
2 teaspoons salt
4 eggs
1 tablespoon plus 1 teaspoon vanilla extract
2 cups (4 sticks) butter, softened
3 cups sugar
1 pound semisweet chocolate, chopped into large chunks
3 cups coconut
2 cups pecans, coarsely chopped

Mix the flour, baking soda and salt together. Beat the eggs and vanilla in a small bowl. Cream the butter in a mixing bowl. Add the sugar and beat until light and fluffy. Add the egg mixture and mix well. Add the flour mixture and mix well, scraping the bowl occasionally. Stir in the chocolate chunks, coconut and pecans. Drop by large tablespoonfuls 3 inches apart onto nonstick cookie sheets. Bake at 350 degrees for 15 minutes or until golden brown. Remove to wire racks to cool.

Makes about 6 dozen cookies

Roux Do: Cool cookies completely before storing, and be sure to store different types of cookies separately so they will keep their original flavors and textures.

Fig Cookies

4 cups flour
2 teaspoons baking soda
1 teaspoon cinnamon
1 cup (2 sticks) butter, softened
1/2 cup sugar
2 eggs
1 cup molasses
1 teaspoon vanilla extract
2 cups fig preserves
1 cup chopped pecans

Sift the flour, baking soda and cinnamon together. Cream the butter and sugar in a mixing bowl. Add the eggs 1 at a time, beating well after each addition. Beat in the molasses. Add the flour mixture and mix until smooth. Stir in the vanilla, fig preserves and pecans. Drop by teaspoonfuls onto greased cookie sheets. Bake at 350 degrees for 10 to 12 minutes or until golden brown. Cool on wire racks.

Makes about 4 dozen

Cowboy Cookies

2 cups flour
1 teaspoon baking soda
1/2 teaspoon baking powder
1/2 teaspoon salt
1 cup packed brown sugar
1 cup sugar
1 cup (2 sticks) butter, softened
2 eggs
1 teaspoon vanilla extract
2 cups rolled oats
2 cups (12 ounces) semisweet chocolate chips
1/2 cup chopped nuts

Sift the flour, baking soda, baking powder and salt together. Cream the brown sugar, sugar and butter in a mixing bowl. Add the eggs and vanilla and beat until fluffy. Stir in the flour mixture. Add the oats, chocolate chips and nuts and mix well. Drop by spoonfuls onto ungreased cookie sheets. Bake at 350 degrees for 12 minutes. Remove to wire racks to cool.

Makes about 2 dozen

Roux Do: Use a cheese grater to make hardened brown sugar manageable.

Pumpkin Bars

PUMPKIN BARS
1 (16-ounce) can pumpkin
1 (14-ounce) can sweetened condensed milk
1/2 cup sugar
3 eggs
1 teaspoon cinnamon
1 (2-layer) package white cake mix
1 cup chopped pecans
1/2 cup (1 stick) butter, melted

FROSTING
8 ounces cream cheese, softened
8 ounces whipped topping
1 cup confectioners' sugar

For the pumpkin bars, line a 9×13-inch baking pan with waxed paper. Mix the pumpkin, condensed milk, sugar, eggs and cinnamon in a bowl until smooth. Pour into the prepared pan. Sprinkle with the cake mix and pecans and pat into the pumpkin mixture. Pour the butter over the top. Bake at 350 degrees for 50 to 60 minutes. Cool in the pan for 5 to 10 minutes. Invert onto a tray and remove the waxed paper.

For the frosting, beat the cream cheese, whipped topping and confectioners' sugar in a mixing bowl until smooth.

To assemble, spread the frosting over the cooled pumpkin layer. Cut into bars to serve.

Serves 15

Roux Do: Freeze bar cookies for 10 minutes before cutting for clean edges.

Cracked Sugar Cookies

2 1/2 cups flour
1 teaspoon baking soda
1/2 teaspoon cream of tartar
1 cup (2 sticks) butter, softened
1 1/4 cups sugar
3 egg yolks
1 teaspoon vanilla extract

Mix the flour, baking soda and cream of tartar together. Cream the butter and sugar in a mixing bowl. Beat in the egg yolks and vanilla. Stir in the flour mixture. Shape into walnut-size balls and place 2 inches apart on cookie sheets.

Bake at 350 degrees for 11 minutes or until cracked and light golden brown. Do not overbake. Cool on wire racks.

Makes about 2 dozen

Roux Do: Spoon flour into a measuring cup and level with a knife for accurate measuring.

Wine Cookies

COOKIES
7 cups flour
2 tablespoons plus 1 teaspoon baking powder
2 cups sugar
$1/2$ teaspoon salt
1 cup baking cocoa
1 teaspoon cinnamon
1 teaspoon cloves
1 teaspoon allspice
3 eggs, beaten
2 cups vegetable oil
$1^1/2$ cups white wine
$1^1/2$ cups chopped pecans

BUTTERCREAM FROSTING
6 tablespoons butter, softened
$1/4$ cup half-and-half or milk
$1^1/2$ teaspoons vanilla extract
Dash of salt
1 (1-pound) package confectioners' sugar
Food coloring of choice (optional)

For the cookies, sift the flour, baking powder, sugar, salt, baking cocoa, cinnamon, cloves and allspice together into a mixing bowl. Add the eggs, oil and wine in the order listed, mixing well after each addition. Stir in the pecans. Let stand for 20 minutes. Shape into 1-inch balls and place on cookie sheets. Bake at 350 degrees for 15 minutes. Remove to wire racks to cool.

For the frosting, beat the butter, half-and-half, vanilla, salt and confectioners' sugar in a mixing bowl until smooth. Tint with food coloring.

To assemble, spread the frosting over the cooled cookies.

Makes about 7 dozen

Syrian Cookies

2 cups ground pecans
$1/4$ cup sugar
1 teaspoon rose water (optional)
1 tablespoon butter, softened
2 cups flour
1 tablespoon sugar
1 cup clarified butter
1 tablespoon milk
Confectioners' sugar for sprinkling

Mix the pecans, $1/4$ cup sugar, the rose water and 1 tablespoon butter in a bowl.

Combine the flour, 1 tablespoon sugar, 1 cup clarified butter and the milk in a bowl and mix well. Knead the dough until smooth. Flatten a small piece of the dough in your hand. Spoon about 1 tablespoon of the pecan mixture into the center of the dough. Fold 1 side of the flattened pastry over the other side to enclose the filling and form a crescent shape, pinching the edges together to seal. Place on a cookie sheet. Repeat with the remaining dough and pecan mixture.

Bake at 350 degrees until the bottoms are very light brown. Cool on a wire rack. Sprinkle with confectioners' sugar.

Makes 2 dozen

NOTE: Rose water adds a distinct flavor to these cookies and can be found in Middle Eastern or Mediterranean specialty stores.

Chocolate Chip Cheesecake Pie

PIE
6 ounces cream cheese, softened
1 (14-ounce) can sweetened condensed milk
1 egg
1 teaspoon vanilla extract
3/4 cup (or more) miniature chocolate chips
1 teaspoon flour
1 (6-ounce) chocolate pie shell

CHOCOLATE GLAZE
1/2 cup miniature chocolate chips
1/4 cup heavy cream

For the pie, beat the cream cheese in a mixing bowl until fluffy. Add the condensed milk gradually, beating constantly until smooth. Beat in the egg and vanilla. Toss the chocolate chips with the flour in a bowl. Stir into the cream cheese mixture. Spoon into the pie shell. Bake at 350 degrees for 35 minutes or until the center springs back when touched. Cool on a wire rack.

For the glaze, heat the chocolate chips and heavy cream in a saucepan until the chocolate chips are melted. Cook until thickened and smooth, stirring constantly. Spread immediately over the cool pie.

Serves 6 to 8

Roux Do: If chocolate begins to harden after melting, add just enough vegetable oil to liquefy.

German Chocolate Pie

1¼ cups chocolate wafer crumbs
1/4 cup sugar
1/3 cup unsalted butter, melted
4 ounces German's sweet chocolate
1/4 cup (1/2 stick) unsalted butter
1 cup sugar
3½ tablespoons cornstarch
1²/3 cups milk
3 egg yolks, at room temperature
2 teaspoons vanilla extract
1 cup flaked coconut
1 cup chopped pecans
1¹/3 cups sugar
1/4 cup water
4 egg whites
3/4 teaspoon cream of tartar
Flaked coconut for sprinkling

Process the wafer crumbs, 1/4 cup sugar and 1/3 cup unsalted butter in a food processor fitted with a steel blade until blended. Pat firmly over the bottom and up the side of a 9-inch pie plate. Chill in the refrigerator.

Melt the chocolate and 1/4 cup butter in a double boiler, stirring frequently. Combine 1 cup sugar, the cornstarch, milk and egg yolks in a mixing bowl. Beat at medium speed for 5 minutes or until thick and pale yellow. Add the melted chocolate mixture gradually, beating constantly until smooth and blended. Pour into a saucepan. Cook over medium heat until thickened and smooth, stirring constantly. Bring just to the boiling point and remove from the heat. Stir in the vanilla, coconut and pecans. Pour into the chilled crust.

Combine 1¹/3 cups sugar and the water in a heavy saucepan and mix well. Cook over high heat to 230 degrees on a candy thermometer, soft-ball stage. Do not stir the syrup until the sugar is completely dissolved. Beat the egg whites and cream of tartar in a mixing bowl until soft peaks form. Add the sugar syrup in a thin, steady stream, beating constantly until the outside of the bowl is cool to the touch.

Spread the meringue over the pie, sealing to the edge. Sprinkle with flaked coconut. Bake at 350 degrees for 10 minutes or until the meringue is light brown. Chill thoroughly before serving.

Serves 8

Chocolate Pecan Tarts

1/2 cup pecans, chopped
2 tablespoons plus 1 teaspoon bourbon
16 unbaked tart shells
1/2 cup (3 ounces) semisweet chocolate chips
3 eggs, well beaten
1 cup sugar
3/4 cup light corn syrup
1/4 cup (1/2 stick) butter or margarine, melted
1/4 teaspoon salt
1 teaspoon vanilla extract

Mix the pecans and bourbon in a small bowl. Place the tart shells on a baking sheet. Cover the bottom of the shells with the chocolate chips.

Beat the eggs, sugar, corn syrup, butter, salt and vanilla in a mixing bowl until smooth. Stir in the pecan mixture. Pour 1/4 cup of the pecan filling into each prepared tart shell.

Bake at 375 degrees for 20 minutes or until set.

Makes 16 tarts

Fig Pecan Pie

1/2 cup sugar
1 tablespoon cornstarch
1 cup corn syrup
1/4 cup Louisiana cane syrup
1 tablespoon vanilla extract
3 eggs, beaten
1 cup chopped pecans
1/2 cup chopped fig preserves
Pinch of cinnamon
Pinch of nutmeg
1 unbaked (9-inch) pie shell

Mix the sugar and cornstarch in a bowl. Add the corn syrup, cane syrup, vanilla and eggs and whisk thoroughly. Add the pecans and fig preserves and mix well. Stir in the cinnamon and nutmeg. Pour into the pie shell. Bake at 325 degrees for 45 minutes.

Serves 6 to 8

The Art of the Lesson

My mother, mother-in-law, and sister-in-law taught me to cook. I learned valuable cooking tools and strategies from each of them. For example, I have learned to perfect my mother's candied apples and my mother-in-law's pies, and my sister-in-law has taught me how to trim the fat but not the taste from a recipe.

—Allie Pierson

Southern Pecan Pie

4 eggs
1/4 teaspoon salt
1/4 cup (1/2 stick) butter, melted
1 1/4 cups light corn syrup
1 1/4 cups packed light brown sugar
1 teaspoon vanilla extract
1 unbaked (9-inch) pie shell
1 cup chopped pecans

Whisk the eggs in a mixing bowl. Add the salt, butter, corn syrup, brown sugar and vanilla and beat well. Pour into the pie shell. Sprinkle with the pecans.

Bake at 350 degrees for 45 to 50 minutes or until set.

Serves 8

Roux Do: Coat measuring cups and utensils with nonstick vegetable cooking spray before measuring corn syrup or honey for easier pouring.

Almond Plum Pie

1/4 cup sliced almonds
3 tablespoons sugar
1 unbaked (9-inch) pie shell
10 plums
1/4 cup sliced almonds
3 tablespoons sugar
1 cup low-fat sour cream
1 teaspoon vanilla extract
1 tablespoon sugar

Sprinkle 1/4 cup sliced almonds and 3 tablespoons sugar in the pie shell. Cut the plums into halves, discarding the pits. Arrange the plums in the prepared pie shell, cutting the plums to fit as needed. Sprinkle 1/4 cup sliced almonds and 3 tablespoons sugar over the plums. Cover the edge of the pie shell with a strip of foil to prevent burning.

Bake at 350 degrees for 50 to 60 minutes or until the plums form juice. Remove to a wire rack to cool.

Mix the sour cream, vanilla and 1 tablespoon sugar in a bowl. Cut the pie into wedges. Serve with a dollop of the sour cream mixture.

Serves 6 to 8

Strawberry Pie with Grandmother's Piecrust

GRANDMOTHER'S PIECRUST
2 cups flour
1 teaspoon salt
1/2 cup vegetable oil
1/4 cup milk

STRAWBERRY PIE
1 cup sugar
1 cup Sprite
1/2 teaspoon vanilla extract
2 tablespoons cornstarch
Red food coloring (optional)
1 quart (4 cups) strawberries, sliced

For the piecrust, combine the flour, salt, oil and milk in a bowl and stir with a fork to mix. Shape into 2 balls. Roll each ball between 2 pieces of parchment paper. Fit each pie pastry into a pie plate, trimming and fluting the edge. Prick the bottoms and sides thoroughly. Bake at 450 degrees for 8 to 10 minutes or until light brown. (If the edges begin to brown too quickly, cover with foil.) Cool on wire racks.

For the pie, cook the sugar, Sprite, vanilla and cornstarch in a saucepan over medium heat until thickened, stirring constantly. Tint with red food coloring. Remove from the heat to cool. Fill the piecrusts with the strawberries. Pour the syrup over the strawberries. Chill until ready to serve. Serve with whipped cream, if desired.

Makes 2 pies

Sweet Potato Pie

3 cups mashed cooked peeled Louisiana sweet potatoes
1 egg
2 tablespoons butter, melted
1/2 to 3/4 cup sugar
1/8 teaspoon cinnamon
1/8 teaspoon nutmeg
Dash of salt
1/2 to 3/4 cup cream
1/2 teaspoon lemon juice
2 teaspoons vanilla extract
1 unbaked (9-inch) pie shell

Combine the mashed sweet potatoes, egg, butter, sugar, cinnamon, nutmeg, salt, cream, lemon juice and vanilla in a mixing bowl and mix well. Beat for 5 minutes. Pour into the pie shell. Bake at 350 degrees for 40 to 45 minutes or until set. Serve with ice cream or fresh whipped cream, if desired.

Serves 6 to 8

The Art of Lighting the Way

Along the Northshore of Lake Pontchartrain, stands the Tchefuncte River Lighthouse. The lighthouse was built in 1838 and is a monument to the Northshore's maritime history. The lighthouse is one of the oldest structures along the lake and is presently being restored to its former grandeur through the efforts of the Lake Pontchartrain Basin Maritime Museum and Research Center.

Tartlets St. Tammany

FOOD PROCESSOR PIECRUST
1 1/2 cups (3 sticks) unsalted butter, frozen
4 cups flour
1 teaspoon salt
6 to 8 tablespoons ice water
1 egg white

LEMON COCONUT FILLING
3 eggs, beaten
1 1/2 cups sugar
4 teaspoons lemon juice
1 teaspoon vanilla extract
1/2 teaspoon lemon zest
1/2 cup (1 stick) butter, melted
1 1/3 cups (3 1/2 ounces) shredded coconut
1/2 cup pecans, chopped

ROUX DO: Grade AA eggs work best for baking.

For the piecrust, cut 6 tablespoons of the frozen butter into 1-tablespoon pieces. Pulse 1 cup of the flour and 1/4 teaspoon of the salt in a food processor fitted with a steel blade to sift. Add the butter pieces. Pulse 2 or 3 times until the mixture resembles coarse cornmeal. Add 1 1/2 to 2 tablespoons of the ice water 1 drop at a time, processing constantly to form a ball. Repeat the process 3 times to form 4 balls. Wrap the balls in waxed paper. Chill for at least 30 minutes before using.

Roll each ball into a circle 1/4 inch thick. Cut with a biscuit cutter. Press each circle into greased 2 1/2-inch tartlet pans to line. Brush the bottoms with the egg white to prevent sogginess.

For the filling, combine the eggs, sugar, lemon juice, vanilla and lemon zest in a mixing bowl and beat well. Stir in the melted butter. Fold in the coconut.

To assemble, sprinkle the pecans into each prepared tartlet pan. Fill each 2/3 full with the filling. Bake at 350 degrees for 20 minutes or until golden brown.

Makes about 56 tartlets

Encore, Encore...Lagniappe and Libations

New Orleans Paled in Comparison

The best bite of a burger I ever had was at the old Riverside Inn at the head of Boston Street. My family had come to Covington to visit my friend Lynne's family at their summer camp, Saggy Springs, on the Little Bogue Falaya River. One morning everyone decided to go to the Riverside Inn for breakfast. This was unusual, for in New Orleans we rarely went out for breakfast, and when we did, we ordered the ordinary fare of eggs, bacon, pancakes, etc. But this time, we were told that we could have anything we wanted. Lynne and I scanned the menu and decided on hamburgers. Hamburgers for breakfast—what a forbidden pleasure!

Lynne and I thought the taste was pure heaven. We wanted the pleasure to last as long as possible, so we took little "mice bites" round and round the hamburger, until it was the size of a quarter. This became a ritual that we established on subsequent breakfast visits to Riverside Inn.

There were other exotica to be found in this sprawling building. Under a wagon-wheel light fixture was a parrot that squawked "Hello!" at us when we entered. And, wonder of wonders, there were nickel slot machines! Our parents would give us a handful of coins, and Lynne and I would indulge in yet another forbidden pleasure. New Orleans paled in comparison.

During the same summer, I experienced a food epiphany with the realization that food could be as pleasing to the eye as it was to the palate. We were often invited to the Barranger home to swim in their artesian well pool. Our parents would relax around the pool as we splashed in the icy-cold water. They attributed this languorous feeling to the "Ozone Air" that Covington was famous for, but the glasses of sherry that they sipped no doubt added to the atmosphere.

There was an eclectic mix of local people poolside, and a starving artist or two. Miriam Barranger, an artist and a kindhearted soul, often would invite them over in order to nourish their bodies as well as their creative spirits.

During the lazy afternoon Miriam would bring out a platter of hors d'oeuvre. She had made the lovely platter in her studio, and every curl of meat, slice of cheese, and sprig of parsley was arranged in a design. It was then that I discovered how much the beauty of food influences and enhances the taste.

SPONSORED BY

—Elizabeth Moore
Author and Columnist,
Times-Picayune

New Orleans

Wine and Food

"Sometimes I have a little food with my wine."

We all know we like the two together, but sometimes the combinations seem overwhelming, and we fear we will make a mistake. A mistake? In reality, there are no real mistakes, just missed opportunities for something better. And the most important thing is to make sure you like the flavor combination you created. Then who cares about "the rules"? All that said, there are a few guidelines to help you:

1. Pair great with great, humble with humble.

A pizza pie does not need a wonderfully decadent Stag's Leap from Napa Valley when a simple $10 merlot will do. On the other hand, a lamb shank with rosemary served among family and friends yearns for something great like that California Reserve Cab.

2. Match delicate to delicate, robust to robust.

A bold spicy dish, something Mexican perhaps, would drown out a light-bodied pinot noir. A peppery zinfandel, on the other hand, can stand up to the task.

3. Decide to mirror or contrast flavor.

To mirror, or match, flavor would be to pair a rich buttery California chardonnay with a lobster in a rich buttery cream sauce. A contrast would be that same dish with a bubbly Champagne. Both are excellent choices.

4. Choose wines with flexibility.

White wines that are high in acidity, like sauvignon blancs or Alsace rieslings, and red wines, like burgundies or chiantis, pair well with many dishes because the acidity balances out most flavors, creating a seesaw effect on the palate between eating and drinking.

5. Saltiness is a great contrast to sweetness.

Try an Asian dish with soy sauce with a sweet riesling, and see how the salt makes the wine seem less sweet and more fruity. Salty cheeses like Stilton are great with dessert wines and ports for the same reason.

6. High-fat, protein-rich foods call for rich, intense, structured wine.

Everybody knows a good steak goes great with a full-bodied merlot or cabernet. Roasted lamb, duck, and aged hard cheeses also work.

7. Dessert goes with dessert.

Dessert wines go great with dessert foods so long as the dessert food is not sweeter than the wine. This tends to make the wine taste dull and flat. Choose a fruit tart instead of a crème brûlée, and see how they pair up better.

8. Country goes with country.

Europe has made wines for centuries that are meant to complement local dishes. When eating French fare, try a burgundy or Rhone wine. When opting for spaghetti, nothing goes better than a chianti.

—Cheers,
Kristen Golden, Hugh's Wine Cellar

Art at the Park

Children and creativity are the focus of Art at the Park, the major fund-raiser for Christ Episcopal School in Covington. Children of all ages enjoy the hands-on crafts at the activity tents, as well as dozens of demonstrations by local artisans. The food is family-friendly, as is the atmosphere, in the shady Bogue Falaya Park by the Bogue Falaya River. The entertainment is also geared toward children with student musicians, local bands, clowns, mimes, puppet shows, juggling, fencing, and storytelling. Festival-goers are invited to enjoy the Juried Children's Art Exhibition and then spend the evening at the Spring Coordinated Art Openings in charming downtown Covington.

Art at the Park is held on the second Saturday in April at the Bogue Falaya Park in Covington. For more information, go to www.artatthepark.org.

Spicy Bloody Mary

6 ice cubes
Dash of Worcestershire sauce
1 to 4 dashes of Louisiana hot sauce, or to taste
2½ ounces good quality vodka
6 ounces tomato juice
Juice of ½ lemon
1 teaspoon prepared horseradish
¼ teaspoon finely ground black pepper
Pinch of celery salt
Pinch of cayenne pepper

GARNISHES
Sliced lemon
Pickled okra or pickled spicy whole green bean

Place the ice in a cocktail shaker. Pour the Worcestershire sauce and hot sauce over the ice. Add the vodka, tomato juice, lemon juice, horseradish and black pepper and shake vigorously until frost forms. Strain into a chilled glass filled with ice. Add the celery salt and cayenne pepper.
Garnish with a lemon slice and pickled okra or green bean.

Serves 1

Variation: To make a Bloody Bull, add 2 ounces beef bouillon and decrease the tomato juice by 1 to 2 ounces.

Creamy Brandy Alexander

2 quarts vanilla ice cream, softened
1½ cups brandy
¼ cup sugar
2 teaspoons vanilla extract
2 cups cold milk
Nutmeg to taste

Combine the ice cream, brandy, sugar, vanilla and milk in a punch bowl and blend well. Sprinkle with nutmeg.

Makes about 64 ounces

NOTE: This is a wonderful dessert course at the end of a brunch, dinner, or cocktail party.

Bushwhacker

4 ounces Cocoa Lopez
2 ounces Kahlúa
1 ounce dark rum
1 ounce crème de cacao
4 ounces half-and-half
2 cups ice
8 scoops vanilla ice cream

Place the Cocoa Lopez, Kahlúa, rum, crème de cacao, half-and-half, ice and ice cream in a blender and blend until the ice cubes cease to exist. Pour into 2 chilled glasses.

Serves 2

Goombay Smash

THIS IS A GREAT-TASTING TROPICAL DRINK THAT IS SURE TO KICK-START YOUR PARTY IN A BIG WAY. ALTHOUGH IT'S A SWEET-TASTING DRINK, IT'S NOT TOO SWEET.

1 part coconut rum
1 part orange juice
1 part pineapple juice
1/2 part good quality light rum

GARNISHES
Orange slices
Pineapple slices

Mix the coconut rum, orange juice, pineapple juice and light rum in a cocktail shaker. Pour over ice in a glass. Garnish with orange and pineapple slices.

Makes a variable amount

NOTE: As long as you follow these proportions, your drink will taste perfect. Don't worry about the drink tasting too rummy—the pineapple juice will cut the taste, as long as you follow the proportions. Also, most people use Malibu rum for the coconut rum, but Bahamian coconut rum gives a stronger kick.

Comfort Cosmopolitan

1 ounce Southern Comfort
2 ounces cranberry juice
1/2 ounce Cointreau
Squeeze of fresh lime juice
Crushed ice

GARNISH
Lemon curl

Mix the Southern Comfort, cranberry juice, Cointreau, lime juice and crushed ice in a cocktail shaker. Strain into a chilled martini glass. Garnish with a lemon curl.

Serves 1

Southern Comfort was created in New Orleans in 1874 by Martin Wilkes Heron, who operated a French Quarter bar. At its inception, Southern Comfort was classified as a cordial but today is more commonly used as a component of mixed drinks.

Sponsored by Southern Comfort

Cranberry Kick

4 cups (1 quart) cranberry juice cocktail
1 (6-ounce) can frozen orange juice
concentrate, thawed
1 (6-ounce) can frozen lemonade
concentrate, thawed
2 cups vodka

Combine the cranberry juice cocktail, orange juice concentrate, lemonade concentrate and vodka in a freezer container and blend well. Freeze until firm.

To serve, place the frozen mixture in the refrigerator for about 12 hours before serving.

Serves about 15

NOTE: For punch without the kick, omit the vodka and add chilled ginger ale or Sprite just before serving.

Cranberry Margaritas

¾ cup tequila
¼ cup Triple Sec
1 cup frozen cranberry juice concentrate
3 cups crushed ice
Lime wedges
Kosher salt

GARNISHES
Lime slices
Cranberries

Process the tequila, Triple Sec, cranberry juice concentrate and crushed ice in a blender until smooth. Rub the rims of margarita glasses with lime wedges and dip in kosher salt. Pour the mixture into the prepared glasses. Garnish with lime slices and cranberries.

Serves 4

Our love for preparing, enjoying, and getting together over food in Louisiana is truly extraordinary, even by European standards. When I left Louisiana in the late '60s for Europe, I was still more or less oblivious to our remarkable food culture, and no one here was really paying any attention to wine—certainly not to wines being produced in America. The quest to produce world-class table wines in the modern era was just beginning in California, and Ella Brennan (of Commander's Palace Restaurant) still hadn't discovered Robert Mondavi (or was it the other way around?). But things were changing, and by the time I returned in 1973, a question was ripe for the asking: Where's the wine?

*—John Seago,
Proprietor of Pontchartrain Vineyards*

The Junior League of Covington's answer is, surprisingly enough, in St. Tammany Parish.

A Perfectly Dry Martini

6 ice cubes, cracked
3½ ounces good quality gin or vodka
⅔ ounce dry vermouth

GARNISH
Olives stuffed with jalapeño chiles or
blue cheese

Place the cracked ice in a cocktail shaker. Pour the gin and vermouth over the ice. Place the lid on the cocktail shaker. Wrap in a bar towel and shake vigorously for 30 seconds. Strain into chilled martini glasses. Garnish with olives stuffed with jalapeño chiles or blue cheese.

Serves 2

NOTE: For a traditional martini, decrease liquor to 3 ounces and vermouth to ½ ounce. For an extra-dry martini, increase liquor to 4 ounces and decrease vermouth to ½ ounce.

Swampwater Martini

6 ice cubes, cracked
3 ounces good quality gin or vodka
1½ ounces dry vermouth
½ to 1 ounce juice from an olive jar
(depending on how dirty you like it)

GARNISH
Olives of choice

Place the cracked ice in a cocktail shaker. Pour the gin, vermouth and olive juice over the ice. Place the lid on the cocktail shaker. Wrap in a bar towel and shake vigorously for 30 seconds. Strain into chilled martini glasses. Garnish with olives of choice.

Serves 2

Peppermint Kiss Martini

6 ice cubes, cracked
3 ounces good quality vodka
½ ounce dry vermouth
1 teaspoon peppermint schnapps

GARNISH
Peppermint sticks

Place the cracked ice in a cocktail shaker. Pour the vodka, vermouth and peppermint schnapps over the ice. Place the lid on the cocktail shaker. Wrap in a bar towel and shake vigorously for 30 seconds. Strain into chilled martini glasses. Garnish with peppermint sticks.

Serves 2

Mint Julep for One

FOR THOSE LONG HOT SUMMER DAYS.

6 fresh mint leaves
1 tablespoon Simple Syrup (at right)
1 cup crushed ice
2½ to 3 ounces good quality bourbon

GARNISH
Sprig of fresh mint

Place the mint leaves and Simple Syrup in a chilled silver mint julep cup or Tom Collins glass and mash with a teaspoon. Add the crushed ice to fill the glass, adding more if needed. Add the bourbon and stir well with an iced teaspoon until the glass is heavily frosted, adding additional crushed ice if necessary. (Do not hold the julep cup or glass while stirring.) Garnish with a sprig of fresh mint.

Serves 1

Frozen Mint Julep

FOR THOSE VERY, VERY LONG HOT SUMMER DAYS.

1 cup crushed ice
6 fresh mint leaves
1 ounce Simple Syrup (at right)
1 ounce fresh lemon juice
2 ounces good quality bourbon

GARNISH
Sprig of fresh mint

Process the ice, mint leaves, Simple Syrup, lemon juice and bourbon at low speed in a blender or food processor until slushy. Pour into a chilled silver mint julep cup or Tom Collins glass. Garnish with a sprig of fresh mint.

Serves 1

Simple Syrup

1 cup water
1 cup superfine sugar

Combine the water and sugar in a saucepan. Bring to a boil over low heat, stirring constantly until the sugar is dissolved. Boil for 1 to 2 minutes. Do not stir. Remove from the heat. Let stand until cool. Pour into a container with a lid. Store, covered, in the refrigerator for up to 2 weeks.

Makes 2 cups

NOTE: You can decrease or increase the equal amounts of sugar and water to make less or more syrup. Simple syrup is added to drinks to offset the tartness of some juices used in making the drink.

Dr. Scott's Postpartum Cosmos

Cracked ice
2 parts vodka
1 part Cointreau or Grand Marnier
1 part cranberry juice
Juice of 1 lime wedge

Place cracked ice in a cocktail shaker. Pour the vodka, Cointreau, cranberry juice and lime juice over the ice. Place the lid on the cocktail shaker. Wrap in a bar towel and shake vigorously for 30 seconds. Strain into chilled glasses. Serve immediately to chase away those postpartum blues.

Makes a variable amount

In Southeast Louisiana, not only do we have the best food, we also have great doctors. During my second pregnancy, the only thing I craved was a big no-no—martinis! When I told my doctor, Scott Striplin, who had also delivered my first child, Jacqueline, about my craving, he informed me that he made the best Cosmopolitans and would make me one after he delivered my baby. True to his word, a day after Scott delivered my second daughter, Camille, he walked into my hospital room with martini glasses and a jigger full of the yummiest Cosmopolitans I have ever tasted. Now, that's what I call a good bedside manner!

—Naz Nawas Butcher

Sponsored by Total Woman Care

Happy Day Punch

1 cup orange juice
3 cups pineapple juice
½ cup lemon juice
1 cup sugar
Ice
2 cups club soda
1 (32-ounce) bottle Sprite

Combine the orange juice, pineapple juice, lemon juice and sugar in a large container and stir until the sugar dissolves. Chill for several hours. Pour over ice in a punch bowl. Add the club soda and Sprite carefully.

Serves 24

Milk Punch

3 cups vanilla bean ice cream
1 cup half-and-half
¼ cup rum
3 tablespoons bourbon
2 tablespoons brandy

GARNISH
Ground nutmeg

Blend the ice cream, half-and-half, rum, bourbon and brandy in a blender. Pour into glasses and garnish with nutmeg.

Serves 4

The Very Best Party Punch

THIS IS THE VERY BEST PUNCH, HANDS-DOWN, NO DOUBT ABOUT IT, NO QUESTIONS ASKED. TRY IT—YOU AND YOUR GUESTS WILL LOVE IT!

1 large can frozen orange juice concentrate
1 small can frozen lemonade concentrate
1 large can pineapple juice
1 large can apricot nectar
1 cup sugar
1 liter ginger ale

GARNISHES
Sliced oranges
Sliced lemons

Prepare the orange juice concentrate and lemonade concentrate using the package directions. Combine with the pineapple juice, apricot nectar and sugar in a large container and stir until the sugar dissolves. Pour into large sealable freezer bags. Freeze until slushy but not frozen solid. (If you let them freeze, remove the bags and allow to thaw at room temperature until slushy.)

Just before serving, place the slushy punch in a large punch bowl. Pour the ginger ale over the top. Float orange and lemon slices in the punch bowl.

Serves 25

Pat O'Brien's Rainbow

To Pat O'Brien's Bar regulars in the 1960s, this drink was known as a Pete's Special, and it was made with 190 alcohol. The name was changed to Rainbow in the 1980s, and vodka replaced the 190. This drink is colorful, tasty, and very popular among locals. It is perfect for the Fourth of July!

1 ounce grenadine
Crushed ice
3 ounces Tom Collins mix
1 ounce vodka
½ ounce blue curaçao

GARNISHES
Slice of orange
Cherry

Pour the grenadine into a lightning glass or a pilsner. Add crushed ice and the Tom Collins mix. Add the vodka. Top the drink with the blue curaçao. Garnish with an orange slice and cherry.

Serves 1

Pat O'Brien's Hurricane

In the 1940s, there was a short supply of distilled spirits because the grains and sugars used to produce spirits went to troops abroad during World War II. However, there was a huge supply of rum coming to the Port of New Orleans from the Caribbean. Bar owners were forced to buy large amounts of rum just to have the opportunity to purchase one case of whiskey. Rum quickly began to stockpile. So, the experts at Pat O'Brien's began experimenting, and the fruity potent concoction was finally perfected. Shortly after, a glass shaped like a hurricane lamp was paired with the drink, and Pat O'Brien's Hurricane was a hit!

For Pat O'Brien's Hurricane, fill a 26-ounce Hurricane glass with crushed ice. Add 4 ounces Pat O'Brien's Hurricane Mix and 4 ounces amber rum. Garnish with an orange wedge and a cherry.

If Pat O'Brien's Hurricane Mix is not available in your market, you can order it at catalog@patobriens.com.

Phoebe's Pholly, or Mardi Gras Madness

1 fifth of white rum
2 (6-ounce) cans frozen limeade
concentrate, thawed
3 (6-ounce) cans frozen orange juice
concentrate, thawed
10 to 12 cups water

Combine the rum, limeade concentrate, orange juice concentrate and water in a large plastic container with a lid. Freeze, covered, for at least 8 hours. (The alcohol will keep the mixture from freezing solid.)

To serve, stir the mixture and place in a pitcher for serving, keeping the remainder in the freezer until ready to serve. (If the mixture becomes too liquid, just return to the freezer.)

Serves 15 to 20

NOTE: This is great to serve for festive occasions. You may add food coloring to fit the occasion you are celebrating.

Apricot Liqueur

Melt 1 pound white rock candy in a saucepan over low heat. Add 1 pound dried apricots and 1 fifth of vodka and mix well. Pour into a glass container with a tight-fitting lid. Secure the lid and age for 6 weeks before straining.

Vodka Slush

1 cup sugar
1 cup water
1 large can pineapple juice
1 (12-ounce) can frozen orange juice
concentrate, thawed
2 concentrate cans water
1 (2-liter) bottle Sprite
2 cups vodka
1/4 cup cherry juice
1/2 jar maraschino cherries

Dissolve the sugar in 1 cup water in a cup. Combine with the pineapple juice, orange juice concentrate, 2 cans water, Sprite, vodka, cherry juice and maraschino cherries in a large freezer container with a lid. Freeze, covered, until firm. Remove from the freezer 2 to 3 hours before serving.

Serves 15 to 20

Sangria

Juice of 6 lemons
Juice of 2 oranges
1 cup sugar
2 lemons, sliced into circles
4 oranges, sliced into circles
2 bottles dry red or white wine, chilled
4 cups (1 quart) soda, chilled
Fruit to float, such as strawberries and oranges

Combine the lemon juice, orange juice and sugar in a small pitcher and stir until the sugar is dissolved. Let stand at room temperature for at least 4 hours. Chill in the refrigerator.

Divide the lemon slices, orange slices and fruit juice mixture between 2 chilled pitchers. Add the wine and soda to each and stir to mix well. Float fruit of choice in each pitcher.

Serves 8 to 10

The Art of the Vine

Contrary to popular belief, fine wines are produced elsewhere besides Europe and out West. The award-winning Pontchartrain Vineyards, located 15 minutes north of Covington in Bush, Louisiana, has been producing distinctive regional wines to complement Louisiana's extraordinary cuisine since 1993. In addition to having daily tours and tastings, Pontchartrain Vineyards also hosts Jazz'n the Vines every second and fourth Saturday from May to October at 6:30 p.m. Jazz'n the Vines is an outdoor concert series, featuring all genres of music, in a vineyard setting. This seasonal concert series has quickly become a Northshore favorite, with people coming from all over the country with their picnic baskets to enjoy the music and fine wines produced by Pontchartrain Vineyards. For more information, go to www.pontchartrainvineyards.com.

Tropical Smoothie

1 banana, cut into quarters
1 (8-ounce) can pineapple chunks, drained
1 cup milk
½ cup fresh or frozen strawberries or raspberries
¼ teaspoon vanilla extract

Process the banana, pineapple chunks, milk, strawberries and vanilla in a blender until smooth. Serve immediately.

Serves 1 to 2

Fruity Yogurt Sipper

1 large banana, chopped
2 medium peaches, chopped, or
1 cup sliced strawberries
1½ cups milk
1 cup vanilla yogurt
2 tablespoons confectioners' sugar
3 large ice cubes

Process the banana, peaches, milk, yogurt and confectioners' sugar in a blender until smooth. Add the ice cubes and blend well. Serve immediately.

Serves 1 to 2

Flavored Butters

Sun-Dried Tomato and Basil Butter

1/4 cup sun-dried tomatoes in oil, drained
1 cup (2 sticks) unsalted butter, softened
1 tablespoon shredded fresh basil
Salt and freshly ground pepper to taste

Purée the sun-dried tomatoes in a food processor or blender. Add the butter and blend well. Add the basil, salt and pepper and blend well. Divide the mixture into halves. Place each half on a piece of waxed paper, foil or plastic wrap. Roll each one into a log and secure by twisting the ends. Chill until firm. Unroll and slice when ready to serve.

Herb and Roquefort Butter

1 cup (2 sticks) unsalted butter, softened
1 tablespoon minced shallots or
green onion bulbs
1 tablespoon chopped fresh tarragon leaves
2 tablespoons chopped fresh flat-leaf parsley
2 teaspoons Dijon mustard
1/4 cup (1 ounce) crumbled Roquefort cheese

Place the butter, shallots, tarragon, parsley and Dijon mustard in a food processor and pulse until blended. Scrape the butter mixture into a bowl and fold in the crumbled cheese. Roll as above and chill until firm.

Lemon and Dill Butter

1 cup (2 sticks) unsalted butter, softened
1/4 cup fresh lemon juice
1 to 2 tablespoons chopped fresh dill weed
Salt and freshly ground pepper to taste

Beat the butter and lemon juice with the paddle attachment in a mixing bowl until light and fluffy. Add the dill weed, salt and pepper and mix well. Roll as directed at left and chill until firm.

Lemon and Garlic Butter

4 to 6 garlic cloves
1 cup (2 sticks) unsalted butter, softened
1 tablespoon fresh lemon juice
2 tablespoons finely chopped fresh parsley
Salt and freshly ground pepper to taste

Purée the garlic in a food processor. Beat the butter and lemon juice in a mixing bowl until light and fluffy. Add the garlic, parsley, salt and pepper and mix well. Roll as above and chill until firm.

Variation: For Garlic Butter, omit the lemon juice.

Aïoli
(Garlic Mayonnaise)

SERVE AS A DIPPING SAUCE WITH FRESH OR COOLED BLANCHED VEGETABLES, OR JUST USE AS A SPREAD ON ROAST BEEF SANDWICHES.

4 garlic cloves, minced, or to taste
Pinch of sea salt
2 egg yolks
1 1/4 cups extra-virgin olive oil
1 to 2 tablespoons fresh lemon juice
1 tablespoon plain white bread crumbs
Fresh lemon juice to taste
Sea salt to taste
Freshly ground pepper to taste

Mash the garlic and a pinch of sea salt in a bowl to form a smooth paste. Process the garlic paste and egg yolks in a food processor until well blended, scraping down the side of the bowl with a rubber spatula as needed. Add the olive oil in a steady stream until thickened, processing constantly. Add 1 to 2 tablespoons lemon juice and the bread crumbs and process quickly. Season to taste with lemon juice, sea salt and pepper. Chill until ready to serve. (You may store in the refrigerator for 7 days.)

Makes about 1 1/2 cups

NOTE: If you are concerned about using uncooked egg yolks, omit the egg yolks and olive oil and substitute 1 1/4 to 1 1/2 cups prepared mayonnaise. Process with the garlic paste until well blended. Add the lemon juice and bread crumbs and process well. Adjust the seasonings to taste.

Gouda Fondue

2 tablespoons butter
1/4 cup flour
1 1/2 cups milk
1 pound Gouda cheese, shredded
2 teaspoons finely chopped garlic
Pepper to taste
1/8 teaspoon nutmeg
1/4 cup dry white wine

Melt the butter in a saucepan. Whisk in the flour using a wire whisk. Whisk in the milk and cheese. Cook until blended and smooth, whisking constantly. Add the garlic, pepper, nutmeg and wine and mix well. Serve hot with vegetables and toasted bread cubes.

Makes about 4 cups

To my wonderful husband, Don Drucker, your culinary skills, coupled with your exceptional taste in fine wine, exemplify your successful career, lifelong ambitions, and loving family.

To my mother, Li-Jiune Lo, who taught me the importance of providing home-cooked meals for our family, especially for dinner. Our traditional family dinner meals facilitated family bonding every evening and encouraged strong family values and love. Also, she has proven that you can cook any type of ethnic food besides Chinese food in a wok and that chopsticks are the most important utensil.

To my mother-in-law, Lillian Drucker, who is a wealth of cooking knowledge since she possesses a library of cookbooks. I believe she owns every cookbook printed. Thank you for providing me with all the shortcuts to preparing a quick and delicious meal.

—Much love, Sharon

189

Blueberry Onion Sauce

2 tablespoons butter
2 medium onions, sliced
½ teaspoon salt
1 teaspoon pepper
2 tablespoons sugar
¼ cup port
2 tablespoons balsamic vinegar
1 cup fresh or thawed frozen blueberries
1 cup chopped sweet grape tomatoes

Melt the butter in a large skillet over medium-high heat. Add the onions, salt and pepper. Cook for 10 minutes or until the onions are golden. Add the sugar. Cook for 3 minutes or until the onions are caramelized. Add the wine, balsamic vinegar, blueberries and tomatoes. Bring to a boil and remove from the heat. Serve over thinly sliced pork or veal.

Makes about 2 cups

Blueberries grow abundantly in Louisiana during the summer and they freeze well, so you can enjoy them all year long. It's best to use frozen blueberries in your baked treats because they do not "bleed" into your dish.

Boudreaux's Blue Cheese Sauce for Filet Mignon

THIS IS A GREAT ADDITION TO BEEF OR CHICKEN. WE TYPICALLY USE IT FOR A TOPPING ON FILETS, AND WHILE THE BLUE CHEESE SEEMS TO SCARE PEOPLE WHO DON'T TYPICALLY LIKE BLUE CHEESE PLAIN, I HAVE NEVER HAD ANYONE COMPLAIN ONCE THEY TASTE IT. IT IS GREAT WHEN TRYING TO CHANGE THAT OLD BARBECUED STEAK OR BAKED BEEF DISH.

4 ounces blue cheese, crumbled
2 teaspoons Worcestershire sauce
¼ cup buttermilk
1 teaspoon Louisiana hot sauce
½ teaspoon freshly ground pepper

Process the blue cheese, Worcestershire sauce, buttermilk, hot sauce and pepper in a blender until smooth.

Makes about ½ cup

NOTE: Place the sauce on top of the meat minutes before done to taste to allow to slightly meld/"marry" with the meat. This can be done in the oven set on low heat or on the grill.

Jeanne's Rémoulade Sauce

2 garlic cloves, minced
1 (16-ounce) jar Creole mustard
1 (4-ounce) jar extra-hot horseradish
1½ teaspoons salt
2 tablespoons paprika
1 tablespoon Louisiana hot sauce
Juice of 1 lemon
⅔ cup cider vinegar
1 cup extra-light olive oil
1 bunch parsley, stems removed and chopped
2 ribs celery, chopped
1 large bunch green onions, finely chopped

Process the garlic, Creole mustard, horseradish, salt, paprika, hot sauce, lemon juice and vinegar in a food processor. Add the olive oil in a steady stream, processing constantly until thickened. Combine the parsley, celery and green onions in a bowl. Add the processed mixture and mix well.

Makes about 3 pints

NOTE: You can use as a dip, or mix with boiled shrimp and serve. The sauce is enough for about 10 pounds of boiled shrimp.

Caper Rémoulade Sauce

Courtesy of The Ritz Carlton Hotel, New Orleans

¾ cup mayonnaise
2 teaspoons Dijon mustard
1½ teaspoons whole-grain mustard
1 teaspoon tarragon vinegar
¼ teaspoon Tabasco sauce
2 teaspoons drained tiny capers, chopped
1 tablespoon chopped fresh flat-leaf parsley
1 scallion with 3 inches of green, very thinly sliced
Salt and freshly ground pepper to taste

Combine the mayonnaise, Dijon mustard, whole-grain mustard, vinegar, Tabasco sauce, capers, parsley, scallion, salt and pepper in a bowl and mix well. Chill, covered, in the refrigerator.

Makes 1 cup

Simple Chocolate Sauce

7 ounces dark chocolate
1/3 cup milk
1/3 cup heavy cream
2 to 3 tablespoons sugar, or to taste

Break the chocolate into pieces. Melt the chocolate pieces in a double boiler over simmering water, making sure the bottom of the pan does not touch the water and stirring occasionally.

Bring the milk, heavy cream and sugar to a boil in a saucepan, stirring frequently. Pour into the melted chocolate and mix until smooth. Serve hot or cold, stirring from time to time to prevent a skin from forming.

Makes about 1 cup

Fudge Sauce

1³/4 cups evaporated milk
1/3 cup sugar
1 teaspoon vanilla extract
5 ounces dark chocolate, broken into pieces
2 tablespoons unsalted butter
Pinch of salt

Heat the evaporated milk, sugar and vanilla in a saucepan over medium heat until the sugar dissolves, stirring constantly. Bring to a rolling boil. Boil for 1 minute, stirring occasionally. Remove from the heat. Add the chocolate and stir until smooth. Add the butter and salt and stir until smooth. Serve hot or cold.

Makes about 2 cups

White Chocolate Sauce

7 ounces white chocolate, broken into pieces
1/3 cup milk
1 cup heavy cream

Melt the white chocolate in a double boiler over simmering water, making sure the bottom of the pan does not touch the water and stirring occasionally.

Bring the milk and heavy cream to a boil in a saucepan and reduce the heat. Simmer for 2 to 3 minutes, stirring occasionally. Pour into the melted white chocolate gradually, stirring constantly until smooth. Serve warm or at room temperature.

Makes about 2 cups

Balsamic Strawberries

1 pound fresh Louisiana strawberries
1/4 to 1/2 cup superfine sugar
1 1/2 teaspoons good quality balsamic vinegar per person
Pepper to taste

GARNISH
Fresh mint leaves

Cut the strawberries into halves or quarters, depending on the size. Place the strawberries in a bowl. Fold in the sugar. Add the desired amount of balsamic vinegar and pepper to taste and stir gently. Chill, covered, for 4 hours. Serve over vanilla or strawberry ice cream, angel food cake or Sallie's Sour Cream Pound Cake (page 160). Garnish with mint leaves.

Makes a variable amount

Fruit Sauce

2½ cups strawberries, blueberries, mangoes,
papaya or pineapple
1¾ cups water
½ to ⅔ cup sugar, or to taste
Juice of ½ lemon

Bring the strawberries, water, sugar and lemon juice to a boil in a saucepan and reduce the heat. Simmer for 20 to 25 minutes or until the fruit is soft, mushy and beginning to disintegrate. Remove from the heat. Process in a food processor until smooth. Strain into a bowl, discarding the solids. Chill until ready to serve.

Makes about 3 cups

Brandied Cranberries

12 cups fresh cranberries
4½ to 6 cups sugar
3 oranges, sectioned and chopped
1 pineapple, peeled and chopped
1 (16-ounce) jar good quality orange
marmalade
3 cups Courvoisier

Layer the cranberries, sugar, oranges, pineapple and marmalade in a large enameled Dutch oven. Add ½ of the brandy and any reserved juices from the fruit. Bake, covered, at 350 degrees for 1 hour or until the cranberries burst. Remove the cover and stir. Taste and add more sugar if needed. Let stand until cool. Stir in the remaining brandy. Spoon into a large jar. Store, covered, in the refrigerator for up to 6 months.

Makes about 12 cups

Note: You may use 1½ cups Grand Marnier and 1½ cups Courvoisier if desired.

Abita Springs (Beer, Water and UCM Museum): Artesian Art

Abita Springs is named for its most cherished resource, its artesian spring wells. The Choctaw Indians used the waters for medicinal purposes, as did nineteenth-century New Orleanians, who escaped the city's oppressive heat and yellow fever to retreat to the piney woods, spring water, and winding rivers. Known as "The Ozone Belt," Abita Springs became the Northshore's most popular local resort spot. To this day, Abita Springs retains its natural beauty, historic homes, and welcoming atmosphere. The artesian waters still play an important role to locals. The Abita Brewing Company credits the pure, unaltered waters of the local wells for the popularity of the famous Abita Beer, and the Abita Springs Water Company has been a Louisiana favorite for years. In addition to its art galleries, antique shopping, and outstanding restaurants, one of the highlights of historic downtown Abita Springs is the UCM Museum. Proudly calling itself "Louisiana's Most Eccentric Museum," this quirky folk art museum is housed in several historic buildings and features local objects, inventions, collections, and memorabilia.

Sponsored by Abita Beer

Citrus Vinaigrette

1/4 cup extra-virgin olive oil
2 tablespoons balsamic vinegar
3 tablespoons orange juice
1 teaspoon lemon juice
1 teaspoon Dijon mustard
Salt and pepper to taste

Combine the olive oil, balsamic vinegar, orange juice, lemon juice, Dijon mustard, salt and pepper in a jar with a tight-fitting lid. Cover the jar and shake to blend well. Chill, covered, until ready to serve. Shake well before serving.

Makes about 1/2 cup

Marinated Artichokes and Mushrooms

2 pounds mushrooms
2 (14-ounce) cans artichoke hearts, drained and quartered
1 (3-ounce) jar capers, drained
1/2 cup sugar
1/2 cup water
1 cup tarragon vinegar
1/2 cup olive oil
1 teaspoon minced garlic
2 tablespoons Worcestershire sauce
1/2 cup Catalina salad dressing
1/3 cup Pickapeppa Sauce
1 teaspoon salt
1 tablespoon curry powder
2 tablespoons lemon juice

Combine the mushrooms, artichoke hearts and capers in a bowl and toss to mix. Dissolve the sugar in the water in a bowl. Add the vinegar, olive oil, garlic, Worcestershire sauce, salad dressing, Pickapeppa Sauce, salt, curry powder and lemon juice and mix well. Pour over the mushroom mixture. Marinate, covered, in the refrigerator for at least 12 hours. Serve chilled with wooden picks or over salad greens.

Serves 8 to 10

Merliton Pickles

Courtesy of Marcelle Bienvenu

6 to 8 merlitons, seeds removed and sliced as for large French fries
2 onions, sliced
2 green bell peppers, sliced as for French fries
3 or 4 carrots, julienned
1 small head cauliflower, broken into florets
3 or 4 bulbs garlic, sliced
1/2 cup salt
1 cup (scant) sugar
1 tablespoon mustard seeds
1 teaspoon turmeric
2 1/4 cups white vinegar
Black, white or red pepper to taste

Combine the merlitons, onions, bell peppers, carrots and cauliflower in a large bowl. Cover with cold water and cracked or cubed ice. Let stand for 3 hours; drain well. Bring the garlic, salt, sugar, mustard seeds, turmeric, vinegar and black pepper to a boil in a saucepan. Add the vegetable mixture and reduce the heat to low. Cook for 5 minutes. Pour into hot sterilized jars, filling the jars with the liquid and leaving 1/2 inch headspace; seal with 2-piece lids. Process in a boiling water bath for 10 minutes.

Merlitons (or Mirlitons)

Merlitons (or mirlitons) are also referred to as chayote squash. Their delicate flavor absorbs the tastes of other foods they are prepared with, making them perfect for seafood casseroles and stuffings. They are used frequently in Creole dishes, as well as in Caribbean and Latin preparations.

194

Grandmother's Cheese Balls

¼ cup (½ stick) butter, softened
2 cups (8 ounces) shredded sharp Cheddar
cheese, softened
1 cup flour
Cayenne pepper to taste
2 teaspoons Worcestershire sauce
Pimento-stuffed green olives

Combine the butter, cheese, flour, cayenne
pepper and Worcestershire sauce in a large
bowl and mix well using your hands. Shape
into small balls. Pat into circles and wrap
around the olives to cover. Place on a nonstick
baking sheet.
    Bake at 350 degrees until brown. Do not
overcook. Serve warm.

Serves 8 to 10

NOTE: You may omit the olives and shape the
cheese mixture into balls and bake.

Louisiana Hot Pepper Pecans

1 cup pecans
2 tablespoons butter, melted
2 teaspoons soy sauce
½ teaspoon salt
6 dashes of Tabasco sauce
1 dash of Creole seasoning

Spread the pecans evenly in a baking dish and
cover with the butter. Bake at 300 degrees for
25 to 30 minutes or until light brown. Mix the
soy sauce, salt, Tabasco sauce and Creole
seasoning in a bowl. Add to the pecans and stir
to coat. Let stand for at least 30 minutes; drain
on paper towels. Store in a tightly covered
container for months.

Makes 1 cup

Sugar and Spice Pecans

1 cup sugar
¼ teaspoon salt
½ teaspoon cinnamon
6 tablespoons milk
1 teaspoon vanilla extract
3 cups pecans

Bring the sugar, salt, cinnamon and milk to a
boil in a 2-quart saucepan. Cook to 234 to
240 degrees on a candy thermometer, soft-ball
stage. Remove from the heat. Stir in the
vanilla. Add the pecans and stir to coat. Spread
on waxed paper. Let stand until cool. Break
into pieces. Store in an airtight container.

Makes 3 cups

Eggplant and Cheese Sandwiches

1 large eggplant, cut into round slices
1/4 inch thick
Salt to taste
4 ounces cream cheese, softened
2 tablespoons freshly grated Parmesan cheese
1 garlic clove, crushed
1 egg, beaten
1 tablespoon chopped fresh parsley
1 tablespoon chopped fresh chives
1/2 teaspoon salt
3/4 teaspoon pepper
1/2 teaspoon Creole seasoning
Olive oil for brushing
Vegetable oil for frying
2 eggs
1 cup toasted bread crumbs

Place the eggplant slices in a colander and sprinkle with salt to taste. Drain for 30 to 60 minutes. Rinse the eggplant and pat dry.

Mix the cream cheese, Parmesan cheese, garlic and 1 egg in a bowl until smooth. Stir in the parsley, chives, 1/2 teaspoon salt, pepper and Creole seasoning.

Brush the eggplant with olive oil. Place on a rack in a broiler pan. Broil until brown on both sides, turning once. Drain on paper towels. Cut each eggplant slice into halves to form half circles. Spread the cream cheese mixture on 1/2 of the eggplant halves. Top with the remaining eggplant halves to form sandwiches and press together lightly.

Pour vegetable oil into a large skillet to a depth of about 1 inch. Heat the vegetable oil to 350 degrees.

Beat 2 eggs in a bowl. Pour the toasted bread crumbs into a shallow dish. Dip the eggplant sandwiches in the beaten eggs, allowing the excess to drip off. Dredge in the bread crumbs to coat evenly. Fry in the hot vegetable oil for 1 1/2 minutes on each side or until golden brown and crisp. Drain on paper towels. Serve hot.

Serves 6 to 8

Northshore Reuben

Toast 2 pieces of fresh rye bread. Slather with good mustard—half Creole and half yellow. Place 5 ounces thinly sliced corned beef on 1 slice of the bread. Place purple cabbage and big-eye Swiss cheese on the remaining slice of bread. Place both bread slices on a rack in a broiler pan. Broil for 3 to 4 minutes or until the Swiss cheese melts. Assemble the 2 bread slices into a sandwich and cut into halves. Enjoy!

—Courtesy of Hugh's Wine Cellar

Basic Chicken Stock

3 to 4 pounds chicken bones, or 1 whole hen,
cut into pieces
8 cups water
1 leek, sliced
2 onions, cut into quarters
4 carrots, cut into quarters
2 ribs celery, cut into quarters
3 sprigs of thyme
1 bay leaf
4 garlic cloves
1 teaspoon whole black peppercorns

Rinse the bones under running water and drain
well. Place in a large stockpot and cover with
the water. Bring to a boil gradually, skimming
off any residue that collects on the surface.
Simmer for 30 minutes, skimming when
necessary. Add the leek, onions, carrots,
celery, thyme, bay leaf, garlic and peppercorns.
Simmer, uncovered, over low heat for 1½ to
2 hours or until the stock has been reduced
by ¼. Remove from the heat to cool slightly.
Strain the stock into a container with a lid,
discarding the solids. Chill the stock. Discard
the fat that collects on top. Store in the
refrigerator for 1 week or in the freezer for
up to 3 months.

Makes about 6 cups

Northshore Caviar

1 (16-ounce) jar medium or hot salsa
2 (16-ounce) cans black-eyed peas, drained
1 (16-ounce) can white hominy, drained
1 cup chopped green bell pepper
1 cup chopped white onion
1 cup chopped tomato
½ cup finely chopped cilantro
¼ cup chopped jalapeño chiles
1 tablespoon sugar
1 tablespoon salt
2 tablespoons pepper
2 tablespoons cumin
Dash of Tabasco sauce
1 large avocado, chopped

Combine the salsa, peas, hominy, bell peppers,
white onion, tomato, cilantro, jalapeño chiles,
sugar, salt, pepper, cumin and Tabasco sauce in
a bowl and mix well. Marinate, covered, in the
refrigerator for 24 hours. Fold in the avocado
just before serving. Serve with tortillas or
corn chips.

Makes 4 to 5 cups

Definition of Lagniappe

*Lagniappe means "a little something extra" or
"an unexpected nice surprise."*

Recipe Contributors

Betty Adams
Lynne Adcox
Betty Addington
Brandie Allums
Kara Ammons
Nancy Anderson
Liz Andrews
Lauren Arceneaux
Bebe Arthur
Louise C. Bairnsfather
Molly Balfour
Paula Bann
Lisa Barnett
Cecily E. Bateman
Dolores Benoit
Judy Berey
Lesley Bierman
Cole Bird
Joann Born
Shelley and Will Boudreaux
Lyndall Boyce
Monique Brignac
Janet Brooks
Laura Brown
Pam Brown
Wendy Brown
Tricia Bruno
Naz Butcher
Karen A. Capps
Linda Cartwright
Sharon Carughi
Leslie Caldwell Castleberry
Susan Catalanotto
Joanne Champagne
Rebecca Christian

Amelia Coate Curran
Deborah Coburn
Amanda Crettet
Jacqueline Cromartie
Jeanne Crotty
Carol Darley
Joan deLaureal
Ginger Dotter
Rebecca Dougherty
Annette Dowdle
Sharon Lo Drucker
Meagan Dubreuil
Elise P. Dunbar
Carolyn Dunn
Priscilla Durry
Jane Eshleman
Monica Ernst
Lizby Eustis
Denise Favrot
Amy Fernandez
Melissa Flanagan
Shirley Flanagan
Wilhelmina H. Fulgenzi
Carie Pattat Furmar
Beverly Gariepy
Laura and Richmond Galbreath
Richard Ganucheau
Vicki Gatti
Cheryl Gerhardt
Margaret Gerhardt
deSha Gernon
Denise Giangrosso
Karen Gilbert
Janet Graham

Aleen Grieshaber
Dana Guzzo
Kimberly Hahn
Karen Hanna
Susan Hanson
Maureen Harvey
Connie Haydel
Liz Healy
Misty Briley Herpin
Alyson Hessburg
Cinnamon Higbee
Julia Ann Hodgson
Cathy Hodge
Julie and Semmes Hughs
Nancy Huhn-Johansen
Nici Huval
Lynne Adcox Iverson
Melanie Iverson
Susan Ives
Linda Janssen
Cathy Jenks
Marion Johnston
Paula Kastanek
Virginia Kelly
Paula Kelly Meiners
Phyllis Kennedy
Dona Kiesel
Kim Kirby
Sharon Kirk
Catherine Lagarde
Karen Landers
Shaun Landwehr
Caroline Langdon
Cindy Leaber
Stephanie LeBlanc

Susan Leonard

Caroline Lightfoot

Cathleen Lindquist

Susan Livaudais

Ellen S. Lorenz

Lisa Lozano

Alesia Mahony

Leslie Marcello

Gilda Mares

Kristin Mares

Marie Mares

Bernie Marino

Allison Marrero

Sharon Martin

Katherine Materiste

Bond Mathews

Cheryl Mayronne

Kelly McCullough

Debby McDonald

Linda McGovern

Rebecca P. McLeod

Dana McPhearson

Nicole W. Menendez

Allison Mercante

Christian Meredith

Pam Meyer

Susan W. Meyers

Curtis Miklas

Elizabeth Moore

Drs. Sue and Rifat Nawas

Amy Moreau

Kay Noel

Lendon Noel

Missie Arata Noel

Anita North

Joe Norton

Liz and Scott Norton

Katharine Odinet

Sonja Ordoyne

Kellie Osbon

Sue Osbon, PhD

Kathy Oubre

Mimi Owens

Lynn Pablovich

Anita Pankey

Melissa Paretti

Rachel Peak

Jenny Pierson

Lynda Pitts

Andrea Plaisance

Marie F. Porche

Leslie Power

Susan Price

Cynthia Prior

Lisa Quinlan

Pat Quinlan

Stacey Rase

Karen Reisch

Kathleen "Kat" Rhea

Ganucheau Richard

Lea Richerson

Theresa Robertson

Diana Rodwig

Beth Rolinski

Erica Romero

Lynette Savoie

Alicia Seicshnaydre

Rosalind Seicshnaydre

Courtney Shelby

Valerie Sikora

Michaele Willis Smith

Tammy D. Smith

Donna Snelling

Melissa Sproles

Catherine St. Pierre

Michele Stalter

Gaye Lynn Stanga

Bonnie Stegen

B. Strain

Gale Taylor

Valerie Thibaut

Nancy Thompson

Vicki Toups

Benny Trahan

Lillian "Honey" Treadaway

Penny Treadaway

Janie VanDeventer

Leah Vaughan

Sacra and Rex Vaughan

Kim Walker

Leigh Anne Wall

Nancy Wall

Dorothy Wall

Joanna Wallbillich

Julie Walmsley

June Ward

Monique Weiner

Marianna Wells

Phoebe Faggard Whealdon

Laura Williams

Faye Witkowski

Marie Wynne

Hostesses for Tasting Parties

Lynne Adcox

Caroline Blossman

Tricia Bollinger

Naz Butcher

Sandra Chapman

Annette Dowdle

Tara Dragon

Elise Dunbar

Carolyn Dunn and Nancy Thompson
at Morgan-Keegan & Co., Inc.

Monica Ernst

Kim Hahn

Maureen Harvey

JLGC Board 2002-2003

Mary Lea

Christian Meredith

Liz Norton

Kathy Oubre

Lynn Pablovich

Rachel Peak

Susan Price

Provisional Class 2002

Theresa Robertson

Phoebe Whealdon

Index

About The Northshore